No Expectations
A Sociological Novel
1936 - 1954

JOHN HALSTEAD

Copyright © 2018 John Halstead

All rights reserved.

ISBN- 10: 1974504689
ISBN-13: 978-1974504688

DEDICATION

To all Foster Parents

CONTENTS

Acknowledgments

1	War in the East End: Who were Ellen and Percy?	1
2	Name Change and War	23
3	Hill Barton Farm	39
4	Return to London, Bow and Beryl	59
5	Starting School	67
6	51A Tate Street	77
7	The Coakleys and the High Dramas	90
8	The Air Raids Continue	95
9	Enid Blyton and Accident	100
10	Ball and Stabbed	123
11	War Workers	138
12	D-Day, Doodlebugs and Death	146
13	Going Home	175
14	Hopping	185
15	Left of the Law	195
16	World Peace and My Law	204
17	At School in Love with Mary	218
18	Secondary School and Itchie	235

19	Taking Up the Church and Acting	250
20	New Baby and New Barrel	263
21	Radio, Films and Games	282
22	The Night Watchman Seduction	289
23	Thinking About a Trade	299
24	The Driving Lesson	305
25	To Go or to Stay?	311
26	A New Life	329
27	Working Boy with Car Trouble	355
28	Fate Takes a Hand	373
29	The First Girl	385
30	Time to Get a Trade	393
31	A Telegram Boy	415
32	Living in History	439
33	The New Elizabethan Age	454

ACKNOWLEDGMENTS

With thanks to these people who were a great help in writing "No Expectations"

Paula Harris Brett, Lucinda Corby, Suzi Ross, Lisa Pollard, The Book Club Ladies – Kim, Lesley, Anne, Michelle, Teresa

1 WAR IN THE EAST END: WHO WERE ELLEN AND PERCY?

Was I born? That was often the burning question on my mind as I grew up and heard people talking about me as an orphan.

I assumed that I had been born but there is always a nagging doubt, because throughout my life there has never been one single person who could look me in the eye and categorically say, "Of course you were born, you silly bastard. I was there, and you popped out perfectly formed in May 1936."

I often heard mothers talking about their children's birth, while I was playing on the floor or sleeping in the shelters. There was lots of talk of the terrible time they had: of calling for neighbours, midwives and boiling water. Followed by the relief stories of how when it was all over and little so and so was lying safe in their arms it had all been worth it. I never once heard tales about breaking waters or phrases like 'It was the midwife's fault that his belly button look like that,' with regard to me The only information I ever heard about my arrival into the family was, that I had been handed over in the street and because my name Michael sounded too Irish they called me John, after a baby boy who had recently died.

Towards the end of the war, before I got into sex and nicking, I found time to fantasise about where I had come from. My two main fantasies were: the one where aliens had dropped me to Earth in a special barrage balloon and I had landed in the East End of London where I was to become a living experiment that would be collected and analysed later. The other one was an idea I got from a horror comic, in which a hideous monster materialised into a deformed man, from a pile of rags and rubbish that had been left to rot, in a back alley. I identified with the fact that he had been formed from out of nowhere and without the aid of parents.

I grew up fully aware that I was a foster child, although there was never a moment when I was actually told, it was something that I have always known. It never worried or bothered me because as far as I was concerned being fostered was a fact of my life. What did concern me was, that when I was old enough to look after myself my 'Real Mother', as she was referred to among my foster family, would return to take me back to live with her. I assume I was told this not to be unkind but so that I would prepared when the time came for me to go. I believe that this, and not the fact that I was fostered, was responsible for the insecurity and over sensitiveness in my development as a person.

Despite being happy with my foster family I often wondered what my 'Real Mother' was like. This woman I knew nothing about, this woman who would one day appear out of nowhere to remove me from the delicate security of my family and friends. It certainly worried me. because when I was about seven years I found a secret place in which to hide should she ever appear. It was in an outside toilet that had once been in the back yard of a flattened house on the Winterton Street bomb site. The pan had been smashed and the hole was full of bricks, but the door still hung on one hinge and this meant that with a big effort, I could pull it almost shut with just a gap to see through. It was my secret refuge. I even practised living in there for over an hour once by dragging the door shut and sitting on the broken bowl. It was very boring. Nevertheless, I was convinced that if the necessity arose I could pack up some food and water and stay safely hidden from the dreaded 'Mother' who would never be able to find me to take me away from my proper Mum.

God only knows what 'Mothers' circumstances were. Giving me away may have been the last thing she ever wanted to do, and I like to think she often thought of me, but to the little boy I was then, she appeared to be an ogre that would come out of the smoke to take me away. I knew she was called Ellen and the last, and as far as I know, the only time she ever saw me was when I was almost three years old. Naturally I don't remember her. I just know about it because my foster Mum often referred to it, even though, when they met she saw no proof to confirm that the woman who appeared was actually my birth mother.

"Didn't you ask to see a passport or a ration book or a letter even?" I asked when we talked about it, many years later.

"What d'ya mean?" Asked Mum.

"Well without you seeing anything to confirm who she definitely was, she could have been anyone. A go-between who was doing it for money or an older sister or even my grandmother. Didn't you even ask to see a post office bank book?"

"No, of course I didn't. She said she'd been in touch with the church. She knew Miss Glazier. What are you talking about? A go-between? She was a respectable woman of forty-eight. She told me she'd had you in her change. That's why you were so thin. She told me she had met your father at the fairground. She said to me, 'You've done a marvellous job bringing him up, my dear. He's a credit to you.' You looked a picture in your blue linen suit. I'd just britched you. She must have been your mother. Who the bleedin' hell was she if she wasn't your mother? She was sending me money to keep you. She looked a bit like you around the face. Big brown eyes. Course she was your mother you silly sod, who else could she have been? Then she got those people in Portsmouth to send me seven and six a week 'til it all stopped but that was due to all the bombing. It was wartime. I reckon she got killed."

"You should have got some proof. Certainly, from a woman you'd never met. I mean, she just appeared out of nowhere and you didn't even ask to see my birth certificate?"

"We didn't need your birth certificate 'til we was going to adopt you."

She was convinced that that the woman was Ellen, and that was that. But in all honesty, there was never any proof and as no one had ever seen 'Ellen' in the flesh before that how could anyone ever know for definite that it was her? Talk about "Was I born?"

The only other connection I had with her was when I received a small parcel on my seventh birthday. When I was told who it was from, I panicked thinking that it might contain news of her coming to take me away. However, I soon got over that because a parcel was an unusual and exotic happening in our family. I got very excited by the brown cardboard box with its stamps and string and bright red sealing wax. Once it was opened, and the covering saved, due to the war, I saw on the top a card with a boat on it addressed to 'Michael. Many Happy Returns,' Underneath was a brown, pullover with long sleeves, a pair of grey socks, and a children's story book. The book was blue with a black line drawing on the cover and was called, "Sven, the boy from Norway." It didn't have much to do with Johnny, the boy from Stepney and it was obviously second hand. Not that that mattered, we were used to second hand. It was the first book I ever owned. I kept it for years and still find that the smell of book dust and sealing wax, I melted it later, reminds me of that parcel.

But who exactly was this Ellen?

I was thirteen when my birth certificate eventually came to light and it provided a big puzzle of its own. Here are some of the parental particulars. The italics are the hand-written information on it.

When and where born *Thirtieth May 1936 214a Cambridge Road.*

Name if any *Michael Peter.* **Sex** *boy.*

Name and surname of Father. *Percy McDowell ROSS.*

Name and maiden surname of Mother. *Ellen ROSS. Maiden surname unknown.*

Rank/Profession of Father. *Turf commission agent (deceased) of 5 Cricketfield Rd, Clapton.*

Signature, Description and Residence of Informant. *W. P. Greenwood. Resident Medical Superintendent 214a Cambridge Heath Road, E.2.*

When Registered   *28th August 1936.*   **Registrar** *H.J. Hardwick*

Signed as a true copy on 16th day August 1948.

Something was definitely trying to be hidden. It goes without saying that I was illegitimate   Hence the reason why there is no maiden surname of the mother?   Ross could have been her real maiden name.   I have been told that this was often the usual procedure under those circumstances. So, having no maiden surname of the mother, presumably helps to remove the stigma of the deed done out of wedlock.   Or perhaps Ross was just a name of convenience that she used at the hospital?   The father (deceased), could have been just plain Percy McDowell.   Or could the married name have been a complete fabrication, made up on the 28th August 1936 by dear old W. P. Greenwood, the Resident Medical Superintendent.

Note that the birth wasn't registered by my real mother or my father not even any relation!   It was registered by Mr. Greenwood, Medical Superintendent. And note that it wasn't registered until I was three months old - 28th August 1936. Why leave it so long?   The time limit for registration so I am informed was six weeks.   This was three months! Presumably because no one had registered the birth the authorities got in touch with the hospital and Superintendent Greenwood was sent to register the birth using information from the hospital records.   And how reliable are they?   Did Ellen have to show proof of identity there?   Or could she just give a name out of the blue?   And who kept the original Birth Certificate?   And where is it now?

This whole business smacks of a virgin birth to me and we all know where that led.   I want no truck with that sort of thing.

When I was a child the grown-ups were always saying that, 'I was old for my years.' Whereas my own children think I am just a mistake and will never grow up.

It is a common fact that most adopted or fostered children concentrate on the maternal aspect of their birth. Paying little or no attention to who their father might have been. So the other big question is - who was Percy and what's all this about him dying. If Percy McDowell Ross had been my deceased father, you would think that there ought to have been a record of his death at least one year either side of my birth date, wouldn't you? No such record for him or Percy McDowell or Percy Ross or any combination of those three names exists at the records office. Unless I really am an alien.

Now, in answer to the original question 'was I born?' I've learned to settle for the fact, that in all probability, I was. Especially as Superintendent Greenwood, says I was. But what happened after that?

I am now going to tell you how I got fostered. Of course, I don't remember it. All the stories I write about until I get to the age of four, are what I have managed to piece together from either being told, bits of gossip, or from stuff I have heard during slanging matches around the foster family.

It was while I was hop picking with her in Kent, that Sarah often told me the story of how she first saw me lying in Miss Glazier's arms. It began on a warm Sunday morning in July.

At Saint Augustine with Saint Philip's Church, at the back of Whitechapel Road, the Eleven o'clock Mass had just finished. Father Raven, his alter servers and the choir had returned to the vestry to disrobe and to do whatever they had to do there. Miss Glazier, the organist was still at her instrument and continued vamping gentle music as she watched the congregation leave by the north door. She reached the end of her piece, pushed the stops back into their holes and slid the lid over the yellowing keys. As she was putting on her gloves she watched Sarah Skelton, three rows from the front, stand up after her final prayer.

Sarah, whose fair hair was turning distinctly mousy as she entered her forties, straightened her print dress and picked up her handbag. She moved into the centre isle and genuflected to the alter. She looked towards the organ as Miss Glazier give a discreet cough and pointed towards the Lady Chapel. So she moved back through the pews towards the side aisle and both ladies met under the statue of the Madonna, clutching the rosy faced baby Jesus to her blue robe. The women greeted each other with the formality of church going ladies of nineteen thirty-six. Miss Glazier led Sarah towards the side door.

"Let us talk in the garden Mrs. Skelton," she said, as she lifted the heavy latch. "It's far too nice a day to stay inside."

They passed under the low Norman archway into an area known as 'the garden,' which was in fact just a tiny collection of sad flower beds separated by paths of broken paving stones. Nevertheless, it provided a quiet oasis in the dusty streets of Stepney.

"I won't delay your return home longer than necessary, but I had to speak to you," said the organist, as she dusted the memorial seat with her scarf. "It is most urgent."

"That's alright Miss Glazier," replied Sarah. "Alice is getting the dinner on so I've got a bit of time. What's the matter? Is it Father Raven?"

"Oh no. He's fine there are no further complications there thank God. I'm afraid it's about a child again," Miss Glazier sighed as they both sat beneath the statue of the good shepherd, she continued quickly. "It's a little boy called Michael. He is just six weeks old and will have to be taken into Dr. Barnardo's unless I can place him into a home within the next few days. He has already been staying with three different families: but unfortunately, none of them have been in a position to keep him for very long. The poor little mite has been passed from pillow to post and now I'm afraid, unless you can help, it will have to be the orphanage."

"But I'm still looking after Rebecca," Sarah said. "I have got her for another month or so. I can't take another kid on. My husband would ..."

"Yes, I know you have Rebecca that's the reason I've not bothered you until now. But you see my dear the situation has become quite desperate. To get straight to the point. Your daughter Kate is married and has her own flat, hasn't she? And your second daughter Nelly was married two weeks ago wasn't she?"

"Yes, she was, to Ted," said Sarah. "You played for their service."

"Yes, and she looked beautiful," said the organist. "Well I was wondering if it might be possible for one of them to take the baby Michael. Only for a few weeks. Maybe just until Rebecca gets placed in a permanent home and then perhaps you can take him over. Or maybe just until I can manage to find a more lasting alternative. Whichever would be the quickest."

Silence fell between them. Sarah was thinking whether she could, or even should, ask her daughters to take care of a six-week-old baby. She herself felt fine about taking in the occasional child but Kate and Nelly were just kids themselves. Nell was only a newlywed of nineteen. After a few moments of deep thought, she turned towards her companion.

"No, I'm very sorry Miss Glazier," she said. "But I don't think I can ask them. It's not fair. It's not just the girls, there's also their husbands to consider. I'm sure they won't want to take on the responsibility of a kid at this point in their lives."

Miss Glazier drew in a sharp breath. She had been working incredibly hard to get this baby settled and this was her last resort. Her mind urged her not to give up as she stared at the woman opposite her not quite knowing what to do. Suddenly with a tightening of her mouth, she got up from the bench.

"Follow me. Will you please Mrs. Skelton?" She dictated, as she marched down the path and into the side door of the vicarage.

Sarah was completely surprised at the suddenness of Miss Glazier's departure and had little alternative than to do as she was told. She followed her into the house.

It was dark inside especially after the July brightness outside, but Sarah walked quickly as she tried to catch up with Miss Glazier who was already climbing the wide polished staircase to the first-floor landing and disappearing through an open door. Sarah arrived just in time to see her lift a small bundle from the centre of the large double bed. She knew straight away that it was the baby they had been talking about and instinctively tried to turn away.

Miss Glazier was going to have none of that and came towards her cradling the contents of the grey blanket.

"This is Michael," she said as she turned to show Sarah the baby's face nestling inside the bundle. "I left him in the care of Miss Bertha while the service was on."

And there I was. And here I am telling the story many years later.

"He's been very upset since he arrived here this morning," said Miss Glazier. "But mercifully he's asleep now."

As if to defy her I stirred, and my long thin fingers emerged from the top of the bundle and flailed aimlessly around as I tried to find my mouth while tiny disturbed sighs came from between my dry lips.

"There, there Michael. It's all going to be fine. Rest easy now."

Sarah looked down at me and noticed that my blotched face was all creased up as though I had suffered lots of bad dreams.

"He's not very strong you can see that," Miss Glazier said. "He'll never survive Dr. Barnardo's. I have nothing against the place, but it is obvious that this boy is too frail to be left there. He must have a proper home with people who will take care of him. This child has a need to be nurtured and loved. If not, he will never see school age. Don't you agree Mrs. Skelton?"

Sarah looked at my eyelids with their mauve veins above the blond lashes then at my nostrils full of the yellow mucus that Miss Bertha had not wiped away and her maternal instincts came recklessly to the surface.

"All right Miss Glazier," she said. "I'll ask my Kate if she and Harry can take him for a few weeks just 'til you can get him settled properly. I can't ask my Nelly it wouldn't be fair. That's all I can promise. I'll let you know as soon as I can."

Sarah left the vicarage. After doing some shopping in the grocers in Philpot Street, she went straight to Tait Street, and the house where Kate had a first floor flat. She gave two hard bangs on the knocker.

The upstairs window opened, and Kate's face appeared above the chipped unpainted window sill.

"Is that you Mum?' she asked. "Stay there I'll come down and let you in."

Her blond head and blue blouse disappeared. Sarah heard her run down the stairs and along the passage to the front door.

"You'll never guess who's here?" said Kate excitedly, as she ushered her mother through the front door. "Our Nellie! She's just popped round 'cause Ted's gone over Victoria Park. We've been sitting here on our own like a couple of old married women. And now you've come round."

Sarah climbed the newly carpeted staircase into Kate's living room.

"Hello Mum. You just come from church? How are you girl?"

The greeting came from her second daughter Helen, known to everyone as Nelly. She was a nineteen-year old raven-haired beauty. She had a face and bone structure that resembled Jean Harlow. In a yellow blouse and a sage green skirt, she looked a picture of health and confidence. Her dark blue eyes were smiling as she got up from the armchair and crossed to the room to give her mother a kiss on the cheek.

"I'm glad you're here," said Sarah taking off her coat and throwing it on the couch. "I can kill two birds with one stone. Put the kettle on Kate. I've got to talk very seriously to the pair of you."

Kate went into the kitchen.

"You just come from Church?" Nelly asked her mother again.

"Yes. I can't stay long because Alice is doing the dinner and she's looking after Rebecca."

Alice was the youngest of her daughters and still living at home along with her father and brother Arthur, often referred to as 'the boy.'

"How long are you gonna keep Rebecca for? You've had her over a month now."

"I've said I'll have her 'til they can find a proper home for her," said Sarah. "She's no trouble and Alice is very good at helping out with her."

"What's the boy up to," yelled Kate from the kitchen as she arranged the cups and saucers on a tray. "Why can't he do the dinner? Are you still letting him get away with everything?"

"I think he's gone to see one his chum's up Poplar way," her Mother yelled back. "He wants to look at a motor bike. You know what he's like for new-fangled contraptions, worse than you and that new-fangled gas stove. Don't come crying to me when it blows up in your face."

"He's too young for one of them bikes," Kate hollered back. "What does Dad say?"

They talked about Arthur, Alice and their father, until the tea was ready and carried in by Kate. Sarah sipped her tea and let a few more minutes pass before telling them about me.

" I don't know how long it would be for," she concluded. "Miss Glazier will keep on trying to get somebody to take him for permanent, so it might only be for a week or so. Otherwise it will be the Children's Home. As I say, I'd take him meself, but I've promised to keep Rebecca 'til she gets settled with someone proper."

The two sisters sat side by side on the sofa each busy with her own thoughts. Those thoughts mainly being on what their husbands would say about taking on a baby.

"Well I suppose I might as well come right out with it, said Kate. "I just can't see Aggie allowing it. Even if it was only for a few days let alone a few weeks. We haven't really got the room here after all it's only an upstairs flat. We've only got our bedroom and that little room out the back but that's full of all our stuff. Anyway, we might have a kid of our own."

"What are you talking about you silly cow," said Nelly. "You're hardly gonna have a kid in the next few weeks, are you?" Adding, as a new thought struck her. "You're not up the spout, are you Kate?"

"No, of course I'm not! I'm just giving you a for instance."

"Nelly don't use that kind of language if you don't mind," ordered the mother. "You're not in the factory now."

Katy looked at her Mother and said. "Anyway, Mum I don't think I really want the responsibility of a kid yet. After all we've only been married just over a year. It'd be a bit soon."

"Yes, that's what I told Miss Glazier. And it's much too soon for Nelly to even think about it?"

"Course it is," snapped Kate. "She's only been married a fortnight! She can't be expected to take on a baby at this time of her life. Besides she's only nineteen what would she do with a baby? She's hardly grown up herself."

"Just a minute Kate," snapped her sister. "When did I give you the right to do my talking for me? I can make up my own mind thanks very much. I don't need your mouth to tell me what to do and what to think. As a matter of fact, I would like to have a baby. Ted and me were talking about it only last week. Maybe looking after this one will give us a bit of experience. He don't want me to work and I'll go mad sitting in that flat on me own all day. So maybe I could give it a chance. Besides I think I'd make a really good mother."

"Nelly just stop and think what your husband will ..." said Kate.

"It'll be a wicked shame if it goes to Barnardo's," interrupted her sister. "I see them every day from my window. Running around in their little short trousers. Poor little sod's."

"Nelly! Will you stop using that language, it's Sunday!" Said Sarah.

"Well It's true," Nelly continued. "You should see them in the early morning their little legs all bare to the wind and people ordering them about all the time. How can a little baby cope with all that? It ought to have someone to love it and look after it. I could look after it much better than them."

Sarah realised that her daughter had got the bit between her teeth and like any mother who knows her child too well, she began to worry.

"Wait a minute Nelly slow down bit," She warned. "You'd better think about what Ted's going to say. After all my girl you haven't just got yourself to think of now. You've got your husband and he must come first because he's the breadwinner. Do you think he would want the responsibility of looking after a baby? And only just two weeks after getting married?"

"Oh Ted'll be alright," said Nelly confidently. "We'll be able to take the kid out and buy him nice clothes and some toys, it'll be really grand. I'll tell you what. I'll talk it over with 'im when I get home and we'll come over to see you tonight. When he's agreed to take it."

"Oh Nelly!" Was all that Kate could say?

Sarah, on the other hand said nothing but worried all the more.

They finished their tea still talking about the good and bad ideas of taking someone else's child. After which Nell and Sarah left together to walk back to the family home in Planet Street. Nelly didn't go inside the house, instead she left her mother at the street door and went home to her husband.

Ted, or Edward to give him his full name, was a handsome fair haired, well built, twenty-three-year-old. He worked as chauffer and driver at the factory where he and Nelly had met and after ten months courtship they had decided to get married.

Inside their rented flat at Barkingside, on this particular Sunday, the newlyweds were not quite seeing eye to eye.

"You can shut your mouth and get this into your stupid head," said Ted to Nelly. "I am not taking on another bloke's kid! You are not going to look after it and you are not going to bring it into my home. Not if you cry from here 'til soddin' doomsday!"

"Well I want to have him and I'm going to have him," was Nelly's tearful reply. "You are just an unfeeling bastard who cares about nothing and no one except yourself. That little baby will have to go into that horrible place over there if we don't take him. What's the matter with you Ted? Haven't you got any heart at all?"

"Never mind what's the matter with me you silly cow. Have you thought what it means to have a kid around? Nell just think about it. We've only been married a couple of weeks, we want to have a bit of time on our own first."

"We've had a soddin' fortnight on our own and I'm bored to death already of just sitting around the place polishing the bleedin' wedding presents. I'm used to a bit of life with people around me. When I was in the factory there was music and people to talk to and have a laugh with. I don't want to just sit here staring at the four soddin' walls all day while you're off working and enjoying yourself. I'll tell you what Ted, if you don't let me have this kid I'm gonna piss off back home."

"If you want a kid we can have one of our own. We've already agreed on that. We'll have one of our own. You don't have to take someone else's."

"But the poor little sod will have to go to Barnardo's if we don't take him."

"Nelly that isn't our business. That kid is nothing to do with us and I'm not going to have him."

"Well then, you can stick your rented flat up your arse. I am going home to my Mum and I'll look after him there."

"Oh yes? That'll be great wont it? I'm sure your Dad will love having you and Alice in the back bedroom with a baby in a cot screaming it's head off all night. Anyway you can't go back there, your Mum's still got Rebecca so there just wouldn't be any room for you and another kid. Arthur's already sleeping in the front room."

Nelly saw the sense of that and for the next hour or so took a more persuasive way of convincing her husband that it would be a good idea if they looked after the baby for a while. Just a short while. Not that long. Perhaps a week or so. After all Miss Glazier would find him a proper home soon. And; as she always did, Nelly eventually got her own way. So after they had done the washing up they went over to Planet Street.

Later that evening Sarah, Nelly and Ted stood outside the vicarage and knocked twice on the big blue door. It took a minute or two before it was opened by the shuffling Miss Bertha, who just raised her head in a questioning way.

"We've come to see Miss Glazier," said Sarah. "She might be expecting us Miss Bertha. I did tell her I would try to get back to see her tonight."

"Come in and wait her in the hall," said Bertha. "I'll tell her you're here. They're just getting over doing evensong, so it could be a mite difficult."

The difficulty proved unfounded and Miss Glazier emerged smiling from the dining room.

"Sarah," she said over enthusiastically. "And dear Nelly with your handsome husband. Edward isn't it?"

Edward grunted and nodded shaking his thick blond hair.

"I am so pleased to see the pair of you. I am assuming you are here because you have decided to look after baby Michael for a while?"

More grunts and nods

"One thing is certain no little boy could ask for more attractive parents. I am sure it will not be for long. I am still hoping we can get him settled permanently. He is now back with the family who have been looking after him for the past week. So, if you would like to wait just a moment, I will just get my coat and we will go there to collect him. It Is just across the other side of the Whitechapel Road, Round towards the Brewery."

The small group of four, left the vicarage and made their way to one of the back streets in Bethnal Green. I can't be more specific because no one could ever remember the name of the street or of the people who had been looking after me. Sarah always insisted that it was somewhere off of Brady Street and Nelly says it was off of Cambridge Heath Road. Ted could never remember anyway so kept quiet. Wherever it was they arrived at a house, knocked. According to Nelly, a woman came out with me in her arms and after a bit of a chat, handed the baby over to Miss Glazier. Just like that. In the street. The woman gave a paper carrier bag to Sarah, the door was closed and the five of us moved away.

"So this is little Michael," said Miss Glazier as we walked down the street. "I had better give you all the details I know. He was born the 30th of May. His Mother is unable to take care of him because she is in service and has to live in. She is willing to pay you three and six pence a week towards his keep and I will be the bearer of the money. I know nothing of the father. As soon as I can I will endeavour to find him a lasting home. He has had three temporary homes in his short life so he is well travelled already. His mother wants someone to care for him until he is fourteen. Only then, when he will be of working age, will she be in a position to take him back and look after him herself. She will probably want to see him at certain times, but I do not expect it will happen while he is in your care because her present duties keep her away from London. So that is the situation, and this is Michael. Would you like to hold him?"

They stopped in the street and the Miss Glazier passed me over to Nelly who expressed her amazement at how light I was. She looked down at me, just as my dark brown eyes opened and began searching the space around me. Over the years, with constant telling, it has been suggested that I was searching for many things including love, hope, identity, family or something that nobody really understood. However, I think I was just searching for something to eat.

"Oh, look at him Ted," said Nelly bringing me close to her husband. "Poor little mite, he smells a bit. What do you think of him? He looks as though he's going to have blond hair the same as you."

Ted stood at her side and said nothing. He looked down at the child and wondered if they were doing the right thing. He consoled himself that it would only be for a few days and anyway Nelly would soon get tired and be glad to get rid of the boy when a permanent family was found. While he was looking, my scrawny hand with pale folds of skin hanging from the arm emerged from the grey blanket. It formed itself into a fist and my fist was pushed towards my toothless mouth.

They returned to the vicarage, where the details of feeding, access, payment and future meetings, were thrashed out. A short time later the four of us left. Nelly left with a baby and a warm feeling. Ted left with hope that the baby would soon be gone. Sarah left carrying baby food, nappies, and a feeding bottle. I left with my fourth set of parents, my meagre worldly possessions and no expectations whatsoever

2 NAME CHANGE AND WAR

During the next few weeks Miss Glazier would give the three and sixpence to Sarah who would pass it on to Nelly when she was visiting Planet Street and I became a living doll for Nelly and Kate.

Kate was feeling guilty at not taking me herself and was also jealous of the fact that I was now known as Nelly's kid and her sister was getting all the kudos for being a mum. Their husbands on the other hand, didn't really take me to their hearts. There wasn't a lot of time for bonding as they were both workingmen and busy six and a half days out of seven. Ted was doing his driving and Aggie was in his office. I never really knew what Aggie did, just that he worked in an office in the Covent Garden fruit and vegetable market. The men did their best but the inclination wasn't really there. Nevertheless the four of them would get together on Sundays and take me for a day out to Chingford, or Theydon Boys.

It was on the first Sunday after I had been taken, that the problem of my name came up. The four of them had been to show me off to Kate's in-laws in Old Ford Road and then they went back to Planet Street for tea.

Nelly told me the story and it went something like this.

'We'd taken you to see Rosie and June. You looked lovely, I had put you in a pale blue suit, and Dad had borrowed the van so we had transport. We had a lovely time with Beatie and Fred up at

Victoria Park, and then we all went back to Mum's for a cup of tea. Kate and Aggie came in to see Farver, before walking back to their place later. As it turned out the whole family were there, Alice, Arthur, Dad, and even Old Granny came in. The kitchen was full. Well, while we were all talking Alice just happen to call you Michael and when she did Old Granny went mad.'

'What did you call 'im?' She shouted of Alice.

'Michael,' said Alice. 'That's his name.'

'Michael!' Said Old Granny. 'We are not having a kid called Michael in this family. It's an Irish name. Roman Catholic. I will not have have that name in the family.'

'It won't matter,' said Alice. 'He's only staying in the family 'till they can find him a proper home to live.'

'Well while he's one of us we'll call him Johnny,' Old Granny insisted. 'After the little 'un that died. I want none of that Popish shit in this family. John, or Johnny. That's what we call him while he's here. Have you all got that?'

'Well you know what Old Granny's like' Nelly said to me. 'They weren't going to start arguing with her on a Sunday, so we all decided that it would be better and easier to call you Johnny.'

When Nelly was telling me the story, I knew what she meant as far as Old Granny was concerned. She was a formidable woman born in Victoria's reign and had a tongue and temper that would kill you at a glance. You'll hear more of her later, but even then she wore her Edwardian long skirts and a small black shawl accross her shoulders over her shirt.

So 'Johnny' I became and continued to live with Nelly and Ted, until, just over a month later, Miss Glazier found a permanent place for Rebecca and I went to live with Sarah, in Planet Street. That being my fifth home. Although I suppose it can't really class it as a home because I was only there for three days.

Having been looking for almost five weeks, Nelly demanded that I be given back to her because she missed me so much. Ted was still not keen but as Nelly always got her own way and after a lot of arguments with everyone in the family putting their oar in, it was eventually agreed, with the approval of Miss Glazier, that I would return to live with Ted and Nelly. I was to stay with them until my real mother returned to claim me and take me away. There was never any paper work or formal agreement about me being fostered, it was all done by word of mouth.

So that was how Nelly and Ted became Mum and Dad, and Sarah and Charlie became Nanny and Farver. The others became my aunts and uncles.

Now that Mum and Dad had me for the foreseeable future things took a different turn. A pram and a cot was bought, and this meant that more living space was needed. The East End grapevine did its job and a bigger flat was found and we moved to Hoxton. We had moved again not long after that, just before Mum gave birth to their first child. This was my brother Eddy born on the thirteenth of June nineteen thirty-seven. Making only a year between our ages

My first conscious memory was just after we had moved again, this time to a bungalow in Richmond Road, Ilford. Aunt Kate had taken me out for the day and when we got home, Mum was in bed and Nanny told me that the bundle in the cot beside her was called Jeanie who had arrived while I was looking at the cows in Romford Market. I didn't go to see the baby I just climbed on to the bed to kiss my Mum, then Dad came in with Eddy, we were told not to jump about on the eiderdown. That is and I can only assume that the shock was too much for me because I don't remember anything more until a few months later, it was the night we were in Nanny's and all the grown ups were looking stern because some bloke on the wireless said we were at war with Germany. All the men were talking about being called up when the fighting started. I was four years old by then and the dramas began to pile up very quickly.

There were many dramas, not with the Germans, I mean between Mum and Dad. One day they were arguing over the breakfast table. Dad complained that his boiled egg was too runny, so he picked it up, in its cup, and chucked it at Mum. The cup went flying through the air towards her, but the egg left it and hit me on my forehead splattering yellow and white liquid all over my face. Jeanie started screaming and Eddy clung on to Mums legs. I remember standing on a wooden chair as she tried to wipe the gooey mess from my face with a damp tea towel. I don't have any mental picture of Dad during all this. I know he is there, but I don't visualise him.

The first strong imagine I have of Dad is, of him during the heavy raids. It was during the blitz in 1940. We were now living in Hemming Street, Bethnal Green. It was night and the air raid warning had gone. It was a wailing sound that started small and low and grew quickly into a high shrieking out across London. Because it was always coupled with Mum's screaming and yelling as she urged us to move faster to get ready for the shelter it never ceased to make me stiffen and panic, as the adrenalin of life or death went through my veins. The siren wailed for what seemed hours but was probably just a couple of minutes. Soon after it had died away we heard the sound of aeroplanes and bombs and guns filling the night with lots of ear-splitting noise.

Mum was desperately trying to get us three sleepy kids dressed as fast as she could so that we could get to the shelter underneath the arches at the bottom of the street. Dad had not yet been called up for the Army and was on standby ambulance duty, so he was already out of the house. As soon as we had struggled into our shoes and socks, put coats over our underwear and grabbed our gas masks, we hurried down stairs, along the passage and out of the front door which I slammed shut behind us.

Mum ran carrying baby Jeanie and I was hanging on to the tail of her outdoor coat with one hand and clutching the three-year-old Eddy with the other as I dragged him along so that we wouldn't get separated. Mum's job was to run as fast as she could, it was ours to us to keep with her and not get lost. We had done all this before, but this night was really bad. It might well have been the first night of the blitz. Even though I had been told never to look up I looked up, and could see, nearer than the stars, the coloured lights of planes and the blue and yellow flames of bursting shells. Small red and green lights flickering among the flashes and sparks. Shells were blasting across the sky as our ack-ack boys tried to hit the German bombers as they dropped their loads and weaved away from the searchlights. I couldn't see any bombs falling, but I could hear them whistling down and exploding in the distance all around us.

"Run! Run for your lives!" Yelled a man as he dashed past us, away from the arch at the end of the street, towards Valence Road. There was a violent urgency in his voice that made us double our efforts. Eddy's and my little legs, in our lace up boots, going fifty to the dozen as we raced towards the shelter and all the time trying not to fall over, as we staggered towards the arch, which supported the railway line from Liverpool Street Station into Essex.

We arrived out of breath as Mum led us through the tense gathering of mostly women, standing like skirted giants above us. I brushed against their legs in the semi darkness, lit by three or four shaded torches, they murmured whispered greetings as we moved inwards. The smell under the curved, soot stained, brickwork was damp and musty. I didn't want to go right to the back where it smelled even worse and was relieved when finally, Mum came across someone she liked and found a place to settle. She passed baby Jeanie to a woman in grey and reached down to draw us boys closer to her with all the maternal instinct and experience of her twenty-three years of life. We stood like that a long, long time while the noises of violent destruction continued above and all around us.

I can't say I was afraid. Once the horrible warning siren had stopped what came after was just a new way of life that was developing. At four years old I had no understanding of mortality. The shock of understanding about that wasn't to be busted apart for another few years.

There were sounds of movement in the crowd and the quiet whisperings took on a more intense feeling as the grown ups around us divided and the faint beam of a torch was played upon the face of my Dad as he moved towards his family. I see him in a dark uniform with shiny buttons, wearing a steel hat and standing with his hands behind his back. This is my first conscious memory of my foster father Edward William Halstead.

He was a handsome man with a strong tanned face, bright blue eyes and thick fair hair that remained thick even when it had turned completely silver. He was well built and had a worker's muscular body. He had very strong hands that when he walloped me really hurt. His face, on this war-torn night, is twenty-six years old and lined with concern.

"Hello Nelly," he said, not moving his hands. "I went to fifteen and you weren't there, the door has been blown off, so I thought I had better check that you were alright. I can't stop, I'm still on duty. It's a terrible night. Terrible."

His eyes began to widen as they filled with the liquid that isn't quite tears. He was a man and men didn't show tears, nevertheless his emotion affected me as I saw him in the torchlight. I felt very afraid and put my arm around Eddy for comfort as I gripped Mum's coat tighter.

"Right then, now I know you're all o.k. I'll get back to the ... I've got the ambulance at the front. You stay here, and I'll see you as soon as I can after the all clear goes. Alright? I'll get home as soon as I can. Look after Mummy, Johnny. Bye Nelly."

He nodded to us, his lips very tight across his white teeth in the resemblance of a grotesque smile. Then instead of turning to walk away from us and out of the arch as you might expect, he backed away. Backed away! I had no idea what it was all about, but I knew something very unusual was going on.

The story of that night was often re-lived when we sat around the fire and the stories of the war were retold. It was in these times that I learned the reason for the backing away. My father had backed away from us because, his hands and sleeves we saturated with blood and he didn't want us to see them.

He had been driving his ambulance around the East End rescuing people trapped in their bombed houses. It had been a fearful night even in comparison with the worst that followed during the next five years. The stories of that night were; of bodies being trapped behind their front doors that had blown back at them as they tried to escape their homes; of mutilated women and children who had sheltered under stairs that had collapsed on them when their house was hit; of bodies pinned under tables and chairs. One story that was always told was of the woman who had been pinned behind a washing mangle, and found wedged against her yard door with the rollers across her chest and was somehow still alive. The grown-ups told stores of the fires and falling buildings, of the blast that filled the streets with smashed window frames and furniture and curtains and clothes. There were stories of wounded, bleeding people facing further danger to themselves as they tried to rescue other people who were still trapped. There were tales of the dead bodies being laid out on the pavement so that the broken and burned living could be quickly ferried to hospital in anything that moved. Along with these stories came the others about the "Bastards" who looted and grabbed anything they could from ordinary homes. These were the tales told around the fireside about that terrible night and my young ears missed nothing.

I have often asked myself if this first memory of Dad is so strong because of the drama of the occasion or because of the backing away? I don't know.

The blitz worried the family so much they decided that we must all get out of London. So far, they had resisted the evacuation that had gone on because they didn't think it was worth it. But now that the bombing was getting serious something had to be done. As always they insisted that they should all stick together, which meant that somewhere had to be found that would take, Nanny and her three daughters Kate who had Joycie, Nelly who had me, Eddy and Jeanie and Alice who wasn't yet married so had no kids. We needed a place for four grown-ups and four children.

Nanny had a relative by marriage called Mary Batterson, who was looking after a large house in Penshurst in Kent, a county they knew well because they went there every year to do hop picking. Somehow Nanny got Mary, to give the eight of us sanctuary. And a couple of nights later, after lots of whispering and minimal organisation, Nanny, the three sisters and us kids were bundled on the back of someone's lorry, after the all clear went and driven through the night to Penshurst.

Mary Batterson, we never called her Aunt Mary even though at that time everyone was an Aunt or Uncle as a mark of respect, met us inside the dark hall and allotted us two rooms upstairs. One for us Halstead's and another for Nanny and the Skelton's. During the war when we weren't living in our home but with someone else, where we lived was known as our billet.

Me and Eddy never took to Mary Batterson. It wasn't because she was a plain woman in her early forties without a bust or even that she had a rat like face and a moustache. It was just something about her. Perhaps it was because she moved in a strong direct manner and had a masculine haircut. Or perhaps it was because deep down she hated children and Eddy and I instinctively knew it. So it came as no surprise to me and my brother when we found out that she was in fact a German spy. It all came to light during our second week. It was just after I'd learned what a cess pit was.

One night, just after she had finished telling us the story of Aladdin, Aunt Kate had gone downstairs to get some water so that she could take her Daisy powder. As she went along the passage on her way back from the kitchen, had spotted Mary on the wide oak staircase, putting a lighted candle in the corner window. She had kept herself hidden till Mary returned to her own room then rushed upstairs to tell the family.

The sisters and Nanny gathered in our room and in hushed tones, because careless talk costs lives, decided that she was lighting up the window to guide German bombers towards London. Penshurst was on the flight path from Nazi land into England. I was listening as I lie top to toe in bed with Eddy. After much patriotic whispering about whether they should go to the Police, the A.R.P. or deal with it themselves, they decided that the police had enough to do looking for dropped parachutists, so it would be best if they took the law into their own hands. Mum, who was the bravest, was instructed to go down and blow the candle. They watched her as she went along the landing down the stairs drew back the curtain and blew it out. She came back tour room where they all giggled and whispered a lot more; and after that they went to bed.

The next morning me and Eddy were having our porridge when Mary was confronted in the kitchen by the whole family.

"Now listen Mary," said Mum, the chief interrogator. "We want to know what the bleeding hell you think you were doing putting a lighted candle in the window during the blackout?"

"And don't try to deny it because I saw you," quickly added Aunt Kate.

"It really isn't any of your business," said Mary.

"Of course, it's our business," said Nanny. "If you\re showing the Gerry's the way to London."

"If you don't mind me saying so" said Mary talking at the same time, "I think you've got a damned cheek to bring me into my own kitchen and ask questions like that, especially in front of the boys. However, if you must know that light was for my brother. He is a rear gunner in the Air Force and I was putting a candle in the window to guide him home."

"Well you are a silly cow and you must stop doing it at once," said Mum. "It's very dangerous."

"No it is not dangerous! It brings good luck to a loved one far away if one places a lighted candle in a window for them to follow home."

"But if your brother can see the lighted candle to follow it home then so can the Nazi's," Aunt Alice reasoned.

"It is very wrong of you to do that, Mary," said Nanny. "You are putting hundreds of lives at risk. You ought to be ashamed of yourself.

"I've got nothing to be ashamed of whatsoever, "snapped back Mary. "There is no danger to anyone let alone hundreds of people, because before I put the candlestick on the ledge I make sure that the blind drawn inside, and the shutters are closed outside."

It did rather put the kybosh on their accusations. After a bit more arguing about curtains getting caught alight and cracks down the side, Mary agreed that she would stop putting lights in windows. She would just keep a shaded night light in her bedroom. But me and Eddy never believed her, and she became known to us as 'Batto, the spy'.

After a few weeks it was decided that, due to the candle incident along with the fact that Mary was a vegetarian which was more than the grown-ups were prepared to put up with, we would go home and to get further away on a proper evacuation. So, the cases were packed, a lorry was borrowed, and we returned to the East End.

Once back home and with the bombs still falling, while we were there I was convinced that we didn't get bombed because our name wasn't on one. After each explosion the grown-ups would say, 'Well our name wasn't on that one,' and carry on with whatever they were doing. Mostly hoping that the next one wouldn't have their name on it either I suppose. Despite the danger, the family remained determined not be separated even though Mr. Churchill had ordered that to get out of London, on an official evacuation scheme, women had to have a small child to take care of. Our big problem was how to get evacuated together when Nanny and Alice didn't have any children? Kate would be alright because she had Joycie and Mum with us three was almost overqualified, but what about the other two?

Mum, ever resourceful, came up with the plan that she could loan out her spare children to her mother and sister.

"But Nelly," said her mother. "What will happen to us if they find out?"

"They'll put us in prison that's what would happen," said Alice.

"How are they gonna find out?" Asked Mum. "If we all go in together they won't know which child belongs to who. Johnny stands out with his hair, but it would be the same if he was with me as it would be if he was with Alice."

"Nelly," said Kate. "You do get some mad ideas, and you don't bother to think of the consequences. Do you?"

"The consequences are," said Mum. "If we don't share my kids they will stay here and probably get bombed to death, and we will be stuck somewhere worrying about them."

"She has got a point there," said Alice.

"How would we work it out then?" Said Nanny.

After a bit more arguing it was decided that Nanny would carry in Jeanie, who was only a baby so could not open her trap to give the game away. Eddy would stay as Nell's son and I would be rehearsed into calling Aunt Alice, 'Mummy.' The fact that my hair was by now a carrot coloured ginger and Alice's was jet black like Mum's, never daunted anyone for a second.

The night before the interview Eddy and I were sleeping at Nanny's and while we were dozing off I tried to explain the ramifications of our new relationships to him. I had come to the conclusion that we would now be cousins, like us three and Joycie. I had also worked it out that if Eddy had gone with Nanny instead of Jeanie he would be my Uncle. Eddy wasn't able to grasp this no matter how hard I tried to explain. I then realised that if Eddy would have been my uncle it meant that Jeanie was now my aunt; but she was only a baby, so it wouldn't be right. Then I fell asleep.

The following morning, we had to go on a bus to some place up West to be registered. After a lot of hanging around and queuing and moving along passages, the eight of us were ushered into an office. I walked confidently into the room wearing my short trousers and jacket, convinced that 'Mummy,' must get me out of London. This was my first exercise in method acting. Even though I knew nothing about it, I instinctively knew that I should be thinking myself into the part.

We were in a room with some inspector behind a big desk who asked the women lots of questions, and even though I wasn't asked anything I did my best to help by chipping in whenever I could. When it was all over and we were outside, the aunts took the piss out of me by saying that I had over done it and I should not have called Aunt Alice, "Mummy," every few words. I denied it with the true facts that if she really had been my Mum I would have called her Mummy at least five or six times anyway. Whether I did or didn't, I must have been convincing and fooled the checker, because we got the right papers stamped and were to get evacuated together.

We left London on an officially organised train with all the other evacuating families. Wearing as much as we could because we were only allowed one case between us. Us kids had labels pinned on to us and had to carry our gas masks. The two baby girls had big gas masks that they could go to sleep in and you could look through a large cellophane window to check if they were still alive and breathing when the gas fell. Fortunately, we never had to use them to save our lives, instead we used them as toys as we got older.

The journey to our new billet took hours and hours and we had various changes of train. This meant being woken from sleeping on the seat or on someone's lap then helping to drag our cases and bags off of one train after which we were left standing about while we waited for the next train to arrive. While this was happening, we were constantly told to try to keep warm and not to let ourselves get separated before we arrived somewhere. It was always 'somewhere.' We were never told where we were going in case someone overheard about it and then sent a telegram or a pigeon to let Old Hitler know where we were. Once he knew that he would put our names on a bomb and send it over on a plane and that would be the end of us all. So I suppose it was always for the best that we never knew where we were going until we got there.

It was bitterly cold in the early hours of the morning, when we were finally ushered off the train, with lots of other people, and told to get onto a single decked bus that would take us to a reception centre. I was glad we were with the rest of the family, because we could all snuggle up to keep warm. Some women were on their own with only one kid and apart from looking worried and bewildered they were shaking with the cold in the night air.

In trying to find us a billet the people who were in charge, known as The Evacuation Committee, were desperate for the family to separate and go to different places. They argued that to find a home for four mothers, with two boys and two girls in the same billet would be impossible. They used the usual excuse, that there was a war on and that we all ought to pull together, adding that some things just could not and would not be done. Nanny and her daughters stood united beside their collective guns and refused to be split up. They offered to take over any empty shed so that we could all stay together. This meant a day and a night of uncomfortable living in the centre and deep sighs from the men and women of the committee. Eventually the family's stubbornness was rewarded and Miss Lavender of the committee, informed us that they had at last, with tremendous difficulty, found us a billet at Hill Barton Farm, in the village of Berrynarbour, not far from Ilfracombe.

3 HILL BARTON FARM

The eight of us with our cases and bags were put onto the back of a lorry and driven to our new home. It was late afternoon when we drove up a hill, along the track that let to the farmhouse. To my almost five- year-old eyes the place was enormous with its tall chimneys at either end of a long two-story brick building it even had some windows in the roof. In the middle of the house five wide steps led up to the front door which opened in to a large hall that had a parlour on either side and in the centre, was a small maid's room under the large curved staircase leading to the upper floors. After living in the two up, two down with the lavatory out the back, this farm was like a huge palace with its own Zoo.

Mrs. Erwin the farmers sturdy and efficient wife, with her upswept hairdo and brisk way of moving and speaking was at the door waiting to welcome us as we all piled into the hall with noise and talking. She allocated us a bedroom on the first floor. Eddy and I shared a bed and Mum slept with Jeanie. Alice and Nanny were given an attic room on the floor above and Kate with Joycie had a small room facing theirs. The pretend relationships we had used for the committee were now forgotten. They were only called upon when we had a visit from the committee or had to do something official, which was very rare.

"Get you all downstairs to the side parlour when you have settled all your cases and bags and I'll get Mr. Erwin to come and speak to you", said our landlady, as we separated on the first-floor landing. "We're all largely busy with the harvest at this time, so you will be a great help to us. Do any of you milk?"

The women, used to working in the clothing factories gave each other some old-fashioned looks, and chorused 'No!' and we all went to our rooms to unpack. Once she had finished her own unpacking Aunt Alice came to help us and in less than half an hour later we all met to wait for the farmer and his wife, in the downstairs front parlour.

It was a big room with two large windows looking out to the front of the house and one to the back, I couldn't see much out of that one because the hill was still rising behind the house. I noticed straight away that Eddy and I would have plenty of room to run around and that the armchairs were big enough to hide behind. As I looked at the sideboard I was convinced that there would be enough room to get right inside it and play trains. But that would come later. The women sat on matching chairs around the huge dark oak dining table. Nanny told me and Eddy to stop when we tried to make sparks, by stamping our steel tipped boots on the flag stone floor and we were warned that we had to be on our best behaviour otherwise we would be sent back to the bombing. So we sat, on a home-made rag rug in front of the fire which was lit and had a brass guard in front of it. Aunt Kate sang to Joycie as she bounced her up and down on her lap.

The handle on the parlour door clicked and the welcoming party of the Erwin's paraded down the hall. The party consisting of Mrs. Erwin, who was carrying a large tray, her husband and a younger woman. They were all looking very embarrassed as though they didn't know what to do or where to sit, as they marched down the parlour.

"I've got a tray of tea for you me dears," smiled Mrs. Erwin. "You must all be parched. There's plenty of milk for the young 'uns but not too much sugar I'm afraid. Help yourself to cake I only made them yesterday so they should be alright. This is Mr. Erwin, my husband. He is the owner and farmer."

I looked up at the red-faced, bull-dog of a man as he walked towards me and stood with his back against the fire to address the room. He spread his legs in their leather gaiters and leaned over us on his stick like a bombed house about to collapse.

"I have set aside some rooms for you all upstairs and you can use this parlour as your own. The other one, across the hall, well that be for the family and the workers. I shall be expecting you all to help as much as you can around the farm and to keep your part of the house clean. We ain't got no idea how long all this is a going to go on for so we had best make the best of 'un. I don't want to be bothered or worried by any of you. If you have any problems, go and see Mrs. Erwin or our daughter Grace. This is Grace" he said pointing the younger woman who was dressed like a maid in a fairy story. She nodded and moved towards the door as though she wanted to run out.

"Any produce," continued Mr. Erwin. "That you might need from the farm I'll be expecting you to pay for. We go to bed early and we rise very early, so I'll be expecting no noise at night. I think that is all, enjoy your tea."

Having had his say he marched quickly out of the room, followed by Grace neither of them paying any attention to the 'thank yous' expressed by the London women. Other than this opening speech, we saw very little of him during our time there, he kept himself hidden and only came out in times of high drama or festive occasions. I saw him once when I was on my own in one of the fields while I looking for Jeanie's spotted knickers that she had left in a hedge, but he just stomped by with Rex his dog at his heels and continued on his way without a word.

The door closed behind them and the women relaxed.

"Get on with your tea now. I'll join you, if that be alright?" Mrs. Erwin said as she smiled, sat down and they all began to gossip.

Everybody had to work on the farm so within two days of arriving, George Erwin the eldest son, had taken it upon himself to teach the sisters how to milk the cows. He was a good-looking man who must have been nearly thirty-year-old and had been what they called 'exempt from service.' Us kids weren't allowed in the cow shed to watch, but while we were waiting outside we heard lots of screaming and giggling from the girls along with the sound of buckets being kicked over. The cows were also doing a load of heavy mooing. After the first lesson, Basil, George's mate who lived on his own across the yard above the stable, joined in to help. George and Basil were enjoying themselves enormously, and so were the sisters, especially Aunt Alice and Mum, who due to George's expert tuition, eventually became very good milk maids. However, Aunt Kate never did get on with it so she concentrated on doing things with eggs and looking after the children.

I was frightened of the cows to begin with and tried to make my brother aware of the danger.

"What's wrong with them?" Eddy asked. "They look alright to me."

"I've heard," I said. "That they will toss you up in the air and when you land on the ground they will pierce you with their horns and you could bleed to death. No one, not even a proper Doctor, would be able to help you; no matter how many stitches they put into you."

"How do you know?" asked my brother.

"I must have read it in a book." I lied. Not knowing where I had got the information but feeling very important. "And another thing I know is that you should never wear anything red. Something in their eyes see red and they go nuts and want to chase and kill you."

This was something I knew for a fact and it was because of this knowledge, that I saved Jeanie's life for the first time. One afternoon Jeanie me and Eddy were out walking over the fields on our own when a cow started moving towards us. Remembering what I knew about cows and knowing that Jeanie, who was now almost three years old but moving very slowly, would be in mortal danger, I made her take off her red spotted knickers.

"It stands to reason," I tried to explain to the family later. "If she had fallen over, the cow would have pierced her, and she would have been dead forever. But I never told her to throw them in the hedge and forget about them once we had run away and got out of danger."

Despite all that I had told him Eddy wasn't frightened of the cows. Eddy, never seemed to be frightened of anything. Even though he was only four and a quarter and I was five and a quarter, he was much braver than me. As brothers, or rather foster brothers, we presented a strong contrast. I was a skinny, freckle faced, ginger haired and shy whereas he was a sturdy, blond, blue eyed bundle of outgoing personality. We got along very well together because I would be able to work things out and he would be able do them. We were best friends and were always there to help each other as we progressed through the weeks of adjusting to our new way of life.

One afternoon in December because of the rain we were all sitting around the fire in the parlour. Aunt Kate and Nanny were playing 'Beat your neighbours out of doors' with us. And the gramophone was playing a record. Suddenly there were terrible sounds of screaming and squealing coming from the cellar. It went on for ages and we all got very upset. Mum and Alice came into the room and said that they were killing a pig. All the women looked panicked, tried to change the subject and encouraged us to carry on with our game of cards.

Later that day, when everything had calmed down and it was all quiet around the house, Eddy and I were playing in the hall when Basil, who was a bit slow and almost eighteen, asked us if we wanted to go down the cellar to see the draining. I didn't really want to go but forced myself because the women were always telling me to grow up and to 'be a man.' I thought that if I went downstairs with Basil and I saw a bit of draining in the cellar it would help me become a bit more of a man.

We followed Basil down the steps into the dark cellar which had a strange meaty smell all around and after he had hung his hurricane lamp on a nail Basil pointed towards the corner.

"There 'un be," he said.

I saw a huge pink pig and its big dark shadow, hanging from a hook by its back legs that had been tied together. Its eyes were closed and it was dripping blood into a tin bath that had been placed under its head. I didn't like it. Basil must have sensed my fear because he put out his arm and drew me towards him.

"Sod being a man," I thought to myself. "This is horrible."

I wanted to back away but somehow couldn't bring myself to be such a namby-pamby. I just stood there and shuddered. Basil drew me closer to him and stepped behind me. I became very conscious of my body between his thick legs as he put his arm across my chest as if to protect me.

"Don't worry Johnny, there's squit to be afraid of," he whispered, and I could feel his breath in my ear as he bent over me. "That ain't no pig no more. That now be only pork. Just think of how good he'll taste come Christmas."

Being near Basil made me feel better, especially when he ruffled my hair and ran his hand under my chin. I was able to pluck up the courage to look at the dead pig again. As Basil put his hand over my shirt and stroked my chest, I was wondering how they had killed it and then I saw the gash across its neck.

"They cut its throat?" I whispered.

"They must have done it with a big knife," said Eddy.

"That's right," said Basil, "a great big sharp knife, very sharp,"

By now Eddy had got bored and having more courage than I had, he just turned around and back went upstairs.

Basil then went into details of how they had to hold the animal down and how it screamed and again how sharp the knife had to be. All this information made me pull away even further from the pig, and closer to Basil who knelt down and put both his arms around me.

"But don't ye worry, Johnny," he said laughing and nuzzling my neck. "Nothing like that is going to happen to you. You're my brave boy. I'll look after thee."

Then he picked me up and held me close to his chest with one arm, while he took the lamp down with the other and while he was carrying me upstairs he brushed his mouth across my face. We weren't down there very long but when I got upstairs and back into the parlour I felt quite strange. It was as though I had been warmed up by the fire even though it had been very cold in the cellar.

However, when Mum found out she let fly at Basil.

"What the bleeding hell were you doing?" She asked. "You ought to have more sense than to take a couple of kids down to see a thing like that. It could give them nightmares. And what would have happened if he had dropped the lamp? They could have be burned to death.

You need to think about what you are doing with a couple of boys and in future you ask me if you want them to see that sort of thing."

Basil just shook his dark head and smiled. Although I didn't like the blood or the smell, I did like Basil a lot more after that. Especially as he often gave me piggy backs and swings.

As December drew on we children were getting very excited because Father Christmas would be coming. We had sent our notes flying up the parlour chimney very early in the month writing a list of presents and promising to be good so that he would bring us the things we wanted. The women got excited because Mr. Erwin had agreed to let their husbands come to stay at the farm for Christmas.

Our dad was the first to arrive on Sunday. Mum and us kids had walked down the hill to meet him because from the farmhouse you could see the cart coming for ages before it got to the gate. He was carrying a gun, or rather a rifle, but we weren't allowed to go anywhere near it. His regiment was the Royal Engineers and even though I didn't know what an engineer was, I had already made up my mind to be one. I was convinced that when I became an engineer I would be a man at last.

Joyce's dad, Uncle Aggie, arrived in the evening. He had got early leave but hadn't been able to let Aunt Kate know in time. When he knocked at the door Aunt Kate nearly burst her stays with surprise. That night all the grown-ups went down to Berrynarbour for a drink. We children were made to sleep in the ground floor maid's room. All in the same bed, two boys up one end two girls down the other. It all seemed a bit unnecessary to me.

By Tuesday, it was Christmas Eve, and everything got really thrilling when Farver arrived with two accordions, uncle Arthur and his girlfriend Margie plus uncle Ernie, aunt Alice's boyfriend. They had all managed to come down by train which meant that the whole East End family were together. Everyone agreed that the war might still be raging but we were going to have a grand Christmas. We had a great sing song in the parlour and we were allowed to stay up late.

On Wednesday it was Christmas Day. I woke up on a camp next to Uncle Ernie, who had to be kept apart from Aunt Alice because they weren't married. Eddy and Jeanie were in another camp bed on the other side of the room and it was very frosty out.

Father Christmas had left both Eddy and me a painted, wooden policeman that Farver had made, and was put together so that it moved its arms and legs, Farver liked doing that sort of thing. We also got second hand comic book each, plus a sock with fruit in it and a cracker sticking out of the top; it would be a long time before we saw crackers again. As our main present us boys had been promised a trip to Ilfracombe. to see the pantomime 'Cinderella.' We knew the story very well and were really looking forward to it.

We had a great Christmas dinner with lots of meat and vegetables and best of all mince pies and Christmas pudding and Jeanie nearly choked on a silver three penny bit. The whole of our family and all the Erwins were eating together and when the pork was dished up, Aunt Alice known as 'the sausage scoffer,' said that it was the best bit crackling she had ever tasted. In the evening Farver and Uncle Arthur played the accordions, and Eddy and I took it in turns to wind up the gramophone when the records were played, and the grown-ups danced. They all had a drink so that they could to toast a victory, and hoped that it came very soon. I had a dance with aunt Alice and we all did knees up Mother Brown and the Hokey Cokey, which made us laugh when Mum held her bosoms so that they wouldn't bounce when she put her whole self it. I was just about awake when we were carried to bed and it was well past nine o/clock. As it turned out and due to that Bastard Hitler, that was the last time the whole family would ever be together.

The men all left on Boxing day to go back to their units, and Aunt Margie went back to London with Farver. Unfortunately, the day after that me, Jeanie and Eddy caught the measles and were forced to stay in the house for three weeks. Most of that time in a darkened room to protect our eyes otherwise they said we would go blind. We never did get to see Cinderella. We heard all about it from the grown-ups who did get to see it, but it wasn't the same somehow. I didn't see a real live show until 'Soldiers in Skirts,' in which a lot of men pretended to be women.

In the new year, Mum and Aunt Alice got a job at the gas mask factory in Barnstaple and I had to go to the village crèche. Eddy, Jeanie and Joycie didn't have to go; just me. I was there from half past nine till four o/clock when a grown up would be at the gate to take me back to the farm. I hated it. No, that's an understatement. I positively loathed it. I still get a desperate feeling of isolation when I think of that square, grey building and its bleak, grey yard where I was harassed something rotten.

The local kids all spoke a different language and took the piss out of me. They called me 'London Rummage.' Rummage being a local word meaning useless or a load of old shit. They didn't ask me to join in any of their games and when I tried to play with them they just pushed me away. There is nothing more desperately lonely than being rejected by a playground full of kids who were pointing and laughing at my skinny legs in my scuffed boots as I stood on my own against the wall. I hated the place and everyone there. Especially the teacher who insisted I eat the mess they called a school dinner. It was made of mixed up porridge oats, cocoa and sour milk that had been cooked until it was burnt and tasted like it might have been made from damp firewood mixed with rat's turds. I felt utterly alone without Eddy and I realised for the first time in my life that I needed him because I was too shy to make friends and he wasn't. My other big worry was the ongoing one: that my real Mother might have found out where I was and would come to collect me and no one would ever know where I had gone.

I was there just over a week before the grown-ups realised how terribly unhappy I was and took me away from my tormentors. Mum told the teachers that I would be educated back at the farm and they didn't make much of an objection as far as I knew. In my own mind I did find it hard to cope with the indignity of being taken away from the school. But I learned to cope with that because it was still a massive relief to get away from the daily bullying and torment.

At the farm I was taught by Nanny. She was a good teacher at the book stuff and I was quick to learn. But she really got on my wick when she kept repeating, "Now come along John you've got to stand up for yourself and be a man." I know she meant well but it didn't really help. It just made me more aware of what a weakling I was. Of course, I wanted to stand up for myself. Of course, I wanted to be a man. I wanted to be tough and not frightened of anything. Nobody wanted it more than me. But I couldn't do it. I was shy, I was often worried and scared. Scared of what? I didn't know. What's more I was painfully aware of these shortcomings. Somewhere deep in my five-year-old gut, I was conscious of the fact that I was a sissy. I knew it but I couldn't actually do anything about it. Well not overnight anyway.

Now, as a grown man, I wonder what it is in our makeup that will make some kids from the earliest age reclusive and unsure while others are secure, gregarious and utterly confident. Having been around many children over the years, I have come to no conclusion about what mysterious programme of genes and circumstances cultivates the introvert from the extrovert? Or why some introverts become extremely extrovert as a defence mechanism, as I eventually did.

We stayed at Hill Barton for over a year. During that time Dad, Farver and the Skelton Uncles came down whenever they could, as did other relatives and friends from the East End. As far as I can recall none of Dad's relations from Hendon, ever came down. Not many memories linger, considering such a long stay. Perhaps because the time was mostly happy with very little drama. Looking at the map while writing this I found it strange that we never went to the seaside which is curious when we were so near the coast. Presumably because it was all blocked off due to the war, there were restrictions on access to lots of beaches due to the threat of invasion.

Back to being a child again; one memory I have was when dad had come down for Easter. Mum, who was not the best cook in the world by a long chalk, had promised to make us a spotted dick. This was a suet pudding stuffed with currents and sultana's. We were going to have it for tea with Birds custard after our corned beef sandwiches. I was looking forward to it because I loved cakes and buns or anything with currents in it. Unfortunately, when she took the steaming pudding from the pot on the fire, everyone was shocked to see that she had boiled it in a bright blue head scarf. Her sisters screamed with laughter and we had to content ourselves with having condensed milk sandwiches instead. It was years before Mum lived that down.

"After all," said Nanny trying to help. "No one wants to eat a blue spotted dick."

One of my favourite stories was the one when Aunt Alice, walking the fields with Nanny, stopped to do a bit of a piddle by the hedge while her mother kept a look out. While she was peeing, there was a sharp shot from a gun that frightened Aunt Alice so much, she fell back into the ditch. The screams of both women must have frightened the gunman because no one came anywhere near them. It was only in the evening when George and Basil popped in to our parlour they admitted it was them.

"We're very sorry Alice m'dear," said George. "But we were out hunting and suddenly saw this white thing bobbing up and down in the bushes across the meadow and though it was a rabbit,"

"You saucy sod, you trying to tell me you took me for a rabbit?" said Alice. "The trouble is, when I fell in the ditch, I landed on some nettles and now I've got a rash all over my arse!"

Then they all fell about laughing.

Mrs. Erwin was always far too busy to have much to do with us kids, even so I did get a bad telling off from her on the occasion when I had somehow escaped the attention of the grown up and filled an enamel bowl with water from the duck-pond. I was showing Eddy how to make the day-old chickens swim in it and two of them had drowned before she happened to pass and saw what I was doing. She pulled me away, still clutching wet feathers and in no uncertain terms told me what a dreadful and cruel boy I was. She then marched me up the front steps and returned me to aunt Kate, who more or less said the same thing and gave me a clump round the head.

The most vivid and long-lasting memory I have of that time happened in the early Autumn, not long before we returned to London. It concerned Mary Batterson, the German Spy, who must have got herself back into favour because she had come to stay in Devon for a fortnight. She was given the maid's room under the stairs, which by then had been turned into a small bedroom for the friends and relations who occasionally came down from London. We kids often played in there when it was not being occupied, so I knew that it was furnished with just a single bed, a chair and a pink marble wash stand by the door with a bowl and jug on it.

The drama took place on a dull Saturday afternoon. It was far too wet to go out to play so Eddy and me were confined to the parlour. We had played Ludo, tiddly winks, snakes and ladders, snap as well as beat your neighbours out of doors until even the grown-ups were bored and fed up. In an effort to ease the monotony, Eddy and I had got into a race up and down the parlour. The race track was from the mat in front of the fire then running down the room and into the hall to touch the closed front door which was the winning post. This meant that we had to run past the maid's room in which, unknown to us, Batto the Spy was trying to get a bit of afternoon shut eye.

After the third race, which I won, we turned away from the winning post ready to go back to the parlour to start again. Suddenly we were stopped in our tracks by the maid's door being thrown back and Mary bursting into the hall. She was wearing a short cream flannelette night dress and pink bed socks. With her glasses on the end of her nose and her short, cropped hair all spiked up, she looked like Keyhole Kate from the Beano Comic having a nightmare.

"Will you two boys stop making that dreadful noise," she commanded. "This is not a playground, it is a place of residence and I am trying to get some rest. Now go back to your mother and annoy her if you must aggravate someone. I've had enough!" She then crossed to the parlour door and called down the room to the women. "Nelly, when are you going to teach these boys some discipline. They are a disgrace." With that she turned on her pink socks and returned to her bedroom, slamming the door behind her.

Subdued and a bit wide eyed at this sudden turn of events, Eddy and I returned to sit back on the mat in front of the fire. After sitting quietly for a little while we started to see the funny side it. In all honesty, she did look a bit of a sight. We kept nudging and giggling with each other and after a brief whispered conversation we got up, ran back to Batto's room and knocked on the door.

"Bed sock rummage," we called. Now fully conversant with the local dialect. "Bed sock rummage!"

We shut the door behind us so that she wouldn't know who had said it and ran back to sit on our mat. We waited for the apparition to appear again. Nanny told us to sit down and stop it and Aunt Kate said she would tell us a story. But we were not in the mood for a story. We repeated our game which was much more fun despite the grown-ups nagging us. Still nothing happened. So after one last run and still no reaction we got bored and gave it up.

Aunt Kate, with Joycie sitting on her lap, began reading to us about 'Jack and the Beanstalk.' She had just got to the bit where they decide to sell the cow when suddenly the door was thrown open and crashed against the wall. 'Batto The Spy,' came padding fast down the parlour towards the family group. When she got to Eddy and me she grabbed us by the hair and lifted us up. We were about six inches off of the mat. Then without saying a word she dropped us back onto the floor. That done, she turned with a loud grunt and swept out of the room slamming the door behind her.

There was a stunned silence. All the women sat still, not believing what they had just witnessed. Eddy and I started to feel the pain and began to whimper as we rubbed out heads.

"She's hurt your soddin' kids, Nell," said Aunt Kate, in a shocked quiet voice.

"That bloody cow," said Mum, as she jumped out of her armchair, threw aside a shirt she was mending and ran down the parlour after Mary.

"Nelly, don't you hurt her," warned Nanny, as she ran around the table to follow her daughter.

The warning fell on deaf ears. By now the full animal instinct of a protective mother was upon Nelly. She burst through the parlour door and rushed to the maid's door which had been slammed shut. From behind it came the sound of furniture being dragged across the floor.

Mum turned the handle and began to push the door open but the bed inside was restricting it. She managed to force just enough space for her to get an arm in as she tried to reach Miss Batterson. By now Nanny, Aunt Alice and both us boys were in the hall, Aunt Kate, Jeanie and Joycie were on their way. Mum, unable to hit the woman with her arm managed to find the jug on the wash stand and aim it at her adversary. She withdrew her arm and reached towards the umbrella stand against the wall where she grabbed one of the heavy walking sticks and got it around the door as she tried to hit Mary. It must have landed hard because we heard a solid crack on some bony part of Mary followed by a loud yell.

"Take that you bastard bitch", Mum screamed through the gap in the door. "You hurt my kids! I'll fucking kill you!"

"Don't Nelly! Don't you will kill her," yelled Nanny as she wrestled with her daughter from behind reaching into the room and dragging the stick from Mum's hand. "Nelly, stop it! Stop it!"

Mum immediately seized another stick and sent it flying into the room towards Batterson. This was followed by two more sticks, a pair of Wellington boots and a broken umbrella. After those went a large torch and two seventy-eight RPM records. There was a satisfying crash as they hit the back wall splintering vinyl around the room and over Mary who let out a scream.

"Got you, you bloody cow!" said Mum, who was now in such a frenzy that it took her Mother, both sisters and Grace Erwin to drag her away from the door.

Miss Batterson left quietly later that night. Goodness knows where she went but I am sure she felt that she was far safer with the Nazi bombs than she would have been with our mother.

Eddy and I had sore heads for over a week and had to have our hair combed very carefully.

In late October nineteen forty-one, uncle Ernie came down on embarkation leave and proposed to Aunt Alice, who must have agreed because before us kids knew what was going on, we were thanking the Erwin's for a wonderful year and returning home in time for Christmas. Mum had begun to get fat and there was talk of another baby coming.

During our stay in Devon the bombing of London had eased but George Erwin's assault on Nell's affections had increased. It was rumoured around the family for years afterwards, that the child on its way might have had something to do with George. When I was grown up I asked her directly if these rumours were true.

"He asked me to marry him lots of times," she told me. "He even promised to buy a bungalow for me and you kids. But I loved your Father, so I had to tell him 'No', even though he was a good-looking man and always held my coat up for me to put on. Anyway, you only have to look at her now to see that she looks more like Eddy than any of 'em."

4 RETURN TO LONDON, BOW AND BERYL

On our return to London we weren't able to go back to living in our house in Hemming Street because it had been severely blasted by explosions and bombs was completely uninhabitable. Having nowhere else to go we moved in with Nanny and Farver. This meant that we all slept in the upstairs front bedroom. Alice, who hadn't got a place of her own had Arthur's room at the back while Nanny and Farver stayed where they were in the front room downstairs. It was a bit cramped but there was a war on and everybody had to do their bit, and pull together, including us kids. They constantly reminded us of this whenever we complained about anything. I think they used it as an excuse to shut us up a lot of the time.

There was a lot of talk about Pearl Harbour being bombed. Being just over six I couldn't imagine why anyone wanted to bomb a harbour full of pearls which I knew were very valuable. Especially those worn by Queen Mary, the old girl in a long frock whose picture I had seen in the Picture Post. It turned out to be the Japanese that had done it and they were now our enemies as well as the Nazis and all the Americans were now our friends. Which I thought was good because they made the best films.

In early December, not long after Pearl Harbour, we heard of a flat going at Bromley-by-Bow. We got very excited about getting a home of our own again and Mum took me with her to Hemming Street so that we could have a look around to find what was left of our belongings to salvage for our new home.

It was a real shock to see the state of number fifteen. The whole of the downstairs front window had been blown out and the gap had been filled by our front room carpet, which was all ripped and filthy dirty. The street door was hanging on two of its three hinges, but it was stuck. This meant that we had to push it real hard until eventually we moved it just wide enough for me to slip through the side and get in. Behind the door was a pile of bricks and a broken chair that looked as if someone had piled them there to keep it shut or maybe to keep people out. Possibly Farver or a friendly neighbour. I moved the rubbish out of the way as quickly as I could so that Mum could get inside and join me.

We walked down our dusty passage and looked into the front room. It was lit by beams of light coming through the holes in the carpet that was pretending to be a curtain. This had been our best room, cut glass dishes had stood on the polished sideboard, a black marble clock and bronze ornaments had stood on an embroidered runner on top of the mantelpiece. A china vase had stood in the centre of the oak table covered by a cream linen tablecloth. Mum had always taken great pride in keeping everything shining and polished. Now only the heavy furniture was left, the ornaments, cloths and photographs had disappeared or lay smashed to bits on the floor smothered in dust and rubble.

"We've still got the dining room suite," said Mum, as she closed the sideboard door. "Although the three piece is ruined. You wait down here Johnny. I'll have a look upstairs."

We carefully trod our way further into the house. The coal cellar, under the staircase, had had its door ripped off and was empty of fuel. I waited at the bottom while she went upstairs to check the two bedrooms. Standing there on my own it all felt a bit strange because although it was our house it didn't feel like home anymore. I could hear mum going into her bedroom in the front.

"The furniture 's still here but there's no bedclothes only the mattress," she called down as she explored her cupboards. "They've taken daddy's clothes from the tallboy. Sod it! My glass dressing table set's gone as well. That was a wedding present from Arthur and Alice," Then her voice cracked. "Oh no! Those bastards! They've nicked me wedding dress and all me clothes and shoes."

She said no more. I listened to her moving around her room and then go into ours. When she returned downstairs. Her eyes looked hard and her lips were pressed together as she went past me into the back room. I followed.

We stood in the doorway and looked at what was left of what used to be our living room. Table, chairs, the baby's high chair, cupboards and the wringer were all lying across the floor. Covered by ripped clothing, torn tea-towels, letters, smashed crockery, saucepans, and even bits of our toys, everything had been broken and thrown around the room.

The curtains were hanging and ripped from the window with its cracked and broken glass.

I heard Mum take a deep breath as she moved into the room and picked up the table. I helped by turning the chairs the right way up. I found the spout less teapot under an old newspaper and put it on the dirty table. Mum found our tin kettle and when she went to put it on the grate she saw among the soot and broken fire bricks a sheet of paper. She knelt on the floor and removed the paper. I watched as she straightened it out on her swollen baby filled belly.

"It's me marriage lines," she said.

She stayed where she was, and I could see her shoulders shaking as she knelt in front of the fireplace.

I stood there for a while not knowing what to do. It is a bit difficult when you are not quite six years old and these things are happening. You know you ought to do something but have no idea what it is. In the end I just put my arm across her back. Because she was kneeling she wasn't much bigger than me and I patted her on the shoulder just like I'd seen grown-ups do that when people were upset. She turned and pulled me roughly to her and gave me a hard cuddle.

She was a strong woman and we were all having to get used to bad times, so it wasn't long before she stopped crying and stood up. As she did she caught sight of herself in the splintered mirror above the fireplace. She looked down at me and gasped. I looked up at her. She was covered in black streaks and blotches where her sooty hands had spread tears across her face. She picked me up and in the crazy angles of the mirror, I saw my own soot stained face next to hers. We both burst out laughing at the sight of these two peculiar faces staring back at us.

"Not only have they looted the house, but the bastards have made me look like Al Jolson," she laughed, as she put me back on the floor. "Come on, let's put what we can in a carrier and go home to Nanny's."

We didn't stay long with Nanny and Farver, in early December we moved to Bow. The furniture, that hadn't been looted from Hemming Street, was brought to our new flat in Coventry Cross. Sheets, towels, curtains and clothes had all been pinched and as there was no money or coupons available for new, second hand things had to be bought, borrowed and given to us.

"It's not gonna be much of a Christmas for the three of you this year," Mum told us. "So, expect much. The army allowance don't go far and I can't get a job 'till after the baby's born."

Our gifts from Father Christmas were for me, a silver cannon gun that shot matches from its barrel when you pulled back a wire lever. Eddy got a cowboy suit, with a gun and Jeanie was given a small doll dressed in a pink knitted hat and dress who lay in a dark brown Bakelite bath. We had other bits and pieces that the family managed to get for us but those are the things that stick in my mind. I showed Jeanie how to change and bath her little doll on our first-floor balcony I also shot Eddy with my cannon and he got me with his cowboy gun. We had to shout out, 'BANG' when we used that because we couldn't get caps.

Beryl, our new sister, arrived on 13th of January and we were now two boys and two girls. Everyone came to see us. Nanny was at the birth and was soon followed by the aunts. As well as them there were also the great aunts from East Ham and Hackney, On the third day came the aunts from Hendon, along with Nell's school friends and friends of the family. They all wanted to coo over the new baby and see for themselves whether she looked like George Erwin or Dad. They all had to kiss us children when they arrived and then kiss us again when they left. Sometimes I was given a treat of a three- penny bit pressed into my hand with a warning that it was for all of us. I liked the money, but I definitely didn't like the kissing. Although I didn't know at the time it was the kissing that caused the trouble that continued between Mum and Dad through the next thirty years.

It started when two friends of Nanny's, May Carol and her sister Stylish Dora, came on a visit from Dalston.

"We've come to see the new baby and to wish you all a happy nineteen forty-two," said May as Nanny opened the front door.

Dad, who was home on compassionate leave, was serving tea and a home-made cake left by his mother, Granny Hendon. As well as bread and margarine which was being passed around on the new, second hand, plates. Mum was in the bedroom being yelled at and us three were roaming around the flat getting in the way. There was a lot of activity as five or six visitors wandered between the bedroom, the kitchen, the passage and the living room.

However, when it came time for May Carol and Stylish Dora to leave, us kids were called into the bedroom to say our goodbyes. Dora didn't kiss us because she was wearing her new Christmas coat and didn't want kids all over it, so she just ruffled our heads. May Carol, an ample woman with glasses and tight dresses, was definitely out to enjoy a long farewell. She picked up Jeanie and gave her a big shaking cuddle as though she was a rag doll and as she bent down to return Jeanie to the floor she grabbed my face, in her podgy hands, and planted a wet kiss on each cheek. I hated it. Especially as I could feel one of her rings digging into my chin. Lastly, she turned to Eddy, and with a squeal, like a rat running around the brewery, she picked him up and hugged him close to her chest before kissing him full on his mouth. I knew Eddy didn't like it either because I could see his naked knees trying to bash into her breasts.

"Oh, you naughty little man you!" she squealed in satisfaction, as she plopped him back on the lino. "You kiss just like your father. Ta-ta then Nelly. She's a beautiful little girl and we'll see you when you're over your Mum's. Come on Dora, 'bye everyone! Thanks for the tea, Ted."

With a lot more of that sort of chat the Dalston dames left the bedroom and eventually the flat, seen out by Nanny.

Nothing was said at the time but later, when everyone had gone, and we were in bed, I heard Mum yelling at Dad, about kissing other women and saying that she will murder May Carol as soon as she can get up and about again. This was the first time I had heard them rowing for ages. I hated it. I snuggled up to Eddy, who was dead asleep and buried my head between his back and the covers, just like I always did when I was worried or disturbed.

Whether there was any truth in Nelly's accusation I never found out, even though the arguments continued, and the accusations became and more vitriolic over the years.

As I got older the following questions often nagged at me; did Dad have a snog with May Carol, in the kitchen, while his wife was bearing his child in the bedroom? Had they had amorous knowledge of each other before? Was it just May Carol showing off or could it have been a deliberate malicious slander to get Mum angry because they had never liked each other? On the other hand: perhaps it was just an off the cuff bit of banter that May Carol was unaware that she had uttered. However now, as I write this years later, I come to the conclusion 'No, I don't think May was unaware. I can still see a malicious glint in her eyes as she put Eddy down on the floor and looked at Mum over her glasses. For the rest i.e. did they ever have an affair? God alone knows. Even now I Would not hazard a guess.

5 STARTING SCHOOL

We lived in Bow just long enough to start school, which due to the birth and everything else meant that our beginning came after most of the other kids had already completed their first term

Towards the end of January, when Mum had got up and about again following her confinement, we were told that we were going to have to start school at Blakeley Street Primary, in Stepney. We were informed that we would start there rather than at a school in Bow, because Mum was determined to return to live near her family in Stepney as soon as possible. It also meant that we could be looked after and cared for during the school term by the aunts and Nanny.

On the Monday when we were due to start it was freezing cold. Mum had put the electric bars of the fire on to give us a bit of warmth as we boys dressed ourselves and Mum sorted out baby Beryl. As soon as I was ready I helped Jeanie to dress while Eddy had a wash. Then I had a wash and helped Jeannie to wash. I had to yell at her to make her stand still. We all ate a bit of porridge and got our big coats on. Then I put up the push chair and helped mum carry it down the stairs into the street where she strapped Jeanie into it. By the time I'd pushed it to the bus stop I was exhausted because apart from all that physical activity there was also the emotional wear and tear. After my experiences in Devon I was dreading what might happen to me at this new school but there was no getting out of it this time. I was well over six now and the bombing was no excuse for me to stay at home any longer because everybody had to carry on and do their bit. The consolation was that Eddy would be starting with me this time. He trotted along beside me holding on to the side of the push-chair while Mum carried Beryl and the bag.

"Get off at Watney Street Market and ask for Nanny," Mum had instructed me in case we got lost.

When we got to the bus stop there was no queue which meant that we had probably just missed one. We waited ages for the number forty which was going all the way to Aldgate. Mum, as usual started telling everyone all her business as soon as they joined the queue.

"They're both starting school to-day only the two boys, she's only three. The baby's called Beryl. Yes, it is an unusual name isn't. it. We're going to Stepney, I was brought up there, we moved here after we got bombed out. The ginger one? Yes, it's a lovely colour. He takes after his grandfather; he had ginger hair. They do all have different coloured hair don't they and all blue eyes apart from the eldest. No, he gets them from my husband's side of the family. Be-low here comes the bus."

The rush again. Mum gave me Beryl to hold while she got Jeanie out of the push chair and folded it up. Eddy was given the carrier bag with Beryl's baby stuff in it. The bus pulled up and we waited on the kerb while Mum tried to squeeze the pram under the stairs. Her new best friend from the queue called Iris, a skinny woman with a massive bum, tried to help but only managed to hinder and hold up the other passengers who were trying to get past me and Beryl inside the lower deck. The conductress came down from upstairs and had to get off the bus to sort things out. By this time this was done the whole of the bus knew that we were aboard and everything there was to know about us. Talk about embarrassing! Eddy and Jeanie who were still on the kerb were heaved aboard by desperate passengers and people swapped their seats so that we could all sit near each other. Eventually the bell was rung, and we moved off as the conductress who we got to know as Lena, took our fares. One adult and two halves.

Eddy and I were given our tickets. They had been clipped by a metal thing hanging around Lena's neck that made a pinging sound and produced a small perfectly round hole on the side of each ticked. I desperately wanted that machine and straight away decided that I would be a bus conductor when I grew up. The girls were too young to have tickets of their own, and anyway they didn't need seats because I was holding Beryl and Jeanie sat on Mum's lap. Our tickets were orange and Mum's was a white one but they both had lots of very small printing on them with the price, in a big red letter, on top of the printing. I felt very grown up and held my ticket with pride as I examined it. Jeanie, who had by now got the miseries was given Mum's to hold, which she tore and made all wet when she put it in her mouth. I got really frightened that Mum would be thrown off the bus if Jeanie swallowed the bits but I didn't dare say anything in case Lena saw what was happening and chucked us off straight away.

Mum didn't seem at all bothered. We had hardly got to the Blackwell Tunnel before she was telling everyone, whether they wanted to hear it or not, the history of our family. All about how we had been bombed out: all about Devon, how long she had been married and even how she had been brought up in Planet Street. Most of the passengers were women and by the time we got past Poplar, everyone in the downstairs of the bus was talking to everyone else.

'Watney Market, coming up love," said Lena, when we were half way along Commercial Road.

"Johnny give me the baby and you take Jeanie's hand 'till I've got the pushchair off, Eddy hold on to the carrier bag and don't run away," said Mum. "When we get off you boys wait on the pavement. Johnny, you take care of Jeanie till I get off then take the baby while I put Jeanie in the push chair. Stay where you are now and wait 'till the bus stops, otherwise you'll get flung off. Eddy hold on to the rail!

Some passengers who were getting off said they would help, but as the bus pulled up a lot of people who were sick of waiting tried to get on, as the other people tried to get off so that everything and everybody got in a terrible muddle. Mum then managed to get the pushchair stuck in the hole again and passed Beryl to a lady who was just getting on I thought the bus would go and we would never her again. But Lena yelled at the driver to wait till we were all off which he did while an old man with a wheezy chest helped mum with the pushchair and Beryl was returned to us as the bus moved away.

Once we were on the pavement Eddy started swinging on the chains that were hanging between two small pillars at the side of the road and Jeanie wanted to let go of my hand and had to be forcibly strapped into the pushchair.

"Now come on all of you, let's get a soddin' move on and get to that school. You're gonna be late on your first day!"

We walked as fast as we could past the bombed-out shops along Commercial Road then turned left into Watney Street Market. The top end had been completely devastated. Across the road we could see right into Winterton Street, the next turning along. There was nothing left standing in that street apart from the ovens of a bombed-out bakery and two air shafts for the Metropolitan Line. The Nazis had been trying to land bombs down them to stop the troops getting to the docks.

It was on the Winterton bomb site that I would later loose my virginity.

"That's where I got married," said Mum, as we passed what was left of Christ Church on our left. "That was a fortnight before I took you Johnny, I was dressed all in white satin just like Jean Harlow. Come on step it out we're nearly there. Don't forget, I'll meet you at the gate after the morning classes and we'll have dinner at Nanny's, before you have to go back this afternoon."

We turned left into Blakeley Street went through a gap that had once been a gate and crossed the deserted school playground.

"They've all gone in," Mum said. "Never mind you'll just have to be a bit late. Come on."

We struggled through two swing doors with windows on the top so that I couldn't see what was beyond them. Inside the floors were stone and the walls brown tiles half way up with cream ones above. All the doors were brown with four panels of glass in the top and a brass handle in the middle. Considering all the bombing it was a wonder that any of the windows were still in, they must have been saved by the wide brown paper crosses that were stuck on them. We walked down the passage to a door without any windows marked 'The Head' and knocked.

"Come in." A woman's low voice said.

"It's me Miss Goss," said Mum as she opened the door and the five of us went into a small office. "Mrs. Halstead with Johnny Ross and Eddy Halstead. Sorry we're a bit late it's due to the bus being late but we're here now. But I don't know what class they've got to go to."

"Oh!" replied Miss Goss surprised at being disturbed. "Well, It is unfortunate that you have arrived so late. However, that being the case we had better get you to the correct classroom as soon as possible. You have missed assembly, I did warn you Mrs. Halstead that it might prove a little difficult to come all the way from Bow every day. Now if you would go to 'class one' at the end of the second corridor on the right. There you will find Miss Rough, who is going to be the boy's teacher. I'm sure you will be able to find it easily enough without my assistance. I would escort you, but I am expecting an urgent telephone call. The corridor is just along there."

There was no questioning her authority. Mum closed the door and we laughed as she pulled a face at Miss Goss behind it. We found 'class one' knocked at the door and after a sharp 'Enter!', turned the shiny handle and Mum ushered us in. About twenty-five mixed infants watched Eddy and me as we tentatively approached the desk of Miss Rough. A curved woman in blue with a pale face and frizzy hair. Beryl started to cry in Mum's arms.

"It's me Miss Rough, Mrs. Halstead with Johnny Ross and Eddy Halstead, we're a bit late due to the bus over running and me not knowing what class they had to go to."

Miss Rough, not a comforting name, got up from her desk and waddled towards us on fat ankles. She looked down and informed us that we had missed assembly but not to worry.

"Now which is John Ross, and which is Edward Halstead?"

We were identified, and she assigned us seats away from each other. I felt as though I was naked as I walked to a desk in the second row from the back and Eddy went to one by the wall at the front.

"I'll be going now boys," yelled Mum, from the front of the class, as though she was addressing an army. "Don't' forget you're coming to Nanny's for dinner. I'll meet you at the gate. So, wait for me there and don't run away. 'Bye Miss Rough, they're good boys and won't be any trouble."

Mum, turned the pushchair round and started to cry. She searched for her hanky in the brown carrier bag hanging from the push chair. I could feel the tears stinging the back of my eyes and my mouth made the shapes they often made when I wanted to cry. I tried to hold back my tears by pressing my lips together under my teeth. Miss Rough had opened the door for Mum and was standing waiting for her to go.

"Mummy loves you and I'll see you at the gate dinner time, don't worry it is only for a few hours. Jeanie let go the door. Bye boys."

She disappeared as Miss Rough closed the door behind her and turned towards her wide-eyed pupils. Our school days had begun.

It proved to be a simple routine to follow. In the morning we had assembly in the hall where we sang hymns and prayed for the King and Queen and for Hitler to be punched in the face. After that we went to 'class one' where we did sums, writing and other work play-time. At dinner time we went to Nanny's to eat. The afternoon was taken up with painting, plasticine or the sand table. Followed by a lie down on the bed for half an hour. The day was finished off by us doing a bit of reading and a story from Miss Rough. After school Mum, would finish her work at Nanny's pick us up and we would get the bus back to Bow.

One day was much like another. After a few weeks Mum, managed to get an outdoor job and began working from Nanny's house. This meant that we had to get up quite early followed by the usual scramble to get out and rush to the bus stop. There Mum always managed to get people to help her on the journey. The passengers often talked among themselves and we heard about the latest raids and of the people who had died or gone away. The war was still raging, but it wasn't as bad as the blitz. The sirens would send us rushing into the shelters, but it didn't matter too much because after only being at school a few weeks, I fell in love for the first time.

I fell in love with Colleen Lack. She was four weeks older than me but very pretty with soft brown hair, round chubby cheeks and big brown eyes. We did actually kiss; on the lips! Which, in our mixed infant minds was tantamount to being married and setting up home. I told Nanny that I loved Colleen when I went home to dinner one day. She went and told Aunt Alice, who thought it was a big laugh. Well it was no laughing matter to me because I really loved Colleen. The problem was that she lived in Jubilee Street which was on the other side of Commercial Road, and I was not allowed to cross it on my own. This fact alone made living together impossible. I did my best, I'd walk her to the top of Watney Market and then along to the traffic lights and kiss her goodbye when they turned orange. But it proved too difficult and the relationship dwindled until it was just touching hands over the sand table. It finally finished when we were sharing the same milk bottle at play time. She passed me her milk and I took a swig. Unfortunately, being thin and an orphan, I had to have cod liver oil to build me up. When I passed the bottle back to her she took a swig and then pulled a face. We never kissed again and gradually drifted apart. I suspect it was doomed from the start.

Mummy continued to hate living so far away from her mother and sisters. She constantly moaned about it complaining so much and so loudly that half the population of Stepney were doing everything they could to find us somewhere to live there. Everyone we knew was putting the word round the market and among the grapevine of families who might know someone who might know of somewhere for us to move to. Whatever they were doing it must have paid off, because before long we were leaving Bow and moving into three rooms and a kitchen on the top floor of a three-storied condemned house in Stepney.

6 51A TATE STREET

The air raids were a lot less frequent now although the Nazi's were still sending some planes over just to keep us on our toes. From what I managed to gather from the grown-up conversations "Gerry was a bit busy elsewhere.' Consequently, we were not too worried about the bombs when, on a bright Saturday morning, we woke up ready to move into our new home in Tait Street.

Dad had managed to get home on leave and drove the borrowed truck with all our belongings piled on the open back. Despite all our pleading and trying Eddy and I could not get permission to ride on the back of it. Instead we went, as usual, by bus and had to wait at Nanny's till the lorry arrived and everyone was needed to help get the stuff into the flat. Everyone that was except Jeanie and Beryl who were to be looked after by the two Andrews Sisters across the street from Nanny's at number fifteen.

Us boys walked round to find the new house with Aunt Margie and Aunt Alice. Our walk didn't take long because our new home was only just around the corner from Nanny's. Turn left at the bottom of Planet Street and past a couple of corner shops and into Bigland Street.

"That's your new house," said Aunt Margie, letting go of my hand and pointing to a three-story building with the lorry parked outside. "That one on the corner."

"Not the whole house," said Aunt Alice. "Just the top floor."

The front door was actually in Bigland Street, even though the address was Tait Street. This was because the ground floor used to be a carpet shop that had its two-door entrance across the corner. Our door had 51a, and a big black knocker on it, which you had to bang three times to get us. It was painted in chipped green paint just like the boards that covered the big windows and the padlocked doors belonging to the shop. Next to the front door was the side door that led into the yard and a small bit of earth called the garden. I always remember the hole that appeared in this door, when it was hit by the flying shrapnel that nearly killed Aunt Margie just before the following Christmas.

We ran down the middle of the street in time to watch Mum's large wardrobe, wrapped in blankets to stop it getting scratched, being hauled up the side of the house. Daddy and Uncle Arthur, pulled it in through the middle window at the top accompanied by a loud cheering from a crowd of about ten people who were watching the goings on. Mum, Farver and some men who I didn't know, were on the back of the lorry moving our sideboard forward and looking up at the rope coming down. Two rolled up blankets were slung out of the top window frame and as they unfurled they look like huge barrage balloons floating down. One fell on the pavement and Eddy and I rushed towards it only to be beaten by a young woman, who picked it up and handed up to the men on the lorry. Nanny came out of the front door.

"Don't you two start causing trouble," she said, as she walked towards the lorry. "You can give us a hand. There's lots you can be helping with instead of larking about out here."

We were given a box each and told to carry it up to our floor. We followed Aunt Alice, who was carrying our bed head, into the passage. It was quite wide with a bike resting against the wall underneath the open fuse boxes. There was torn lino on the floor and no carpet on the stairs. We got to the top of the stairs and crossed the first-floor landing smelling of cabbage and bad onions. I saw the open door of the lavatory, on the left, as I went on past it and up a narrow staircase to our own top floor. There was an awkward narrow bend in these stairs, which was why they had to bring the big furniture up through the window that was at the end of a small hall. I could see Daddy and Uncle Arthur leaning out of the window that had had its frame removed.

"Put your boxes in the kitchen," Aunt Alice told us, pointing to the room on the right. "I'll take this to your room."

We dumped out boxes just inside the door and ran out to watch the sideboard being dragged through the hall window. We saw them begin to untie the ropes and then rushed down the stairs to watch the blankets fly down again. As we ran across the first floor we both heard a scratching and growling sound from behind the door facing the lavatory.

"A dog!" we said, almost together, as we swung round the banister and scampered down the uncarpeted stairs to the front door.

Back in the street, we just managed to see the blankets fly down then ran back into the passage. I looked through a crack in the partition wall, into the disused shop. Once my eyes got used to the sunlight that shone through the boarded-up windows. It looked full of promise. I could see; display stands, counters with drawers in them, a big till and loads of things all covered in dust. We could have a really good game with all that if we could only get in there, I had just moved out of the way so that Eddy could have a look when Aunt Margie passed with an armful of bed clothes and told us that we ought to be outside helping and not messing around getting in everyone's way.

We were given a drawer each and told to put them in the sideboard in the front room when we got to the top. I had the knife drawer, which was lined in green felt, although we never used it to put knives in because the cutlery set had been looted when we got bombed out. We only had the second-hand ones now and they were always in the washing up bowl because we used them every day. We paused on the first floor to listen for the dog. There were two dark brown doors with a glass door in the middle leading to a small kitchen that was under our hall, but there was no sound of the dog now, so we carried on up to our flat.

At the top of the stairs facing the kitchen was a green wooden coal bunker. We went around behind it into the room on the left where the sideboard had been placed under the window that looked out over Tait Street. I had trouble getting my drawer in, but Eddy put his in with casual ease and then helped me. He was always much better at doing things like that.

'Let's see what's out of the window." I suggested, getting all excited.

We quickly dragged one of the dining room chairs towards the window and climbed on to the sideboard. In Bow, we had been on the first floor but now we were even higher up. By standing on the sideboard and leaning against the window we could see across all the roofs of the two-story houses towards the rail track that ran along Chapman Street at the bottom of Bigland Street. I'd always wanted a train set and now just by looking out of our window on top of the arches, was a real live one.

"What the bleedin' hell are you doin' up there?" shouted Mum, as she came in carrying a small drop leaf table. "You'll fall out of that window and brake your bloody necks. Get down, this minute, the pair of you! Get Down!"

She had that tone in her voice that brooked no argument and if either of us did it would be followed by a good hiding. We scrambled of the sideboard and got out of her way as she carried the table to a corner at the side of the tiled fireplace.

Back in the hall, we went to look at the room next door. This was obviously going to be our room because Aunt Alice and Aunt Margie were trying to put our bed together. We nipped in to help. The room had no fireplace, but it had two sets of windows facing in two different directions. Our old blue lino was already on the floor and Aunt Alice was standing at the back of the room holding the wooden bed head. Aunt Margie was trying to get the iron side of the spring base into two clamp things, that were on either side of it, at the top of each leg. She wasn't having much success because as she got one side in she couldn't balance it to drop the other side in. It seemed that the two sides had to drop straight, or they wouldn't go in at all. Both women were getting frustrated. Alice was much more frustrated than Margie who was more refined and worked in an office.

"Right, you two are just who we need," said Alice. "Take the side of the bed next to the wall, while Aunt Margie holds the other." This we did. "Now all of you lift. A bit higher, bring it towards me. Watch it boys, be careful. No! Lift it a bit higher. Down a bit Margie. That's it. Now slowly let it drop into those crevices. No, you've moved it out of the way, hold the soddin thing straight Johnny. Margie don't pull on it. Eddy, stop pulling it that way. That's it, now up and slowly down - that's it - go on! Done it!"

We gave a cheer, and all laughed. The bottom end was simple after that, it was just a case of lifting it up and placing the two crevices underneath the bits sticking out. We had done it and were feeling good.

Before they could ask us to help make the bed we ran out across the hall into a big room where the wardrobe was now standing. This would be for Mum and Dad as well as Jeanie and Beryl. Dad's tallboy was just being winched through the window as we came out and we were ordered to go down again for more stuff.

Nanny gave us saucepans this time which we banged with their lids as we ran up the stairs. Mum was coming behind us with a bowl full of crockery, tea towels and cutlery. One of the doors on the first floor opened and an old lady came out.

"Hello Nelly," said the lady. "Sorry I can't help you. I'd be willing but not with my leg. But I am keeping the dog out of the way."

"That's alright Mrs. Coakley," Mum said. "We've got lots of help, these are my boys. Johnny and Eddy. Say hello to Mrs. Coakley boys."

"Hello Mrs. Coakley."

We ran up our stairs to the kitchen and put the saucepans in the cupboard that was not ours but had been left behind. It had two glass doors at the top and flap, called a dipper, that pulled down to make a work surface. When the dipper was up it kept all the food fresh and away from the flies. Underneath this was a set of drawers and another small cupboard where we put the saucepans. We shut the cupboard door and ran down for our next load.

Ages later, when we were practically dead for need of food, Nanny arrived with spam sandwiches and doughnuts. The table and our chairs were now in the kitchen, so we ate in there. Over the sink was one cold tap and we were warned, that we must not put tea leaves down the plug hole or it would block the pipes. A bucket would be kept for that. A kettle was boiling on the gas stove which stood on four legs in the corner next to the door. While we ate we looked out of the window onto a row of back yards and at, what we were told was, the workshop roof. We had a cup of tea and then were allowed our doughnut.

When we had finished, and the grownups stopped to have their dinner, Nanny took us for a walk round to Cable Street Park. It was only a small park, but we had a good time playing on the swings, the slide and the maypole. Later we had a look inside St. Georges in the East Church, that had not been bombed but badly blasted. Through a big crack in one of the walls we saw coffin's in the crypt.

Nanny called us away because it was time to be making tracks.

"You'll be able to join the Children's Library when you get settled in," she said, as we were leaving the park. "There it is, right outside the gates."

When we got back, the lorry had gone, beds were made, curtains were being put up, furniture being organised and on the bare boards, mats being put down, lifted up and then put down somewhere else. We were kept in the kitchen and after a late tea, were put to bed in our new corner room. Jeanie slept with us because Daddy was home. Looking out of the side window we could see the dark shape of Bigland Street School. It was closed and unused since the Blitz. Eddy and I were talking about this before we fell asleep and decided that maybe there just weren't enough kids to go around anymore because so many of them were evacuated in the country. Some had even gone a million miles away to America and some were already dead. As the three of us snuggled up in bed on that first night we had no idea, that by the time we moved out; some of the family would be dead and new ones would be born.

I fell asleep trying to figure out if a million miles was further than Devon and found it very difficult to decide.

Dad had to go back to the Army and we had to learn to settled in. While we lived at 51A most of our time was spent in the kitchen which was partly for economic reasons of warmth and partly because our noise would not get on Mr. Coakley's nerves. It wasn't a big kitchen and by the time the table and chairs, the dipper and Beryl's high chair were in it, there was hardly any room for the five or six of us when Dad was on leave. It was a multi-purpose kitchen also used as our dining room, bathroom, playroom, where we did sums, jig saw puzzles, read Sunny Stories and played I-Spy. It was in the kitchen that we washed ourselves, our crockery and clothes at the sink in a white enamel bowl containing water boiled on the gas stove. In the Summer we would have a cold wash under the tap by standing on a chair and leaning over the sink.

Once a week, usually on Friday night, we were scrubbed clean in shared water that had been boiled in the kettle and two pots on the stove and poured into the tin bath. The same stove was used for cooking, baking, and warming us on bitter mornings while our clothes heated in the oven or under the grill. OI don't know how two grown-ups and four children managed to cope in that small space. Perhaps it was because we knew no different and were small for our age.

Our change of clothes Mum washed by hand but the big washing load, which would include our bedding, was done by putting it into a sack with our number on it and taking it to the bag-wash shop near Watney Street Market. The charge, in nineteen forty-two was about six pence. Mum would hand the bag over to Norah, behind the counter who would give her a ticket with the bags numbers on it. A couple of days later we would collect the bag although the washing was never completely dry, so had to be hung out in the yard or on lines around the kitchen ceiling.

When I got older one of the ways I worked to make money was to collect the bags from the women I was working for and using a pushchair wheel the various bags I had collected to the bag wash shop and later return them to their various owners. I would get paid two pence or three halfpence a bag.

Back to the story of 51A. Our warmth in the kitchen was provided by the gas stove and in the rest of the flat by two fireplaces. A grey pink tiled one in the living room and a black iron one in Mum and Dad's bedroom, but that one was only used if one of us kids slept in there when we were ill. The fires were fuelled from our big wooden coal box at the top of the stairs. If we were running low to re-stock, Mum and I would have to go to the coal merchants and then wheel a half hundredweight sack home on the pram. Or if the coal man came we would have a hundredweight, because he would carry it up on his back and pour it into the box, making the coal dust rise up and float around the hall. The lid fitted very well and was used as a shelf or high table to throw coats or bags on. When the fire needed 'making up' we would shovel coal from a sliding flap in the front at the bottom and carry it straight to the fire place. Over the years the box got so clogged up with damp coal dust that the flap became useless and coal had to be shovelled or picked out from the top. When coal got scarce we had coke, but it never burned as good as the coal.

That gives you a picture of my new home and I settled into it and to my new routine quite well. I was now six and a half and because there was a war on I had to pull my weight.

My first job was to get to know the shops so that I could help Mum with the shopping. I was good with the ration books and could do money and adding up and taking away but being a bit thin I had to have Eddy to help me carry any heavy things I bought. Our nearest two shops were Gussie's, where we could get groceries put on 'the bill,' and Katz, where they didn't do credit. Both of these shops sold everything from kosher bread to Brasso and vinegar by the pint. They did not sell meat, bacon or fruit and veg. When we wanted that sort of thing we had to go to Watney Market.

It still exists to-day but in those days, there wasn't much going on at the Commercial Road end because it had been bombed flat. The bottom end, near Shadwell Station, was mostly still standing and had butchers, bakers, shoe shops, and Fielding the stationers. In the road there were lots of stalls. Lots of fish and vegetable stalls and the well-known cat's meat stall. The fruit and veg stalls sold English-grown apples, plums and cherries in season but never oranges or bananas or anything from abroad. My favourite shop was Anderson's the bakers. They baked their own stuff on the premises and I loved the smell of freshly bread that came from the windows under the ground when I was queuing for a loaf.

Food was bought as and when we needed it because we didn't have the money to buy ahead and when the weather got warmer nothing stayed fresh for long. Even when it was left outside, on the kitchen window sill. No one had a fridge in those days, most of us had never even heard of them. Mum or me often had to go to rush to the market when we heard that there was something special on sale because most things were still in short supply, so we had to get there fast and join the queue. Sometimes women, who ought to have known better, would elbow us kids right out of the way in order to get whatever was going.

I was queuing once at McCarthy's packet grocery stall, when they had tins of Bartlett pears to sell. I was on my own and about three from the front, when Mrs. Firth eased her big fat arse in front of me. She was a florid woman with had two grown up boys who could have done me over and given me a black eye, so I let it pass and kept my mouth shut. But not so Nanny who just happened to see what she had done while she was searching through stuff on the second-hand clothes stall across the road.

"Oi, Johnny," she called. "Don't let that woman push in front of you. Stand up for yourself. You mustn't let people push you around like that."

I was really embarrassed and went as red a hot poker.

"It's alright Nan," I called back to her.

"No it's not! You mustn't let people take advantage of you!"

"Oh, is he in the queue?" said Fat Mother Firth. "I thought he was with you love," she said to the woman behind me. "I wasn't trying to push in Sarah I just got mixed up. Go on Johnny you can go ahead of me."

"You've got to learn to be a man," Nanny screamed. "You'll be pushed around all your life if you don't stand up to people."

I don't know why she had to yell it out so loud. People would have heard her up in Aldgate. I just wanted to be blown away because everyone was looking at me. Even Mrs. McCarthy took pity on me and said that she'd serve me first. I grabbed the tin of pears paid her the four pence ha'penny and fled back to Tait Street, as fast as my worn-down boots would carry me.

7 THE COAKLEYS & THE HIGH DRAMAS

During our stay at 51A we got to know Mrs. Coakley much more than we did Mr. Coakley who tended to keep himself to himself. They had a daughter called Ruby, who was about the same age as Mum and had no children "because she was plain." To overcome her looks she wore vivid lipstick and big hats. Except when she was going out to a dance then she would always wear what they called a two-piece suit. This was a short coat and a skirt that matched, and Ruby's was plum coloured with a pink blouse under the coat. To top the whole outfit off, round her neck she wore a thin, silver fox fur stole. I really liked this because it had two black glass eyes and a leg that clipped onto a tin clamp in its mouth to keep it round Ruby's neck.

When we were a bit rowdy it was always Missus who would bang on their ceiling with her broom handle and tell us to 'shut our bloody noise up there.' She never came upstairs due to her leg. I made Eddy laugh fit to burst when I told him that – 'She couldn't come up the stairs because she was too bleedin' big to get round the bend.' I said that soon after the tea incident when we badly needed a good cheering up.

The Tea Incident happened while I had been looking after the kids, because Mum was doing a bit of work round Nanny's. Jeanie had been a right little mare all the evening and wouldn't let me wash her so that I could put her to bed. While I was trying to grab her to get her to the sink, she had ran out of the kitchen and into the living room. I chased her and without thinking of what I was doing, I had grabbed the slop bucket, which was outside the kitchen door and ran after her. Eddy, who was taking her side in the row, put a chair in my way, so that when I ran into the room I slipped and slung the bucket full of tea leaves all over my younger sister. Which was rather unfortunate because we only had a couple of mats in the living room and the brown liquid that hadn't soaked into Jeanie or her clothes quickly seeped through the floor boards onto Mrs. Coakley's ceiling below.

Three children all went horribly quiet. I picked up the bucket and tried to scrape up the tea leaves as best I could without making too much noise. Eddy helped by getting the bits off of the furniture. Jeanie went quickly back into the kitchen and stood by the sink waiting for me to wash her. Which would take a lot longer, now that her vest and knickers were soaked in tea and leaves.

"Johnny! Johnny!" Mrs. Coakley yelled up our stairs about ten minutes later. "What the bleeding hell are you doing up there? There's a load of piss coming through my ceiling."

I pulled a face at Eddy, stopped washing Jeanie and leaving her naked in front of the sink, I went to the kitchen door.

"It's alright Mrs. Coakley," I answered. "It isn't pi…. It isn't wee. It's only tea leaves."

"Well what the soddin' hell are tea leaves doing coming through my ceiling? You shouldn't have that bucket in the front room! Come down here and see what you've done."

I quickly dried Jeanie's face and gave her a clean pair of knickers and a vest to put on before down.

Mrs. Coakley, was standing with her arms on her hips and leaning against her living room door which was on the jar. I had never been in her living room, so apart from being a bit worried I was also dead curious.

"Where's it comin' in?" I asked.

She opened the door and I stared quickly round the room as I went in. It was as big as our living room and our bedroom put together. Her furniture was big and dark. She had glass oil lamps, red cushions and a big picture of a deer on the wall between the two windows.

"Stop your nosing around and look up there." She pointed upwards to a brown circle on the ceiling at the edge of which some dark drips were falling into an empty fruit bowl on the floor. "You wait till your mother gets home."

"No, I'm sorry Mrs. Coakley it was an accident. I was just emptying the teapot and Beryl crawled over the floor and pushed the bucket over. It was a compete accident. I'm very sorry."

"You lying little sod. I heard you fighting. The three of you. What was the bucket doing in the front room anyway?"

"I was gonna make us all a nice cup of tea," I lied. "Would you like on?"

"Get up those stairs you saucy little git. You wait till I tell your mother and Gawd knows what Ruby is going to say."

Ruby by now had taken a liking to me and once or twice had let me stroke her silver fox when she was all dolled up and going out.

"I can't see her letting you run her errands for a couple of pence when I tell he about this." Mrs. Coakley continued, as if to push her advantage.

I turned to go upstairs with her threats ringing in my ears.

"I'm really very sorry Mrs. Coakley, "I said and I meant it. "It was a accident and I promise it won't happen again. Would you like that cup of tea?"

"You can bet your bleeding life it won't happen again." She slammed our staircase door behind me. "Stick your tea up your arse you tricky little sod."

It was later, after I had been walloped and made to clean up the stain on the front room mat that I made Eddy laugh about her being too fat to get around the bend to chase me up the stairs.

We shared the only lavatory, which was on their floor, with the Coakley's. Obviously not at the same time even though it was quite big. Each family had their own paper. Due to the war we didn't have real toilet paper we used torn up newspaper or bits of an old telephone book when we found one on a bomb site. If we were going to do number two's, we had to take our own three sheets with us. A sheet to wipe, a sheet to polish and a sheet to dust. Once when we were playing around in the yard of a bombed-out shop in Watney Market, Eddy found a roll of real toilet paper. It was damp and dirty on the outside, but it wasn't rough like the Evening Standard, or Izal tissue paper that felt like tracing paper. What he found was soft like crepe paper used to be. I got a real thrill when I carried it home and presented it to Mum. We used it vary sparingly, allowing one sheet per person. The sheet to dust.

When I got older I used to sing while I was having a sit down in there and became known to the Coakley's as 'Singing Poop.' I heard from Ruby that Mr. Coakley once said that he liked the singing but not the smell. How he had the cheek to say that with all the cabbage and cheese smells that came from their kitchen beats me. He must have had a special filter in his purpled veined nose that only smelled me. And what about their dog, Blackie? A greasy, dirty, grey haired old mongrel who lived to be nine hundred and sixty. When that dog farted, which he did all the time, you could smell it as far as the Blackwall Tunnel. When we moved in Eddy and I had got very excited about having a dog about the place, but this mutt turned out to be a real nasty piece of work who growled every time we passed the door and was always trying to jump on top of Baby Beryl to eat her.

8 THE AIR RAIDS CONTINUE

The war carried on with the German's still bombing us but not as much as they used to. Air raids were mainly seen as an inconvenience to us children who had no conception of mortality, except when sometimes at school no one answered their name and didn't come back. If we were out walking or playing away from home and the 'warning' went, we had been taught to find shelter or stick closely to the walls. This happened once when me and Eddy were on our way home from Arbour Square, after we had been to the church of St. Mary's and Michael's, to look at Jesus hanging on the cross outside on a bit of grassy mud. We were strolling along Commercial Road when the siren went. We got into a huge argument as to how close to the wall we ought to stay and where to look for a shelter meantime trying to see the planes. It was daylight, so the raid didn't last long, and I didn't see any planes that I remember so it might well have been a false alarm.

The raids were different during the night. At 51a we had our big yard, with its small bit garden and a paved area. In the garden part they had put an Anderson shelter. This was made by the grown-ups digging a big hole miles down into the ground. When they had done that they put curved corrugated pieces of very hard metal over it to make an underground room with an entrance at one end to climb down into it. It was a sort of buried iron igloo. The outside was then covered over with earth to protect it from the blast which was a dangerous thing and could kill you leaving no marks at all. You just died bang bosh. Once we were through the small doorway we had to climb down steps. Inside we had some iron bunks so that we could sleep in it, but because it was so horrible and smelled, we only used it when the raids got bad. Every night before we went to bed we would arrange all our clothes and shoes and coats and gas masks in neat piles on the chair by our bed, so that we would be able to find them easily in the dark and calmly get dressed before going to the safety of the dig out. As it was known. That was the theory.

The reality was that as soon as the wailing of the warning started, and we were dragged from a deep sleep we all got in a panic and muddle. We slept with our vest and pants on, so it was just a case of trying to find our shirts and trousers. Before everyone got out of bed someone would have knocked the chair over. Mum in the meantime, would be trying to light the candle or the oil lamp. We couldn't put the big light on because the German Pilots would see it and put our name on a bomb. Before we got any light Jeanie would be crying and Beryl would be screaming. Mum would start to yell at us boys to hurry up and order me to get Jeanie dressed while she saw to the baby. Our toes would get stuck in the holes of socks, shoes would be put on the wrong feet and laces would get knotted and have to be undone. Shirts would be done up with the wrong buttons and wrong arms would be put in wrong coats and everything would have to be taken off again as the drone of the planes, the banging of the guns and the whistling of the shrapnel would be urging us to move faster.

Half-dressed we would stagger downstairs and past the Coakley's, who never went to the shelter, and arrive on the ground floor. The five of us would make our way, in the dim light of the oil lamp, through the pass door leading to the yard go past the cellar door and the workshop before eventually getting out into the garden. Facing us would be a thin fig tree growing against the wall between our house and the ruins of the bombed house behind it. Once in the open air we would be screamed at to turn left as Mum put out the lamp so that it could not shine up to the sky. Half asleep and frightened we would stumble our way across the few yards to our Anderson shelter. All muddy and smelly but it was our own and offered us a promise of safety and life tomorrow.

Mum would pull back the blanket, hanging across the doorway and go down into the hole first. Once she was there I would pass Beryl down to her and she would be put on a bunk bed. While we were doing that Jeanie would go into a tantrum and would try to run away from me. Meantime, the guns would be starting to ack-ack and the searchlights would be sweeping the sky for the Nazi bombers. I would have to chase Jeanie grab her and almost throw her down into the hole so that Mum could get her sorted. While all this was going on, Eddy would want to look for the Hurricanes and Spitfires and Mum would be doing her nut trying to get the pair of us down and out of danger. All this would take place in the pitch dark if there wasn't a moon out. It was only when we were all down and the blanket drawn across the opening, that the lamp could be lit again. This became such a palaver that after a few regular raids we eventually decided to sleep down there every night. Unfortunately, Mum couldn't stand the spiders and baby Beryl got a bit of a chest, so after a week we were upstairs again, back into the old routine of panic and confusion. Secretly I was relieved because although I never said anything, I didn't fancy the idea of being asleep when the house got bombed and the ruins fell all over the garden and trapped us alive in the shelter.

Once we were in the Anderson we were by then so full of adrenalin that it was impossible to get back to sleep. So Mum would have to tell us a story or we would sing some songs or play cards until the all clear went. Jeanie, favoured 'I spy,' because she could yell out answers that had nothing to do with the letter that had been spied. Like she would say "I spy with my little eye, something beginning with 'T.' Which we had gone through all the things beginning with T she would say she had spied a blanket! She was a silly cow and a bit of a cheat. Although in the small space with its sparse furnishings, there wasn't much scope for a spying anything so there was always a lot of repetition.

When Mum got worried, because the raids were getting very heavy again, we would go around to Nanny's house to sleep. Farver, if he wasn't on fire watch, would listen to the Nine o/clock news on the Home Service. During that time everybody had to be silent. I mean not just quiet but completely silent as though it was the King or Mr. Churchill speaking, which sometimes it was. When the news was over the grown-ups would talk about the battles that were going on around the world. Me and Eddy would sleep on a mattress under the dining table where we would listen to them talking until we fell asleep. Mum and the girls slept upstairs in Aunt Alice's room. Aunt Margie had the front room upstairs, but not all the time because sometimes she would have to work all night at the government office where she did secret stuff at a desk.

Air raids were even more chaotic at Nanny's, especially if Farver was on fire duty. When the warning siren started wailing Nanny would have to strap leads on the two wire haired terriers, Tony and Neene. We of course would be going through our usual routine of losing everything in the panic, only on two levels, me and Eddy downstairs and the girls upstairs. Where we would be aided, in the confusion, by Aunts Alice and Margie. When were almost ready to go, Nanny would have Tony and a large piano accordion in each hand and Aunt Alice would have the bitch Neene and a smaller piano accordion, which was uncle Arthur's, in her hands. It got absolutely chaotic when it was time for the dogs to mate. The yells of Nanny screaming at Alice to, 'Keep Tony away from Neene, for God's sake!' Could be heard even above the crashing of the bombs and shrapnel smashing into the falling buildings. Nanny would then lurch out of number sixteen trying to lock the door behind her and Tony would be trying to mount Neene as Alice dragged them apart. The rest of us would be falling over each other as we tried to hold hands and move fast towards the shelter, which was in the cellar of a factory on the corner of Planet Street and Commercial Road.

Nanny would eventually stagger up the street and totter down the stone steps into the shelter. It was a large, make-shift shelter which had ten bunks in it plus some old chairs and lots of pipes running along the ceiling and down the walls. But it was functional and none of us ever got killed. There was the night when it got badly flooded, but I'll tell you about that later.

9 ENID BLYTON AND ACCIDENT

During the Summer holidays of nineteen forty-three, Mum had taken us with her to Nanny's when she popped round for a gossip and to find out if there was any outdoor work going. Aunt Kate was already there with our cousin Joycie, who was six months younger that Jeanie and being an only child had much better clothes than us.

After we had given a kiss to Nanny, Joycie came out to watch us playing hopscotch in the road. Dennis Stag, Eddy's mate was also playing and said that we ought to let her join in. The problem was that she wasn't much cop at it. It took her ages to get the bit of bottle glass, that was her chipper, into box one. After she had messed up her fifth 'go' I got really bored and decided that we could go for a walk and get a book of 'Sunny Stories,' from Mrs. Midder's in Commercial Road.

Mum, Nanny and all the grown-ups had always told us children in no uncertain terms, that we were not, repeat not, to cross Commercial Road because it was a dangerous and busy place. Especially when a convoy was passing on its way to the docks from up beyond Liverpool Street. When they did come along we would go to watch the tanks, gun carriages and the trucks with soldiers waving at us as they passed. We cheered and waved back at them hoping that they would throw us some sweets which sometimes they did, but being on the other side of the road we didn't always get them unless the soldier had strong arms.

'Sunny Stories' was a comic written on thin paper by Enid Blyton and was what Mum would read to us when we were in bed at night because it helped us get to sleep. It came out once a fortnight and yesterday was the day it was due. I reckoned that Mrs. Midder should have it in by now and ran up the passage to tell the grown-ups what I was going to do.

"Where are you gonna get them?" asked Aunt Kate.

"Up to Mrs. Midder in Buros Street," I replied. "I'll take the others with me for a walk."

"Well you're not taking Joycie with you," said her Mother. "I'm not having her up on that main road!"

"We're not going to cross the road," I said with my full cockiness. "Mrs. Midder's is on this side,"

"Like I didn't know that because I've only lived here all me life. Oh, you're a saucy little sod," said my aunt with a twinkle in her eye.

"Here's twopence ha'penny," said Mum, closing her purse with a snap. "And only get Sunny Stories. If they haven't got it at Midder's, don't you dare cross the road and go to O'Connor's."

I took the money from her.

"Try Fielding's round by Shadwell Station," she droned on. "And don't be all day. I'll see you back here. And make sure you hold Jeanie's hand."

"And leave Joycie here," said Kate.

Joycie looked really sad sitting all alone on the step with big blue eyes watching us go. But we didn't care, the four of us just left her and went up to the top of Planet Street and along Commercial Road until we got to the top of Buros Street where the stationers were.

I went into shop leaving the other three outside playing around the model of a huge ice cream cone with a Walls Polar Maid stuck in the top. That model always got on my nerves because you couldn't get ice cream anywhere, so it seemed like they were just taking the piss. It was the same with the red, green and lemon iced drink bottles that Midder still had hanging upside down in her window. What was the point of that? There were never any bloody drinks in it to buy!

"I'm vedy soddy Johnny, I've got no Sunny Stories, left," said Mrs. Midder in her strong accent. "I say to Nelly, 'Vy don't you order?' But no, they don't listen, nobody listens anymore. . . Like I don't know vot I'm talking about. . .They should live so long . . .."

I'd heard all that before and many times, so I went back into the bright sunlight while she was still moaning on in the background.

"She ain't got none," I informed the others.

"That don't matter, we can get it at O'Connor's. They'll have it there." said Eddy.

O'Connor's was a newsagent in the middle of Philpot Street, facing the toilets. But, and this was a very big but, it was on the other side of Commercial Road. The big road! The road that I was not allowed to cross and should certainly not take Jeanie, Dennis and Eddy over. Nevertheless, I did give it some thought.

"No, we'd better not." I decided after a pause. "I promised Mummy we wouldn't go over to O'Connor's."

"How's she gonna know?" Eddy said. "We can tell her that we got it at Midder's if she asks. Oh, come on Johnny it's too hot to go all the way round to Shadwell. We'll be sweatin' if we have to go all that way up Watney Street."

I could certainly see the sense of this. It was either a quick run across the road to Philpot Street, or a long hot walk to Fielding's at the Cable Street end of the Market.

"Alright," I said after a pause for effect. "But we've got to cross on the crossing outside the Palo."

Our little band walked towards the Palaseum Cinema in front of which was a break in the railings and a set of studs across the road which provided a crossing area. It had no island in the middle. I was holding Jeanie with my right hand and took Eddy in my left. He snatched his hand away.

"I can cross on my own, thanks."

"Give me your hand or we won't go," I ordered, very determined. "Dennis, you stay close to us and wait for me when I give the word to cross. Alright?"

"All right!" Said Dennis the man of few words.

I grabbed Eddy's hand and I looked up the road. There was nothing coming for ages on our side and on the other, there was just a van then a long gap in front of a bus.

"O.K. Now listen," I said. "Get to the middle and wait. Let that van pass, then cross the rest of the road behind it. And no dawdling because of that bus."

I set off with Eddy still struggling to get loose from my hand. We got to the middle and waited for the van which shot past, hooting at us, then we all ran to the safety of the kerb on the other side.

It felt really strange being over there on my own. It was like being an explorer in another part of the world. I had only ever been there with Mum, when she drew her Army Money from the post office. We turned into Philpot Street we crossed to the middle where the toilets were and then over to O'Connor's which was next door to the post office. I made the other three wait outside.

As we had suspected all along, Mrs. O'Connor did have a copy of 'Sunny Stories,' I gave her the twopence ha'penny and a polite 'Thank you.' All the time hoping against hope that she wouldn't mention it to Mum when we next went in there.

I came out of the shop and we all gathered round to flick through the pages and have a look. On the front, it had a border of red around a picture of well-behaved, well-dressed, middle-class children, preparing for another adventure in their village. I was holding it but before I knew what was happening, Eddy had snatched it from my hand had started laughing and ran away towards the big main road.

"Eddy bring that back here and stop larking about you little sod," I yelled. "We've got to get back over the crossing."

"No we ain't. Don't be so bossy," he shouted back. "Come on Den."

Dennis ran towards him and I grabbed Jeanie's hand and followed. At the top of the street they turned into the main road but instead of going right towards the crossing they went left towards Cavel Street. This was not good for me. It was miles before we would get to the Watney crossing. And then we would have to walk back to Planet Street.

"Eddy, come back! Come back here, you little git!" I screamed in my high pitched girlie voice. "Don't blame me if you get run over."

Both boys were whooping and yelling and larking about and showing off trying to worry me. They ducked under the railings and balanced along the bit of kerb stone that was on the edge of the main road. There was too much traffic for them to cross the road, so they had to stop. I soon caught up with them. Leaving Jeanie on the pavement, in front of the florist, I ducked under the chain and tried to grab Eddy's hand, but he moved quickly away and started waving the comic at me. A car blew its hooter as it drove past.

"Eddy, give me your hand and we'll all cross together," I was pleading with him now because I had started to get frightened of what might happen to me if Mum found out. "Come on. What are we gonna do if someone see's us and tells Mummy. She'll soddin' well kill me and you. Come here. Give me your hand!!"

Then there came a short break in the traffic as a black van passed and a dark blue car was still a bit further off. I don't know what got into them, but before you could say Jack Robinson, both boys had scooted across the road as fast as their legs would carry them. Leaving me with my mouth and eyes opened wide and with my breath stopped. I didn't dare follow them because I still had Jeanie to look after. I turned to get her from the other side of the chain. She wasn't there! My four-year-old sister had disappeared! My six-year-old brother had just ran across a main road and I was supposed to be in charge of them. Fuckin' 'ell! I spun round the other way and found Jeanie, on my side of the chain waving at Eddy who was now waving the copy of 'Sunny Stories,' taunting us from the other side of the road. I put my hand out to take Jeanie's while yelling at Eddy to stop waving. The dark blue car sped past furiously blowing its hooter. But Jeanie didn't take my hand. She just stepped off of the kerb without looking and ran towards our brother.

My eyes were riveted on her and I began to tingle all over with fright. I suppose it must have been shock or something. It was lucky for me that everything started to slow down. I saw her tiny legs in their white socks and sandals moving across the tar blocked surface of the road. The skirt of her pink frock was bouncing up as, I sensed rather than saw, the bus bearing down towards her. I threw myself off the kerb. As I landed on one leg behind her I could hear the screech of brakes and the sound of a hooter as well as people yelling, screaming and shouting. I put my hand out towards Jeanie's back as my other leg came in front of me and she moved further away. Her pink dress started to get redder and I could smell the engine and feel the heat of the bus quite close to us; worst of all I could see that my sister was level with the off-side wheels that were going to squash her.

I thought, "Mummy'll murder me if she gets killed!"

By now I could only hear the screeching brakes and the throbbing of the engine. Bright red seemed to be everywhere. I jumped forward as hard as I could, reached out with both hands and as Jeanie, was almost under the wheels, I pushed her with all my might. I felt the warmth of her back as the bus knocked me up into the air. I travelled forward a bit and then landed on the ground just as it went over me.

Actually, I don't remember all that about being hit by the bus. I only know what happened because it was told by witnesses.

After I pushed Jeanie's back I knew nothing until I woke up in the cave. Well I thought it was a cave. Not that I had ever been in one because you don't get many round Stepney, but it was how I imagined a cave to be when I'd read about them in a book. When I opened my eyes, everything was black. As my eyes grew used to the dark I could see that the roof was just above my face. I focussed and saw that it wasn't a roof but a load of pipes all smothered in grime or something. I realised it wasn't a cave, so I didn't have a clue where I was. My head was hurting, and I felt bewildered. My main thought was that I had better try to get out and go home. I struggled to turn onto my side but something was caught on the front of my shirt. I wriggled and pulled until I managed to unhook myself from a bit of metal that was hanging loose. I turned over onto my side and then onto my front. The pain in my head got a lot worse.

I lifted my head and looked towards the end of the passage where I was lying. In the distance I saw a bright white light. I don't know why, but I knew I had to get out and into that light. I started to crawl forwards even though my arms were hurting and so were my knees. As I moved I could feel something dripping around my face. The pain in my head and body made me want to stop moving but I knew that I had to keep going. It took ages. I couldn't hear anything because there was a deadness in my ears as though I'd gone deaf. I wasn't crying but I could feel something wet whenever my hands got near my head. 'Keep going.' I thought as I urged myself on, 'you'll soon be home.'

When I eventually got out of the tunnel and into the light the first thing I saw was loads of people standing about. Men, women and children as well as a Policeman who was standing by the kerb holding a sack. They were all staring at something behind me.

"There he is!" a woman screamed as she turned from the front of the bus. "He's crawling out from the back of the bus!"

I looked down to heave myself forward and saw that my arms and hands were all covered in blood. I passed out.

When I opened my eyes the next time, it seemed that I was in a deep hole looking up to the sky, with a load of people standing around an iron fence looking down at me. I slowly came to the realisation that I had been carried down the steps into the Gentlemen's toilet and laid on a blanket. A few moments passed as I tried to get my bearings. I saw the white tiles of the toilet and could hear my Mother's voice.

"What the bleedin' hell are you talking about, I can't go down there," Said Mum from a distance. "I'm his mother!"

"And I'm his aunt," said Aunt Kate from the same direction. "So, get out of the way and let us get to him."

I looked to where their voices were coming from and I saw them at the top of the toilet stairs arguing with a policeman!

"I'm sorry ladies but this is a gentleman's toilet," said the copper. "The ambulance is on his way. If you wait there you'll be able to go with him to the hospital."

"Well, we're sorry an' all that but we don't care whose toilet it is. We are both married women and we want to get to him now. So get out of our way." Said Kate, as she pushed the policeman to one side and both women ran down the steps towards me.

What were they thinking of? My Mum and my Aunt were coming down into the Gentleman's toilet! And there was a policeman watching them! I passed out again!

I heard the bells in the ambulance and came round to see Mum leaning over me and a man standing behind her who was holding a lot of blood stained bandages. I couldn't see out of the ambulance windows because they were all blacked out. Then I did the same. I woke up in a bed. I was in a dark room with a small amount of blue light and a strong smell of disinfectant. There were sounds around me that I couldn't understand, it was as though they were trying to keep themselves quiet. I tried to move to see and hear more but my head and body hurt too much.

"Mummy," I groaned. Then a bit louder because there was no response. "Mum."

"Ah, you're awake now," a lady's voice whispered as it come towards me. "How are you feeling?"

"Alright thanks," I said. Even though I was feeling awful and in pain. "Where's Jeanie? I must see Jeanie."

"I'm going to put the light on now to have a look into your eyes," said the voice.

A hand was put over my eyes as light appeared from a lamp that was hanging out of the wall above my head. The hand was slowly removed from my face and I saw a nurse in a big white hat.

"Now how about a sip of water?" she said, as she leaned over my bed looking deep into my eyes.

I was lying flat with a pillow behind my head. Everything around me was clean and very tight. The nurse picked up a small white cup with a spout like a teapot then she put her hand behind my shoulder and raised me up, very gently, so that she could put the spout into my mouth.

"Have a nice cool sip now," she said.

The cold water came into my mouth and felt good. Then I coughed. The pain in my head was very sharp and not good at all. "Aaaagh. Shit!" I whimpered because it was too painful to cry or eve yell out. I thought my head must have been blown up.

"Good boy. It's alright," said the nurse, as she placed me down again and wiped my mouth with a piece of dry lint. "Try to get some sleep now."

She took my wrist between her fingers and looked at her watch, counting, under her breath. She gave me little smiles, but I could tell that her mind wasn't in it until after she stopped counting. She stayed with me and stroked my hand as I closed my eyes.

When I woke up it was morning and I had no idea where the bleeding hell I was. It all came back to me when a nurse, carrying a jug and a bowl, passed at the bottom of my bed. I was in hospital. Jeanie had been run over and I had been trying to save her. That's how I had got here. Did I save her or was she dead? I looked around for someone to ask. On one side was an old man sitting up in bed washing his face from a bowl resting on a table thingy in front of him. He was too engrossed with his cleaning to look at me, so I turned towards the other side. Bloody hell my head was hurting. I saw another man lying on his back with lots of pillows round his head and shoulders. I tried to sit up but the bedclothes were too tight for me to move.

"I'll leave your tea on your locker Harry, 'till you've finished having your wash," said a woman's voice which was quite loud. "This is the boy that got knocked down isn't it? Oh, you're awake, are you? D'ya want a nice cup of tea?

Her round face with lots of curls under a grey cap came into my view across the starched sheet. She disappeared towards the end of my bed and returned holding a clipboard.

"I see you're Michael. Well dear, I'm auntie Dolly and I do the teas. Would you like a cup? Do you like sugar?"

"I can't sit up." I said.

"Never mind you can have it in your beaker. Nurse Daldrey!" Dolly called out as she disappeared again. "Can Michael have a cuppa?"

I was left staring up at the dusty ceiling with questions going around in my aching head. Why was she calling me Michael? They must have got me mixed up with someone else. I started to panic! If they thought I was Michael, it would mean that when Mum came to find me she wouldn't know where I was, and I would never get home. Perhaps she didn't even know I was in hospital. How long had I been here? I could have been in here for days or even weeks. Perhaps she thought I had been killed in an air raid and had given up looking for me. Or perhaps because I had let Jeanie get run over, she didn't want me anymore. Tears started to prick the back of my eyes. No! No, wait a minute: things started to come back to me. Mum and Aunt Kate, hadn't they been in the ambulance that brought me here? They must know where I am. They'll find me soon. I closed my eyes telling myself that I mustn't cry otherwise everyone would start looking at me. Dolly came back into view.

"Now try getting a drop of this down ya," she said lifting me up and putting the teapot to my mouth. "I've put lots of milk in it, so you won't burn your lips and I've given you a big spoon of sugar. That's it Michael dear, go on 'ave a good swig."

" Johnny," I said after having a good swig of the tea and coming up for air.

"What?"

"My name's Johnny."

"Oh. Alright then Johnny. Now be a good boy and finish this last little drop for Auntie Dolly."

I finished the tea and was told I was a good boy and placed back flat on the bed. Then away went Dolly with her beaker and trolley and even though she was out of my sight I heard her say,

"Poor little bleeder. He must be delirious. Don't even know who he is. It's a shame ain't it. Come on Barry, it's about time you were having your wash, it's getting on for five-and-twenty to seven."

The next few hours passed in a mixture of pain and bewilderment. I was Sat up, washed, laid down, sat up, had my temperature taken and laid down again. After a while a doctor come to write on my chart and tell me I would be alright and could now sit up. Pillows were put behind me and my bed was moved further down the room, which I learned was called a Ward. Once I was settled, at about ten o'clock, a selection of old and younger men as well as nurses come over to my bed to have a chat to me. I think they meant well and were very nice: but I was too shy to talk to them, so they all thought that I was much worse than I was. During all of this I was wondering if Jeanie was alive or dead and who the bleedin' hell Michael was? I couldn't understand why they all thought I was him. Surely two of us couldn't have been run over on the same day by two different busses.

It was not long after eleven in the morning when a lady who they called Sister and who wore a dark blue frock plus a huge white hat, looking like a bride's veil, swept towards my bed like a whirlwind.

"Michael," she said. Talking as though she was a headmistress. "To-day and only to-day you are being allowed special visitors. This is because we have had to put you up here in the men's ward instead of in the children's. In future you will only have visitors at three o/clock in the afternoon the same as the rest of the patients. I will bring them to see you when they arrive. Now try to rest and keep relaxed."

It wasn't long after this, although it seemed as if I had been there for weeks, that I heard Mum coming along the passage leading to the ward.

"Oh look! There he is Kate," she said to the World. "Aw, look at his little face and look at the bandages round his head. Don't worry Johnny, Mummy's here now. I've got you some strawberries and Aunt Kate's got you some flowers. You alright darlin'? Oh, I hate the smell of hospitals. Mummy's here Sweetheart."

Everyone was staring at her and Aunt Kate, as they came through the open door and down past the other beds. Sister was trying to keep up with them as they almost ran down the ward to get to me. I was a bit embarrassed, but it really was smashing to see them.

"Please Mrs. Ross," said Sister quietly. "There are some very sick patients in here, could you please keep your voice down. This visit is a special privilege. You must understand that."

"Sorry Sister," Mum, said as she got to the bed and cuddled me up in her arms. "Hello darlin'. Mummy's here now. Gawd, you gave us such a scare. I thought you was a gonna. They told us that when you crawled out of the back of the bus, it was like a miracle the whole crowd went mad. We was just coming across the road to get to you. And when I saw that copper, standing there with a sack to carry you over, I nearly died. I was almost knocked down by a motor bike, wasn't I Kate?"

"Nelly don't pull him about like that you'll do him a damage," warned Kate.

The ward Sister came to the other side of the bed.

"Mrs. Ross," she whispered. "This lady is right, don't shake Michael, he has a serious head wound. You can stay for just ten minutes. There are some chairs in the middle of the ward please take one. The boy has some wounds and abrasions on his legs and his arms, and some heavy bruising on his back and chest. But he's going to be fine, aren't you Michael? I will be back to escort you out in ten minutes."

She returned to her office as Aunt Kate put a chair on either side of the bed.

"I'll put these flowers on your locker and they will put them in water later," said Aunt Kate. "We got them on the Waste. How are you Johnny love?"

"I'm alright," I told her. "Is Jeanie here? Is she alright? Why isn't she here?"

"Children aren't allowed to come visiting in the grown-up wards," said Mum. "But she's alright. We've had to come to see you, so she's round Nanny's with Eddie, Joycie and Beryl. You pushed her from under the wheel. Mr. Keaton saw it all and said she would have been dead if you hadn't run out and pushed her from under the bus. But what were you doing going over the soddin' road in the first place. I've told you time an' time . . ."

"Alright Nelly, don't start all that again," said her sister. "The boy's not well."

"He's put bleedin' years on me, he has."

"Mum," I said. Desperate to change the subject. "They keep calling me Michael. Have they got me mixed up with someone else?"

"No, they haven't got you mixed up, you silly sod. That's your real name," Mum said, "I had to give it to the police and the ambulance men yesterday."

"Nanny called you John, after our brother, that she had just lost," explained Kate. "Old Granny said Michael sounded too Irish."

"So you've been John since I took you," Mum said. "Your real name is Michael Peter Ross. Not John Ross. That's what you real mother called you. 'Mickey wanna biccy,' that's what she said when she come to see you once."

"Will she call me Michael, when she comes to take me back?" I asked.

"No! She's never going to come back for you now," said Mum. "It been over a year since I've heard from her or had any money. She must have been bombed or killed or something. Those people in Chetwyn Road haven't sent a word. No, I reckon she's bought it in a raid somewhere. Mind you the porter that wheeled you in last night, said that there was a bloke discharged the day before yesterday who was the spitting image of you. He reckoned he could have been your father. That's what he said didn't he Kate?"

"Yes he did," Kate agreed. "But I don't think it could have been anyone or anything to do with Johnny. It was probably just because the fella had ginger hair. You was telling him how you'd taken Johnny as an orphan, Nelly. So, I think you was just putting ideas into his head and then he started putting ideas into yours."

"It could have been his father! You never know."

"Is Jeanie alright? Can you bring her in to see me?" I asked. "Please Mum. Ask that Sister woman, she might let you, if you ask her nicely. I just wanna see her. You can bring her in when it's proper visiting time."

"I'm not coming in again to-day," Mum said. "I can't stand this hospital smell, it makes me feel sick. I can't do it twice in one day. I'll pop in again tomorrow afternoon. Jeanie's alright, she missed the wheel by inches. Don't you start fretting over her. I'll get Nanny to come in this afternoon, but I don't think they'll let Jeanie in. Do you Kate?"

"We'll ask the Sister," said Aunt Kate. "I think he's fretting. So it will do him good to see her."

"Alright we'll ask her on our way out," said Mum. "But Johnny don't go getting all aeriated. You mustn't start fretting about Jeanie. It's a bad thing having a bash to the head. You could have got concussion. As well as that you've got the scrapes on your knees and your arms. Is it sore?"

"I don't know, I can't really feel much," I explained. "Unless I move."

"It's the drugs," the two sister's said together and nodding their heads towards each other.

I was feeling a bit tired, so when the Sister came and told them to go I wasn't completely disappointed. I fell asleep before they got to the end of the ward. I was woken up later and told by Dolly, "To try to eat a 'little bit of dinner'. I tried and was given some water before I dozed off again.

Afternoon visiting time was three o/clock. The bell rang, the doors at the end of the ward were opened and a crowd of women came in and went to the beds of their men. I was obviously the talk of the ward because so many of them kept glancing over at me as I sat up in my bed alone. I felt terrible because I was imagining that they thought no one cared enough about me to come and see me and were pitying me because I didn't have a visitor. After a few minutes a woman, who was visiting a man with his leg in the air, left his bed and came towards me.

"Oh shit," I thought, she was becoming my visitor because I didn't have one.

"You're Michael, aren't you?" she said with a smile, showing only four brown teeth in the whole of her mouth. "My husband was just telling me."

I nodded. I wasn't going to speak to her. I didn't need a visitor that bad.

"You are a very brave boy," she said. "Here's a bit of chocolate for you. I'll leave it on your locker and you can save it for later. You get some rest now. I won't disturb you anymore. Your Mummy must be very proud of you"

I pushed my cheeks up into a sort of smile and nodded my head to say thank you for the chocolate.

"Oh yes," I thought, "my Mummy must be very proud of me. Too proud to put up with the smell of bleeding hospitals."

I lay back on the pillow and shut my eyes so that they couldn't see me and when I opened them again, who should be coming down the ward but Nanny. She had a little blond girl with her. It was Jeanie. It was true, she didn't go under the bus after all! No. It wasn't Jeanie. It was Joycie! Joycie, in her yellow dress with the blue ducks on it. This was terrible. Jeanie must be dead. They were just telling me she was alright this morning so that I wouldn't fret. I hadn't cried much with all the pain in my head and the other places, but this was different. I couldn't help the tears that started running down my cheeks.

"Hello Johnny," said Nanny, as she got near the bed. "Look who I've brought in to see you. It's Jeanie. Give her a kiss. She's walked nearly all the way to come and see you."

She lifted the little girl up on to the counterpane and then I could see that it really was Jeanie. I rubbed away the tears with the back of my bandaged hand and reached out to cuddle her as she put her arms round my neck and rubbed her cheek into mine. I felt much better straight away and was thoroughly pleased that she hadn't got run over after all.

"You're looking alright now Johnny give me a kiss and I'll read you something out of Sunny Stories." said Nan, with a twinkle in her eye. "Jeanie had to borrow Joyce's dress 'cause her own was a bit shabby to come to the hospital in."

The Sister came and told us that Jeanie had to get down from the bed, and as soon as she'd gone, Nanny made my bedclothes a looser so that I could move a easier which made me feel a lot better.

I was kept in the hospital for six days and soon started enjoying all the attention as well as the gifts my visitors brought in. I quickly became the pet of the ward and loved the fact that we got pudding every day with our dinner. Although I found it a bit strange when they had to write my name on the egg that Farver had sent in for me. One thing I didn't understand was why they woke us patients up so early and then, after getting us washed and cleaned up we, were allowed to go back to sleep again. It just didn't make sense to me.

When I was first told I could get out of bed for a short walk I was amazed at how giddy I was. My legs just didn't belong to me, it felt like I had become a bit of jelly on a plate at a Sunday School party. Standing up got easier after a few attempts and by the time I was fit enough to walk round the ward, it was time to get discharged. Aunt Alice came to collect me to go home where I was quick to tell Eddy all the stories of stitches, needles, old men piddling in bottles and sitting on the bed to do a poo in a bowl.

There had to be an enquiry into my accident, but I wasn't called as a witness. Aunt Margie told me that the bus driver didn't blamed because he never stood a chance of stopping in time and anyway he had got a big scare when he run me over. A witness had stated that Jeanie left the kerb and run directly into the path of the bus and that I had had ran to push her away from the wheels. Too late to get out of the way or to stop, the bus had hit me, and I went under the middle. Another witness said that I had been dragged along until the vehicle had managed to come to a halt. The driver and the other witnesses had waited but as they couldn't hear me screaming or see anything, because the trolley bus sides were so low to the ground, they had assumed I was dead. The conductor had made a phone call for something that would lift the bus off of me and while they were waiting a Policeman found a sack to cover me over with if a ambulance didn't arrive in time. The witnesses had all been standing around and were given a big shock when I crawled out from the back of the bus, with my head all covered in blood.

After that everyone was going around saying that I was a little hero. It didn't seem to matter that I had taken the kids across the road and Jeanie had nearly been killed. The important thing was that I was alive and had saved Jeanie's life. All the kids round the streets wanted to know what it looked like under the bus. No one in the history of the world had ever been under a trolley bus and lived. At least no- one any of us knew. I was the only one. Grown-ups were saying that I had a 'charmed life,' Whatever that meant. I came to the conclusion that it meant everyone would be nice to me for a few days because that's what happened. But it didn't last long. Once the stitches were out and the scars were healing, I was back doing the shopping, making the beds, looking after the kids and doing whatever was needed. So, the charmed life came to a standstill.

Even though I was a hero, there was still a war on!

10 BALL AND STABBED

While I was in the hospital I could have had anything I wanted, but as soon as I was out it was the usual excuse of 'No!' or 'We haven't got enough coupons' or 'There isn't enough money for that,' or any excuse that came to hand. The trouble was that the excuses were all true. Even though I was very grown up for my age, I was just too young to appreciate just how difficult it was to be bringing up two boys and two girls on the money we got from the Army. that broke.

Three weeks after my discharge, I went with Mum, on one of our usual trips to see uncle Percy in the pawn shop. It was a Saturday and we needed a few bob to get us through the week-end. I waited outside while she went in to talk to Uncle Percy. It got on my nerves when she was in there trying to haggle for another few pence on the article she was pawning. Sometimes she would have to pawn something else to pay the interest on something that she had pawned almost three months earlier which she was in danger of losing because the time was running out and we still didn't have the money to get it back. When the time ran out the article would become the property of the pawn shop owner and be put up for sale. When I got a bit older, I would have to go down to 'Percy's' on my own, with bedclothes, blankets, overcoats, a wrist-watch, daddy's camera, or whatever we could raise money on and I would have to learn to haggle. On this occasion I was too still young. Although not too young to know what is was like constantly living from hand to mouth.

I stood in Cannon Street, looking in the window of Bernstein's the toy shop next door to Uncle's. Through the glass I saw lots of boxed games and books, but it was the bright red ball that caught my eye. It was what we called a dog's ball, meaning that it was made of a hard rubber that caused it bounce very high. It had a label next to it telling me and the whole of the East End, that it cost six pence. There was something about it that took me under its spell. It called to me and I wanted it. The longer I looked at it the more I yearned for it. By the time Mum came out of the pawnshop I desired it with complete and utter longing and I dragged her over to Bernstein's window.

"Mum, come and have a look in this window. Look there it is. Mum, can I have that ball? It's only six pence. That's not much, is it? I'll do all the errands and wash up and clean the place, and look after the kids. Could I have it mum? Could I? I promise I'll be good all the week."

She looked at the ball through the glass, surrounded by all the other bits and pieces laid out to tempt the young, then she looked back down at me. The expression on her face looked as if I had asked for a hurricane bomber and enough petrol coupons to fly it to Germany.

"Don't be a silly Pratt, Johnny," she said. "I've just come out of the fuckin' pawn shop. What makes you think I've got money for balls?"

"It's not balls Mum, it's just one. I'll work for it Mum, I promise. Go on Mum. What would I have to do? I'll do anything, I promise."

I carried on like this as we went to get some vegetables and a bit of fresh fish down the Jew's Market in Hessle Street. I carried on all the way home and for the rest of the day. That night after a lot of argument and when the other three were in bed, she eventually gave in.

"Alight," she said. "I'll give you the bleeding six pence. You can have it next Thursday when I get my Army Pay. Provided that you do all the things you've promised and behave yourself. Now don't keep going on about it and driving me mad otherwise I'll smack you in the mouth and you won't get nothing. Now get to bed."

I was ecstatic and went down stairs for a wee. When I came up I gave her a big kiss. She gave me one of her resigned looks and then she put her arms out to give me a special cuddle. I only ever got one of them when she had a minute to spare and all the others were in bed. She then stood up and we walked into the living room. She took a sixpence-penny piece from her purse and placed it on the tiled mantelpiece.

"And there is stays," she said. "Until I get me Army Pay on Thursday and you've done everything you said."

When I went to St. Augustine's, with Nanny, on Sunday, morning I said a special prayer that she wouldn't change her mind or forget all about it. She was prone to do that once she had got what she wanted. During the next five days I slogged myself silly and was on my utmost bestest behaviour. I never gave her no cheek or did anything wrong. Everything she asked me to do, I did without arguing. I hardly even swore. The silver sixpenny bit remained on the tiled mantelpiece. By the time I got to Wednesday afternoon I only had to wash up the dinner things to be followed by tea things later. Mum had gone to see Lena Whitmarsh about getting some outdoor work. The others were with her or out playing. I finished the washing up and put all the stuff neatly in the dipper cupboard and made the kitchen look real tidy. Then, I thought I might as well take the six pence and go to Bernstein's to buy my ball. I knew it wasn't Thursday and Mum still had to get her Army Pay, but it was only a few hours away so it wouldn't matter if I bought the bal now. So, I did.

It was a nervous moment when I walked over the bombsite, at the bottom of Tait Street, and went across Canon Street to Bernstein's. Terrible thoughts were going through my mind. What if it had been sold? What if the price had gone up? No, I couldn't bear it. The happiness of the rest of my life depended on it being there. It had to be there! I got to the shop and looked in the window and there it was, all shiny and red. I quickly went into the shop and gave Mrs. Bernstein my six pence. She passed the ball over the counter to me. It felt terrific. I immediately wanted to bounce it up and down, right there in the shop. I wanted to bounce it real hard. But I resisted the temptation and waited 'till I got outside. As the door shut behind me, I let my ball drop out of my hand onto the pavement and it sprang up back to me like a well-trained Jack Russell. It was fantastic. I had worked hard for it and now I was going to enjoy it.

I almost ran back to Tait Street knowing that just past number fifteen, Aunt Kate's house, there was a large brick wall which was the side of a house in the next street. The wall had no doors or windows in it to smash or anything get in the way of a clean throw.

Once I got there I played at throwing the ball against the wall from different positions and then catching it. After a few minutes of this I elaborated by throwing it at the pavement so that it bounced forward, hitting the wall and then curved back to me so that I could catch it. I elaborated further by adding a counting game, to see how many I could catch it before I dropped it. I then bounced it through my legs at the wall and practiced catching it in either hand. I wasn't very strong but according to my teachers I did have good co-ordination, which meant that I was good at catching things. Even when I missed the catch, I got pleasure in running after it because it bounced so beautifully.

While I was playing, Aunt Kate came by, with Joycie, and asked me in for a drink. Before we went upstairs I showed Joycie my ball and even let her have a throw. She threw it at the wall but not having any co-ordination at all she missed catching it when it came back so quickly. I ran after it and returned it to her as we went indoors to have a drink and spend a bit of time playing LUDO.

The snag was, that I spent a bit more time than I had meant to at Aunt Kate's. Before I knew was happening, it was past tea time and I knew that Mum would be home. I thanked Aunt Kate for the drink and ran, two steps at a time, down her stairs out into the street and home to fifty-one A.

I could hear that there was trouble as soon as I arrived on Mrs. Coakley's landing. Mum was doing her nut, Eddy was crying, Jeanie was bawling, Blackie was barking, Mrs. Coakley was brooming the ceiling and I wished I was back in the peace of Aunt Kate's house. I opened the door and climbed our stairs wondering what had happened for Mum to be in such a bad temper.

"Where the bleedin' hell have you bin?" Mum demanded, as I put my head round the kitchen door.

"I've bin up Aunt Kate's," I replied. "I did all the work before I went out."

"Have you taken any money of mine?" She asked.

"No, I haven't why?"

"I told you," she shouted, at Eddy. "I said Johnny wouldn't take it. It's you! You've had it. You lying little sod!"

She went for Eddy again.

"I never touched your money," said Eddy trying to dodge her flying hand

"I could bleedin' murder you," she continued, shaking her fist at him. "I wanted that tanner for potatoes for tonight. I was gonna do chips. Christ knows what we're gonna have now. You'll just have to have corned beef sandwiches. Johnny, have we got enough bread."

"Yes," I said quietly. Quietly because a terrible truth was beginning to dawn on me. "Yes, there's enough bread if we cut it thin. Mum, that six pence that was on the front room mantelpiece, was that the money Eddy took?"

"Course it was. It was all I've got 'till I go to the Post Office tomorrow." She sat down at the table and started banging her fingers on the baize cloth.

My thoughts started to fly around like a barrage balloon in a storm. "Oh shit! Oh No! There had been a mix up, she's saying that money was for potatoes. But she promised it to me. It had been on the mantelpiece for days. Don't say she's forgot. I didn't nick the money. She said it was mine. That was my money. I earned it. She must have forgot that she had promised it to me and now I was for it."

I started to work out how I could avoid a walloping. As luck would have it, I was still standing in the kitchen doorway at the top of our stairs, so I realised that my escape route was clear. But before I could do anything, I had to explain what had happened. I couldn't let Eddy take any more blame, not if I was ever to be a man.

"Mum."

"I've been round Lena's and sorted out some work," she wasn't even listening. "It's making batteries. You'll have to help me, the pair of you."

"Mum!"

"What?" She snapped at me. "What d'ya want?"

"That six pence on the mantelpiece in the front room was mine. You said I could have it when we came back from Uncle Percy's last week. You said it was mine if I did all the work."

"What the fuck are you talking about, yours?" she asked. "It wasn't yours it was mine. It was for our tea tonight. Are you telling me you took it. After I've just paid him for doing it. You little bastard! You've nicked that money." She stood up. "You've robbed your own Mother and let that poor little tyke take the blame? I'll fucking kill you."

There seemed to be no reason to stay there any longer. I'd done my best. I was running down the stairs before she managed to push past Beryl's high chair and get to the door. I knew if I could get out I'd be safe. She'd never chase me through the street and leave the girls on their own with Eddy.

"Come back. Come back here you robbin' little git."

I got to the bottom of our stairs as she got to the top.

"I'll smash your soddin' head in. I'll give you another crack to match the one you got from the bus, you lying, robbin' little fucker."

I raced across the landing and was down the bottom stairs, as Mrs. Coakley came out and got in Mum's way.

Once out of the front door I flew like a Spitfire. Up Bigland Street, round the corner past Gussie's and the Star pub, into

Planet Street and instinctively raced towards number sixteen and the safety of Nanny's.

Unfortunately, just as I passed the chapel steps, who should come out of number eighteen, but Old Granny Skelton. Farver's Mother. She still lived in the olden days and wore a bonnet, a long skirt and took snuff. She was a hard woman who had reared four sons with a rod of iron and stood no nonsense from anyone. She was carrying a jug and was on her way to get her 'half penny worth of stout from the Star.

"Where the bleedin' hell you running too?" she demanded, looking at me hard through the best of her eyes. "You've bin up to no good. I can see it in your face. You're trouble, you are. I know you are. I warned her not to take you. What you bin' up to?"

"I ain't bin' up to nothing," I said, as I ducked under her outstretched arm and into Nanny's ever open front door. I ran up the passage and straight into the back room.

"OI! Be-low!" said Farver. "Calm it down a bit. Where's the fire? There's no incendiaries in here so what's your rush."

"Mummy's gonna do me in. She gave me a tanner that she put on the mantelpiece and I did all the work and bought my ball and when I got home she was bashing Eddy up for nicking it and when I told her it was mine she started to chase me for making her hit him and now we ain't got no money for chips for tea because she forgot that she gave me the money last Saturday when she come out of the pawn shop and she's gonna kill me if I go home. So, I wanna live here?" I explained.

Farver, started laughing and called through the open window for Nanny to come in. She was washing some tea cups under the tap in the yard and when she finished she came in and sorted me out.

I was told off for taking the money without telling Mum. However, her parents knew what she was like and understood that she said one thing one day and then contradicted herself the next. So, after a cup of milk I was given six pence and told to go to Bernie Goldstein's, get six of chips and take them home to the family. Which is what I did. When I got back home, the smell of the chips and vinegar must have calmed Mum down a bit. She told me off again, but I didn't get a walloping.

That night when we had gone to bed, I apologised to Eddy, and explained that it wasn't my fault. He was growing up and getting to know what Mum was like, so he forgave me, and we had a cuddle before we went to sleep.

The 'ball' incident was soon forgotten because there was a heavy raid that night. In the morning we were all still alive, the house hadn't come down on top of us, the Anderson shelter hadn't flooded and nobody we knew had been killed. We had a lot to be thankful for and Farver said we could keep the six pence.

Years later that it would be occasionally thrown up in my face as to how I had lied and had watched Eddy being punished for stealing the money. It was often used as ammunition to start another row. She would never face the fact that she was the one who caused the wrong boy to be beaten, because she had a great capacity to utterly forget her involvement in any occurrence for which she might be blamed.

It was the same with blackout incident. Even when I was a grown man and showed her the scar she would still refuse to admit that she was to blame.

It was on a Saturday night that the stabbing occurred. We had been round at Nanny's, for to a bit of a do, so it was dark by the time we got home. Everyone was tired, and we were going to have one drink before we went to bed. I had put the kettle on and we had all gathered in the living room to get undressed while the water boiled. There was the usual muddle over clothes and shoes. Jeanie was getting in the way because she was half asleep and Beryl was wailing and moaning because she needed changing.

Mum had got the blackout blanket from behind the armchair and was going to hand it across the window because we had put the light on and if the A.R.P. saw it they would be knocking at the door to complain. She was standing on the top of the sideboard and me and Eddy were watching her from the other side of the room by the door while she nagged us to get undressed.

She managed to get the first corner of the large blanket hooked on to the nail that was on one side and then stretched out to the middle one. The trouble was that as she walked along the cluttered sideboard towards the far hook, she somehow managed to pull the middle one out of the wall. Well to us boys, the blanket falling off its nail was very funny. It seemed even funnier because we were tired. However, it was not at all funny to Mum as she tried to cover up the window in case there might be an air raid. Me and Eddy went into roars of laughter when, in her desperation, she pulled the blanket off of the first nail and it came out of the wall so that she nearly toppled off of the sideboard.

"Stop taking the piss and shut up," she yelled. She was very angry. "It's no laughing matter. More to your credit to come and help me before the soddin' German's start bombing us."

By now we were at the stage when everything was funny. So that sent us into hysterics, especially as there hadn't been a raid for days and days. We fell on each other and laughed all the more.

She screamed at us to shut up and in her rage felt around the top of the sideboard for something to throw at us. She could have grabbed one of the glass dishes, a saucer, books, scissors, coat hangers or anything, but the thing she happened to find was a pointed bread knife which, without thinking, she threw at the pair of us as we clung together.

It was in the air before she realised what she was doing, and I saw the look of horror on her face as I watched the knife leave her hand. For once her aim was on target and I saw it moving towards my brother. I let him go and as he bent forward to laugh it was coming towards his head. I stood up and somehow stuck out my left leg. The knife went into it, pierced my skin just above the knee before falling on to the floor. Blood appeared, and I screamed.

"Aaaagh! She's done it now. She's stabbed me to death." I yelled.

Mum jumped down from the sideboard, leaving the blanket draped over the sideboard and ran towards me.

"She's gone and killed me. Look Eddy, I'm gonna die. I'm bleeding to death!"

She reached me, and I thought I was going to get a good slosh in the face but no; she seemed quite concerned.

"Sit still," she sounded scared, "I'll get a wet flannel to stop the blood."

She ran into the kitchen and came back with a wet dish cloth.

"Hold that over the cut, I'm gonna go over the road to get Louis Patmore. Stay there. all of you stay where you are. And Johnny make sure you keep that cloth over your leg to staunch the blood."

Strangely we all stayed where we were. I suppose we were in some sort of shock. None of us said anything. Eddy and I just looked at each other and at the cloth, slowly getting red through the dampness. Jeanie who had undressed herself so was now ready for bed in vest and knickers, was sitting on the armchair with her arm on Beryl's leg. Beryl still hadn't been changed but had somehow sensed there was no point in crying anymore, so she had shut up. We heard Mum and Louis running across the downstairs landing and up our stairs. Mum rushed into the front room dragged me from the chair and started to cuddle me.

"Oh, Johnny," she said in a crying voice and shaking me to death with her apologies. while I tried to hold the dish cloth on my knee. "Mummy loves you darling. I didn't mean to do it but you were driving me mad the pair of you. I had to get the blinds up before the warning went. You never know when they're coming over. But I shouldn't have done that to you."

"Put him down Nell," ordered Aunt Louis. "And let's have a look at what you've done."

"What am I going to say up the hospital if he needs stitches?" said Mum. "They could take him away from me for this. Couldn't they Lou?"

"We don't know if he needs stitches yet," said Louis. "Sit him back on the chair so that I can have a look."

Mum put me on the chair while Louis, her old school friend, knelt in front of me to examine the stab wound. As she removed the tea towel I expected a welling up of sympathy for my suffering.

"No, that look's alright. It should probably have one stitch in it but we can hold it together with a plaster," she said, just before she slapped me round the head. "And as for you little bugger, you ought to learn how to behave yourself instead of driving your mother mad so that she has to start throwing cutlery at you."

"But I was saving Eddy's life," I insisted.

"Rubbish, you lying little git," said Louis. "Nell open my Oxo tin and get one of those big plasters out. We don't want to have to go all the way to the London with just that, do we."

The edges of my wound were pushed together to save on the stitches and Louis put a big plaster on my knee. She also put a bandage round it, to hold it in place. That done she stood up in front of me and wagged her finger in my face.

"Now listen Johnny," she said, "take it easy on that leg for a couple of days. And if I hear that you're playing your mother up any more I shall be up those stairs and it will be more than a knife you'll find in your legs." She turned to Mum and said. "Get me a hammer Nell and I'll bang that nail back in for ya. You should knock it in the wood not in the brick. It won't stay in the brick unless you plug the wall."

She banged the nails in the window frame, put the blanket up and jumped down saying, "I'm off now Nell, Mr. Bennett will be wondering where I am." And out she went clutching the Oxo tin with her medical supplies in one hand and giving me a final clip round the head with the other.

That night when Eddy and I were in bed and I was finding it difficult to get off to sleep I said to him, "That's bleedin' good ain't, I save your life and stop Mummy getting hung and all I get is a soddin' telling off from pratty Patmore. Fuck 'em!"

"Yeah. Fuck 'em," repeated Eddy quietly as he fell off to sleep. As I said before Mum always refused to admit that the scar on my leg, which I have to this day, was due to her stabbing me.

11 WAR WORKERS

The lack of money was a constant problem to Mum, who had to try everything she could to get a few bob extra each week. One of her enterprises was making batteries in the garden. This came about because Lena Whitmarsh's brother Danny, knew some bloke whose cousin Bert, had a contract with the war office to deliver to them hundreds of batteries every month. Bert was finding it hard to keep up with the orders because the way the war was going they were wanting things done quicker and quicker. So he was being forced to recruit more outdoor workers to keep the demand flowing. Lena, who knew that Mum always needed money. managed to persuade Danny to get Bert to give her a try.

The weather was very warm, so Mum had set up a workshop in the back garden which consisted of two wooden tables and six chairs for her team of workers. The workers were, Nanny, Aunts Kate and Alice, Lena and Louis Patmore with occasional help from me. Mum had also set up the gramophone on an orange box for music while we worked. 'I've got a girl in Kalamazoo,' was my favourite because I could go 'Zoo Zoo, Zoo, at the end of the chorus. Eddy liked 'Deep in the Heart of Texas,' because he could do the three claps just before he sang the title line.

The work consisted of wrapping bits of cloth around a black stem, like a pencil lead, and sticking it inside a box that contained black jelly that was smothered in soot. A Bakelite plate, which had connectors on it. was banged on top to seal it in. I never understood how it all worked but when we had finished making millions of them and put them in boxes, they took them away to do something else with them at a factory. We all got covered in soot and after ten minutes I found it very boring. I did everything I could to get away from the table and play.

Since Aunt Kate was working, it meant that Joycie was with us in the garden all the time and when I wasn't at the table I was put in charge of minding the others. This meant that I had to organise things for them to do and games for them to play. We played mothers and fathers in the shelter and 'gobs,' now called five-stones, on the step by the back door. We had the run of the garden and the yard area but were forbidden to go into the shed at the back of the yard because it was falling down. I found this a great pity because we were increasingly drawn to the interesting rubbish that was in there. We only kept out of it because the door had a catch at the top which none of us could reach.

After three days, when Eddy, Jeanie and Joycie were getting thoroughly bored with I spy, hide and seek and hunt the old teapot spout, I managed to get then amused by trying to get their hands into the shed to see if they could get any treasure. Eddy managed to get the rail of an old train set, Jeanie found half of a broken saucer, and Joycie got nothing because she was afraid a spider would kill her. I did the best because when I got my hand in between the broken boards at the bottom of the door, I managed to grab a tin of paint. Bright green paint.

It was a good haul which I was pleased about. I quickly realised that it could benefit me two-fold because as well as keeping the others busy I could get in Mum's good books by painting the shed door green which would be a nice surprise for the grown-ups later in the day.

We didn't have any brushes, but I thought we could make some out of bits of the battery rag. I went down to the work table and stuck a few stems in for a while and when no one was looking, I put some of the cloth in my trouser pocket and up the front of my shirt. A little while later I left the table and returned to the shed. While I had been working, Eddy and the two girls had been digging up the earth and had found some bits of an old kettle with its spout still on. Eddy was using this to open the lid of the paint tin which took a bit of doing but eventually he managed it.

I gave Eddy, Jeanie and Joycie a bit of cloth each and showed them how to roll it up so that it could be used as a paint brush. We carried the tin to the door and put it on a brick so that it wouldn't get knocked over on to the earth. I, being the foreman, decided that Jeanie and Joycie would do the bottom and us men would do the top and we all set to work.

It went quite well, except for the fact that it was supposed to be green and when we put it on the wood it was just a lot of oily stuff. This meant that we had to put our hands right in to get the actual paint on to our cloths. Unfortunately, some of it went on our arms and hands, and as we were painting it dripped on to the girls below. The green colour looked rather nice in their hair because they were both blonde. It wasn't long before I came to the conclusion that we would need something to stand on so that we could paint the top part of the door.

Fortunately, no one noticed when I borrowed one of the chairs, because the grown-ups were busy having a break and chatting to each other. Aunt Kate was turning the record over and winding the gramophone. Mum was changing Beryl's napkin, Nanny had gone upstairs to make some tea while Lena and Alice were moving the full boxes nearer to the open yard door. Louis had popped back across the road to check on Mr. Bennett.

When I got back with the chair, Eddy thought it would be a good idea if we got on to the shed roof so that we could have a look over the wall at the ruins of the house next door. He was a much better climber than me so we both got on the chair and I gave him a bunk up. Once he was on the roof he bent down and pulled me up to join him. I was a bit scared at first, but he had no fear of anything. He marched straight over the planks of wood towards the wall until suddenly the roof collapsed and he disappeared. I was shocked.

"Mum, Mummy!" I screamed. "Eddy's fell in the shed. Quick Mum he's gone through the roof!"

I think it must have been a worry to them all when they looked up and saw me standing on the roof of the shed with the two girls below splattered with green dots and no sign of my brother.

Mum had to put Beryl back in her pram, so Aunt Kate was the first to arrive. She wrenched one of the planks away from the side of the shed and looked in.

"He's knocked out." she said as she knocked the wedge from the top of the door and rushed in.

"Is he alright Kate?" Screamed Mum, as she ran up. "Is he alive?"

"He's smothered in blood all over his face" Said Aunt Kate, coming back out again. "Hang on …. Yes, he's still breathing Nell, but he's knocked out."
Aunt Kate disappeared into the shed, as the kitchen window was pushed up and a head leaned out.

"Johnny, get down off that roof this bloody minute. You'll break your neck." That was Nanny shouting from upstairs. "I'll murder you when you do get down."

"Eddy's fell through the roof and is laying in the shed," Mum yelled up at her.

"I'm coming down," said Nanny and disappeared.

I tried to get down, but I wasn't sure what would be the worst; falling and breaking my arm or getting down in one piece and being smashed round the head by my mother. They women stared at me as I turned and balanced along the rotting wood towards Lena who had left the table and was now on the chair and reaching over to lift me down as Aunt Kate came out of the shed carrying Eddy unconscious in her arms.

As this was happening, guess who appeared coming through the back door at the other end of the garden?

Our Dad. He was home on leave standing there in his uniform with brasses shining and kit bag over his shoulder. He looked as though he was trying hard to make sense of what he was seeing at the end of the garden. Three kids splashed black and green, a soot covered woman standing on a chair while his wife, who was also covered in black soot, had her arms outstretched to catch the boy who was balancing on the shed roof. Meanwhile his sister-in-law came towards him carrying his unconscious son who was dripping blood.

Once he got hold of the situation lots of things happened at once. There was a lot of screaming, shouting and confusion. Aunt Kate passed Eddy over to Dad, and Aunt Alice ran to Louis' house to call the ambulance. Mum started panicking and I jumped into Lena's arms and was put on the ground. Soon after that Nanny arrived and after a lot of argy-bargy she took me and the two girls upstairs to be cleaned off. I heard the bell of the ambulance while Nanny scrubbed me with paraffin, hot water and half a bar of Sunlight soap rubbed on with the scrubbing brush. It wasn't until later that I found out that Eddy had concussion and had to stay in hospital overnight while he had got over the worst, whatever that meant.

He came out the next day with a bandage round his head and we swapped stories about what it was like to be in hospital, as we sat in sight of the grown-ups with the gramophone playing and told not to go anywhere.

Dad was only home on a forty-eight-hour pass but while he was with us he urged the women to keep working on the batteries because something big was gonna happen soon. I never found out what was going on because they would keep talking in codes like the grown-ups did. In those times you had to because 'Careless talks cost lives.' That was the saying and it was true. The Nazi's were listening everywhere. Maybe even over the wall of the bombed house on the other side of our yard. And if they found out what was going on they would put a bullet up your arse as good as look at you.

Aunt Margie knew all about careless talk, because she worked at the censor's office. That was the place where they read your letters to make sure that you never told your husband or wife where you were, in case the German's read them. Once the German's had read them they would know exactly where to bomb everyone, including the King and the Queen. That's why you had to be careful in what you said and in what you wrote.

Aunt Margie, who I think liked me best of all her nieces and nephews, took me to her office for a treat towards the end of the war when things were a bit more relaxed and it was a day to remember.

Her office building was somewhere up the West End, a long way past Aldgate and it was smashing! She let me play with rubber stamps that I banged on a pad and then pushed it on to a sheet of paper and the words all wrote themselves in violet ink. There was plenty of paper and envelopes and lots of good things around to play with. There were boxes with cards in what they called files. There were also sticky stamp things to stick on stuff and paper clips, plus a machine that made holes in paper and something else that clipped sheets together when I banged the top of it. It was terrific to be there. The women workers came up to me and spoke in posh voices saying that, I had lovely ginger hair and how I should have been a girl with those curls. Women were always saying things like that to me, silly cows.

We had sandwiches for lunch, which was what we called dinner time but they called it lunch. They gave me a cup of coffee, which I didn't like and after that Aunt Margie took me to a Museum on a special pass. There were models and a plane hanging from the ceiling and cases that when you pressed a button, things would move about. There were lots of Soldiers around and no other kids at all. I was very important, and they made a great fuss of me. We returned to the office and I played with sticky labels marked priority and secret that I put on a wet sponge in a glass dish then stuck on parcels and fat envelopes. I could write and scribble as much as I liked on scrap paper with black printing on it that said On His Majesty's Service. And best of all you could light a bit of string and drip sealing wax on to the backs of letters. It was a day I never forgot it was just absolutely grand.

12 D-DAY, DOODLEBUGS AND DEATH

I was just over eight and Eddy was almost seven when we heard about D-day. I thought it was something to do with Dunkirk again. Dunkirk, was when lots of our men were being killed and all our boats went over to get them away from the Germans. It even included the little boats which were rowed all the way to France and when our men got there they picked up soldiers and sailors out of the water. Even if they were wounded very badly and had blood pouring out of them. Dunkirk had happened years ago when I was still a little boy. Only D-Day wasn't about Dunkirk; it was about some other place. But that didn't matter because wherever or whatever it was everyone was very pleased. Everyone said that 'We were really giving the bastards what for.' The women, in the queue round Harvey's fish stall, were saying that the war wouldn't last much longer, that the men would be home and we would all live happily ever after. That news didn't last very long because before we could get used to the thought of peace, the Nazi's had invented the doodlebug.

The doodlebug was a 'plane that didn't have a pilot. The grown-ups were saying that there wasn't much that could be done about it because it was a rocket. If your name was on it, that was it. You'd had it. The rocket would fly over to

London, all on its own, with a name on it to drop on someone. The engine, which sounded just like an old lorry, would cut out and everything would go very quiet until the person whose name was on it got it. The trouble was no one never knew whose name was on it until it hit them. It could be us and we would never know until we were dead. We would just have to wait until the red light on the rocket went out and it stopped, then bang and someone had got it. The Bosch called them V.1. Rockets, V being for Vengeance but we British called them doodlebugs. Which was one in the schmackers for Hitler, that bastard!

The Nazis must have been making them like mad, because lots and lots of them came over and not just at night they came during the day as well. As there were no Gerry pilots to drive them, old Adolph could send over as many as he liked safe in the knowledge that he wouldn't lose any men.

Eddie and me with Dennis Stag and Lucille Grebe, were on our way back from Cable Street Park one afternoon when warning went. We heard the throbbing of the doodlebug coming which was a bit scary, so we got close to the wall and all bunched up together against the bricks. While we were all breathing in each other's breath, it dawned on me that we would be alright because we were too young to have an address of our own, so our names couldn't be on it. I quickly told the others who saw the sense of it so we came away from the wall, walked in the middle of the street waiting for the engine to stop and listening for the bang. A woman standing in a shelter doorway started screaming at us to take cover. We ignored her, so she rushed over and dragged us into the shelter. Lucille tried to tell her that our names couldn't possibly be on the bomb, but the woman refused to listen.

So, we were forced to stay there until the rocket exploded. It did with a huge noise. After the all clear sounded we all left the shelter to find out where it had landed.

Our gunners shot a lot of rockets down, but loads got through and they started flying to other places in England. The Air Force, our Boys in Blue who were very clever, found their starting points which were in Cherbourg and they began bombing them. Farver told us this and it must have been true, because he listened to the Home Service and they told him everything on the nine o/clock news.

Once the rockets started Mum got too scared to sleep with us on her own so we went back to kipping in Nanny's shelter up Planet Street. Me and Eddy top and tailed in the top bunk and Jeanie and Joycie did the same in the bottom bunk. There were seven other families in there as well as the dogs and the accordions. Lena Whitmarsh always brought a big cut glass rose bowl with her. It had been a wedding present and she didn't want it to get bombed now that her husband was dead. Some people, like the Andrews Sisters from next door to Lena, didn't have bunks so they slept on a chair or on the floor. It got very smelly. Especially when some of the grown-ups had been on the beer and got a fit of the farts. But we had to put up with it because there was a war on.

Some nights it would be difficult to even start to get to sleep - never mind about being woke up! There would be the throbbing drone of the fleets of plane's going across to bomb the Gerry's, then there would be the guns and the warning and just when we were about to drop off there would be the sound of the doodlebugs, doodling around 'up there' followed by the silence. During the silence, which I don't think was very long, but it seemed to take donkey's years, the faces on the grown-ups became very tense. As if they didn't know where to look and tried not to catch the eye of anyone else. Everyone must have been feeling guilty for praying to God that someone else's name was on it. It was always a bit of a relief when the explosions finally came. Then people nodded and smiled and shook their heads, as they thought of the families they had willed to get blown to smithereens instead of them.

It was in the middle of June, just after Eddy's seventh birthday, that a couple of them crashed a bit too close for comfort around Watney Street Market. In the blast a water pipe broke and our shelter got flooded. I was shaken awake to see everyone trying to get things on to the top bunks before they got soaked. Farver was there that night and managed to save the accordions by carrying them up the stairs. Tony and Neene were barking and splashing around in the water but we weren't allowed to join in. When we came out in the morning we found that our school had been wrecked, fifteen people had been killed and six shops had gone. This really scared the grown-ups who realised that it was now very dangerous to be in London.

As more and more rockets came over and the casualties got heavier Mr. Churchill warned people to get out of the city. Which meant that we had to be evacuated again. We didn't have a lot of luggage. The big advantage of not having much was that it made choosing what to take very easy. We had just a case and a few bags for the five of us. On this evacuation, we didn't have the bother with gas masks because the threat of death by gas had evaporated. Being summer we packed light clothes and carried our heavy outdoor coats for when it got colder. We had no idea how long we were going to be away for, so we had to pack for all eventualities. It was Tuesday, July the eleventh nineteen forty-four when we left our house in Stepney we had no idea if we would ever get home again or even if our house would be there when we did.

Aunt Kate, Joycie, Nanny and Aunt Alice went to somewhere in Suffolk while Aunt Margie stayed in London to do essential war work. Mum with us four kids was posted to Middlewich in Cheshire, near Wales. Some people we knew from the East End came with us but Mum loathed being separated from her mother and sisters. When we said goodbye to the family then were taken to a station to board the train that was going to take us to Crewe.

There were millions of people all trying to get on the train, so we had to have labels pinned on to us in case we got separated. Mum managed to get us seats together in the same compartment. I found it very exciting with the whistling, the steam, the engine revving up and slowly pulling us out of the station. At the start of the journey it was impossible to get away from Mum to explore the train. Especially when we had hardly got started and the warning went. No planes shot at us and no rockets hit us. We must have been far from London when it was over because I never heard the all clear.

After we had been travelling for a couple of hours the W.V.S. brought round tea and sandwiches. This meant that me and Eddy could do a lot of going to the toilet at the end of the carriage. Although we had to promise Mum not to open any doors or windows or forget the way back. Jeanie came in handy get out of the carriage because now she was nearly five her bladder was always loose.

The journey took ages and the three of us big ones got very bored. Beryl who was now almost two and a half was being difficult, which meant that I had to hold her a lot when Mum got fed up with her fretting. Mum even allowed me to take her for a walk along the train but the corridor was very crowded and she wanted to wee so it didn't last long. Late in the afternoon I fell asleep leaning against Eddy. When Mum shook me awake it was still light and she told me that we had arrived at Crewe.

I stood up to find that everything in utter confusion. Train doors were slung open and crashed against the carriage walls, people were ordered to get off the train by people who had strange accents. Posh old men carrying clipboards, were telling the evacuees where to get in a line. The evacuees were yelling through the doors and windows as they tried to get their families and belongings together. A man wearing an A.R.P. arm band started shouting at people, telling them that they were going the wrong way. They turned back and crashed into another lot people who were also going the wrong way. As I stood at the train door waiting for a W.V.S. woman to lift me down, it looked as if the whole train had burst its rivets and was spilling Londoners all over the platform. Somehow the five of us all managed to keep together. Mum was carrying Beryl and the case, Jeanie was holding on to my arm while both Eddie and I hung on to Mum's coat tails with one hand and carried a bag in the other.

We were led out of the station and put on to a coach with other evacuees. We were then driven through the countryside to a place called Middlewich, where we were ordered off of the coach and led to a reception centre. Once we got inside there were more people to order us about as they tried to find us somewhere to live. Well I say us, it wasn't us at all, it was just most of the others. The gang from the coach got smaller and smaller and after about an hour most of the other refugees left us with their "T.T.F.N.'s" and "We'll see you laters."

It was getting quite late when the woman in charge came up to tell us the news.

"I'm sorry Luv, we haven't been able to get you a billet yet, so you'll have to make yourself comfortable in the reception centre for the night," she said. "We are trying me duck, but it's proving a mite difficult with you being so many."

There were two other families, that couldn't be found a billet, so we all stayed in the dilapidated church hall dubbed the Middlewich Evacuee Reception Centre.

During the next day the two smaller families, were found somewhere to go. A couple of times during the morning we heard that they might have found us a billet, but it always fell through. It was proving very difficult, to find anyone to share their house with a woman and four children. During the day Daisy Ewer and the Andrews Sisters, from Stepney, came back to see Mum and we met other friends when we went for a walk in the town. It was hard going and by Wednesday night we were in the hall on our own.

Eddie and I shared a brown hard mattress on the floor, covering ourselves with flannelette sheets and smelly blankets. Mum and the girls shared a similar one on the other side of the case which doubled as a bedside table. I watched Mum putting her dinky curlers in by the light of an oil lamp and saying that we would still be there when her hair had turned silver. Somehow, she kept us amused with her stories about how she loved Clarke Gable and another about the that sausage rolled off her plate when she first met Dad. She could always get us laughing when she was in the right mood and wanted to be funny.

But on Thursday a miracle happened, and we were packed up and marched to the house of Mr. Jenkinson in St Ann's Avenue. He was kind enough to give us his upstairs bedroom, share kitchen and facilities. His house was red brick, with two rooms upstairs and two down, with a wash house, stuck like an inflamed wart, on the back. It had a tiny garden in the front and a slightly bigger one at the back. We had put our case and the bags upstairs and were just looking around the back garden, when the woman next door put her head over the wall and called Mum over.

"Are you alright Luv? Got everything you need? I'm Mrs. Kelly," she said. "They asked me to take you but it just weren't possible, what with our Tilley and Ivy in the front and me and Jim in the back. What lovely children. And look at the ginger hair on that one. What a lovely colour, he should have been a girl with those curls."

Mum, as was her way, got talking to Mrs. Kelly and told her all our business and found out the local gossip. That night when we got ready for bed in our room, Mum stuck a chair back under the door handle.

"Johnny, you'll have to help me do guard duty," she whispered. "Two hours on and four off. I'll do the first shift. We don't want 'im comin' in here."

"He won't come in here," I said. "He's told us this is our room."

"It's not that," said Mum. "It's that Mrs. Kelly told me that his niece had recently had a baby and the think he was the father. I wouldn't put it past him. I suspected something when he asked me to talk close to his ear because he's a bit deaf."

We were all dead tired, so it was great to sleep in a proper bed again. I went out like a light and it seemed only minutes before she was waking me up.

"Johnny. It's time to do your shift. I've had no trouble so far. Just look at the clock and when the big hand gets on the two and the little hand gets on the six, wake me up. I'm gonna nut down now. Don't forget to wake me."

I sat up and could see the clock in the moonlight and feel Eddie at the other end of the bed. He was all warm and snug. I was thinking I might wake him to keep me company, but thought better of it. Before I knew it, Mum was waking me up and it was Friday morning July the seventeenth. She didn't nag about me falling asleep on guard duty. I suppose because nothing had happened during the night and she wasn't going to have another baby.

We went down stairs to have breakfast. Mr. Jenkinson had got porridge for us while he had toast and jam. Jam! We looked at it hopefully, but he never offered.

Mum decided that we must now all get clean again. So she lit a fire under the copper in the wash house and when the water had nearly boiled gave the four of us a good wash down. Later, after a bit of dinner, at the fish shop, we went to the town. On the way back, we met Derek and Roger Andrews who were going to play. They asked me and Eddie to go with him.

"Eddy can go, but Johnny you've got to stay and look after the girls. No! Now don't start!" she said as I opened my mouth to protest. "I've got to get all the washing done. You can play with
them in the yard. Eddy tell me where we live now. What's your address?" He told her and went with the boys while we turned the corner towards our new home.

When we got indoors, we sorted out the shopping and raked the embers under the copper. Mr. Jenkinson was out so we felt at ease. I went into the garden to play with Beryl and Jeanie, who was being a bit of a cow because she didn't want to be bossed about by me.

It was a lovely afternoon, we'd been in the garden for a while and although I can never remember the game we were playing, I will never forget the scream that came from the wash house. Of all the events that happened that day and in the weeks, that followed and most of the details are stuck in my mind forever, it is the scream that hurts the most.

"Johnny!" Mum yelled from inside the wash house, happy with her packet of Rinso and half a bar of Sunlight soap.

"What?" I yelled back.

"There's a knock at the door. I've got all me hands wet, go and see who it is will you?"

"Alright," I said, as I lifted Beryl over a fence to keep her from running indoors. "Keep your eye on her while I'm gone." I told Jeanie and went into the wash house.

It was hot and steamy in there due to the fire under the copper which had boiled the washing. Mum was at the low sided sink, wearing her pink dress with the faded paisley pattern. She was wringing out the clothes that were under the cold water in her strong hands. He black curls still springy from her 'Dinky's' were swinging in time to her wringing.

"Find out what they want and tell them I'm busy and Mr. Jenkinson's out," she said, as I went into the passage, closing the connecting door behind me.

After the sunny garden it went suddenly dark in the passage with only a small dirty window at the street end to let in any light. I felt my way past the stairs sliding my hand along the wall until I reached the front door. I stood on tiptoe, pulled back the latch and opened it. I looked up at the silhouette of a woman, outlined against the bright blue sky, standing above me.

"Is your Mummy in Johnny?" It was Vera Briggs. There was a breathless energy in the question. She had been running.

"Yeah," I replied. "But she's doin' the washin' at the minute. What do you want?"

She took a step into the doorway, arched her body over mine and called down the passage towards the closed wash house door.

"Nelly! Are all your kids here?" She took a breath. "Only there's been......" She never finished the sentence.

She was interrupted by a scream, a shout, a groan, or a wail that was a noise of painful disbelief. It was the noise that pierced into me and has stayed forever. It was a wounding, hurting yet pitiful scream: and it was coming from my mother.

The connecting door crashed open against the wall and Mum was running down the passage behind me.

"Come on Johnny!!" she growled, splashing me with water as she tore past and out of the gate towards the canal. I knew she wanted me with her, but Vera caught and held me tight.

"Now you stay here and look after the girls Johnny, there's a good boy," said Vera.

"Piss off. You look after 'em," I replied as I kicked her in the shins with my little black boots. She let me go and I was running down the avenue following my Mum, before she knew what had hit her.

Mum was ahead and going fast but I was determined to catch her. I fixed my eyes on the back of her dress and really ran. I may have been skinny, but I was fast. I began to gain on her. She was slowing down. I doubled the effort in my thin legs and caught up with her. I reached out and grabbed the skirt of the paisley frock. We ran together. She must have felt me because she didn't look at me, she just put her hand behind her as she stared ahead trying to bore into the distance.

"Keep up with me Johnny. Keep up son."

"Mum what's the matter? Where are you going?"

"It's Eddie, Johnny. I know it is." She was gasping from the run.

"What Mum? What are you talking about?"

She collapsed.

She fell on the grass at the side of the pavement. I was pulled down with her and landed on to her arm. I was very frightened. I thought she must have died. I lay on the ground and looked across at her closed eyes. I'd never seen her so still.

"Mum. Mummy!" I could feel tears coming and pressed my lips hard together so that I wouldn't cry.

Grown-ups began to gather around us. Women's voices talking in their local accent. Then a man's voice.

"It's alright lad, she's only fainted. She'll be alright"

I heard the click of a gate latch and above the rest of the murmuring a firm female voice.

"We can't leave the poor lass lying like that, bring her into my parlour. George, you take her top and a couple of your take her legs. Hurry up now.!"

A lady helped me up and the others picked up my Mother. I caught hold of her skirt again as they carried her towards the house feet first. I looked up at the women who were looking very upset.

Our group crossed the pavement and up the short garden path into a house. It was one of those houses that didn't have a passage because the street door opened straight on to the front room. I had to let go of the comforting skirt because there wasn't enough room for us all to get through the door. A lady behind me guided me in.

I could tell straight away it was a posh house. Because everything matched and was green. The three-piece suite, the carpet with a pattern of leaves on it, the runner on the sideboard with matching green dishes at either end. They laid Mum on the sofa in front of the fireplace with a green marble clock on the mantelpiece. I followed them round and got as close as I could to her. George and the others moved away and stood by the front door. Between the green curtains through the window I could see a crowd gathering and trying to look in.

"It's alright my duck, take it easy," the woman who had called us in said, as she held a small bottle under Mum's nose.

"Mum, Mummy," I said, shaking her.

Mum stirred and shook her head away from the bottle. The lady persevered and Mum opened her eyes.

"Hello my Luv, "said the lady. "I'm Mrs. Williams and you're in my house. You were......."

"Johnny!" Mum ignored the woman and pulled me to her. "Eddie? Is he alright? I heard Vera, saying something about my kids and even as she said it I had a terrible presentiment. Is Eddie alright?"

"I don't know nothing Mum, you just run down the street and when you fainted they brought you into this posh house."

She looked at me bewildered, not knowing what she was about and her voice was quiet.

"What am I doing in here?"

"It's alright, I'm Mrs. Williams and this is my house. I'm afraid you fainted outside, and I thought it best to bring you in here. What's your name duck?"

"Mrs. Halstead. Nelly."

"Well, Mrs. Halstead, perhaps you and Johnny would like a nice cup of tea. I'd just made some when I heard the commotion."

At that moment there was a change in the group around the door and window. We looked over and saw someone forcing their way through. Daisy Ewer, Mum's old school friend, burst into the room. I felt a bit better at seeing someone I knew.

"Nelly it's me, Daisy," she said in the rasping voice that she got from shouting out in all weathers on a fruit stall. "Now listen gel, there's bin an accident," she came around to the front of the settee close to my mother. "A little boy has fallen into the lock at the bottom of the road and we think it's your Eddie. They've got him out and he's still alive. They're working on him now."

"I knew it," Mum cried. "I knew it was him, as soon as I heard Vera's voice I knew it. I must go to him. Johnny help me!"

She was desperately struggling to get up. Mum was always such a strong woman that I felt frightened at seeing her so weak.

I stood up to help her, but they sat me down with words and firmness like grown-ups do.

"Sit a while longer Lovey," said Mrs. Williams sounding a bit like a teacher. "I'm just going to pour your tea."

"She's right Nell, you stay here," rasped Daisy. "You' can't do nothing if you go to him and if he sees you the shock might do him more harm than good. I'll see how things are going and come back in a minute." She was up and barging her way out through the crowd before Mum could think; least of all say anything.

Mrs. Williams passed Mum some tea in a cream cup with little orange and green flowers round the rim. But when she took it she was shaking so much that Mrs. Williams had to hold it for her while she drank. More people had gathered around the door and window, but things seem to settle down a bit.

In no time at all Daisy pushed her way back to deliver her report from the canal. She told us that a doctor was there, they'd been giving Eddy artificial respiration and his colour was coming back. I didn't know what that meant but it seemed to please the crowd who smiled and thanked God, as they parted to let Daisy return to the front line. I looked at my Mum. But the concern and pain in her face was too much for me to see. I looked away. She saw me do it.

"Johnny, come here," she spoke like she did when the others were asleep, and she was going to give me a special cuddle. "Look at your dirty face. You've got a black line all down the side of your mouth. Come and let me wipe it off."

She pushed Mrs. Williams and the tea aside and took a handkerchief from her paisley pocket, she licked it and wiped the side of my mouth. As she helps my chin to keep my head still, I noticed that her hands were still red from wringing out the clothes in the cold water.

Then the silence started.

It wasn't complete silence because there were still birds and faint sounds in the distance. It was the silence of a lot of people saying nothing. It crept across the room to us and together we looked towards the street door.

Daisy was there. She looked unfamiliar because her face was all pulled back and her lips were wrinkled up as though she was going to kiss someone. She looked at my mother and said.

"I'm sorry Nell."

She didn't say anything else but now the silence was a really deep silence. My ears hurt with it. It was as if all the grown ups were playing a game of holding their breaths to see who could hold it the longest. My Mum, still holding the handkerchief, pulled me towards her as she told me.

"Eddie's died."

She drew me towards her and buried my head in her chest. I could feel the vibrations of her body as she tried to control her breathing. I could also feel the tears dropping on the back of my neck. I was pleased she was hiding my face, because I didn't know what to do. I didn't understand. Eddy died? He couldn't have. People only died in the bombing or when they were old, like old Mrs. Arnicker. Children didn't die. Anyway, I'd seen him about an hour ago when he was going out to play. He couldn't be dead. He'll be coming in for his tea soon. But our Mum was crying so it must be true. What should I do? I was the eldest; I should do something. But what? If only our Dad was here. But he was in the Army, we didn't know where and I don't suppose he knew where we were.

"He'd gone down twice," I heard Daisy saying in a voice that hurt your throat to listen to her. "There was a man talking on the corner and saw two kids and a woman waving from the bank So he ran up the side of the lock and managed to grab Eddy as he came up for the second time. The bloke pumped the water out of him. He'd only gone down twice so there was a chance, he kept saying. Then a doctor came, and she gave Eddy a needle and they kept working on him. Then his colour started coming back and he looked as if he was gonna be alright." Her voice was getting closer to the settee. "Then his heart gave out." I felt her hand on my shoulder. 'Nelly it's me, Daisy. Nelly? Let Johnny go Nell, you'll hurt him."

Mum let me loose and Daisy slowly moved me away, keeping me next to her with my back to the fireplace. I could feel the warmth of her thigh against my shoulder. I kept my eyes on Mum, because I didn't want to look at all the people who were staring at us.

I knew then that my brother had died. Eddy who was my best friend, who stopped me from being afraid and who I loved. He was dead, and my mother was lying on Mrs. Williams green settee crying quietly. Mum, raised her head and looked over at me. Her eyes were brimming over with tears: tears she didn't bother to wipe away so that they rolled down her face on to her lap like tiny little water babies. Her face was all pink and shiny, just like it had been in the wash house only a little while ago.

As I watched her sitting in this stranger's house, in this strange town, hundreds of miles from our real home and our real relations, I knew what I had to do.

"Come on Mum," I said, as I eased myself away from Daisy's hand. "We'd better get back to the girls, they'll be wondering where we are."

Her eyes closed for a second or two and her mouth crunched up as though she was trying to put her chin on her nose. She took a deep breath and opened her eyes. She nodded her head and her face strained into a shining wet smile. She got up from the settee, took my hand and we began to walk out of the room. She still couldn't speak but I could feel the fight coming back into her. The crowd opened up to let us through. We had just reached the door when I remembered my manners. I turned back into the room and said.

"Thank you for the tea Mrs. Williams."

Mum didn't say anything. She just put her two hands in front of her face and bowed her head.

We walked back up the Avenue.

Everything is a blur about what happened for the next few days because so much happened and I was in a deep shock to remember the details.

We left Mr. Jenkinson's that Friday, 14th July 1944. Mum felt that she couldn't stay there anymore, so we packed up the case and filled the bags and were taken back to the reception centre, while they looked for a new billet. Everyone rallied round us and not just the evacuees. A telegram was sent to Dad telling him that Eddie had died and to come at once. Just as it was beginning to get dark we got a billet. We went to stay with Auntie Rene and her three boys. I was really missing Eddie but felt I shouldn't cry about it. Not that there was much time what with the moving and looking after the girls and Mum. I still expected Eddie to appear any minute, it just didn't seem right without him. I had no one to talk to or to take my part when things were hard. But he didn't come.

On Saturday Mum had a visitor Mr. William Bailey a local man who told her that my brother could be buried in his family plot. This was a special place he had in the Middlewich Cemetery. There was still no sign of Dad. We kept a look out for him all day.

Dad eventually arrived on Sunday morning. The letter telling him that we had been evacuated had never reached him, so he thought Eddie had died in London and had gone there. He had had to change at Crewe, from where he was stationed which was not far away. and could have been with us by Friday night had he known. Mum was pleased to see him even though they cried a lot. On Monday they arranged the funeral.

Tuesday Dad had to go to the Town Hall for the inquest. Here's the report from the local paper.

§ *Lance Corporal Halstead told them that his son was healthy but couldn't swim. The child had been playing at Kings Lock and fallen in. Mr. Davies had been called, ran up the bank and dragged him out. He was giving him artificial respiration when Dr. Bergeimer arrived. She gave the boy an injection, but it failed to revive him. Mr. Daniels, the coroner, gave a verdict of Accidental Death, and expressed his sympathy to the family who had been overtaken by tragedy in this way.* §

The same day, Nanny, Farver, Granny Hendon and various aunts arrived. My brother's coffin was put in Auntie Rene's front room. I wanted to see him to make sure he was actually there, but the grown-ups thought it best if I remembered him as he was. So, I never got to have a look. Auntie Rene's boys said it was bad luck having a dead body in their house, because it would bring in ghosts, but I wasn't afraid.

The weather was warm on Wednesday. They put Eddie's little coffin in a car that had thousands of wreathes all over the place. We stood by the door waiting. People were standing outside the door and some of them were crying. Mummy was crying really bad and Daddy helped her and me get into a big posh car. It was so big that it held Mummy, Daddy, me, Farver and both grandmother's managed to get in as well, that shows you how big it was. The girls didn't come but stayed with Auntie Rene. We weren't in the car very long before we had to get out and go into a church. Eddie was already there with flowers covering him, while some choir boys were singing. Then back in the car, another little drive and then out again. Which was a nuisance because I could have done with a longer ride.

Some men from the cars carried the small white coffin towards a hole in the ground that had some straps across it. There were loads of people standing around the other graves. I had never been to a funeral before and I remember thinking that with all those thousands of people who died in London, I had to wait 'till I was evacuated before I got to go to one.

I stood at the grave between Mum in her borrowed black and Dad in his khaki. Aunts Kate and Alice were there and even Aunt Margie. They were all dressed in black, even wearing

black stockings, like the nurses. They were all crying, even the men who were standing around the hole had tears. We watched the coffin, smothered in sweet peas, as it was lowered into the mud.
The vicar said some prayers and there was a silence and slowly people started to move away.

Mum and Dad didn't want to come away, nor did I, but we had to come away at the end.

It was horrible to leave Eddie there all on his own.

The car ride was a bit longer this time and when we got back, Aunt Rene had done some salmon and shrimp paste sandwiches plus a cake and tea. It didn't feel like anything to do with us. It felt like as though we were in a story which would end soon, and Eddie would come bouncing through the door.

But he didn't.

The next day everyone, except Dad, went home and we had to get on with things. We stayed at Rene's for just one more day then were re- billeted to Big Dora's house. I have no idea what she was actually called but thinking back, it seems a good enough name for her and for the place. One thing is for certain I've never forgotten it. Neither has Jeanie and she was only five.

The first night there, I woke up in my single camp bed scratching my swollen fingers. The light was on and as I looked across the room I saw Mum and Dad standing on a bed killing large bugs that were crawling from inside the mattress and running up the wall. As my parents cracked them dead, traces of blood were left on the distemper. Even baby Beryl was being bitten. We were living in a lousy house! It was a terrible place, but we had to stay there because there was nowhere else to go.

Big Dora had a large family of two boys, three girls and a husband in the Far East who never wrote. She weighed about eighteen stone, had bad ankles and found housework so painful that so she left it to her children to cope as best they could. The children were all very dirty and slept together in a flock mattress. That is actually inside the flocking, which was covered with old coats instead of blankets. On the first Saturday we were there Dora got all dressed up and went off to a wedding.

"Look at the sway on her. All dolled up like a dog's dinner and her kids running alive with lice," said Mum. As we watched Dora waddle down the path looking like an escaped barrage balloon in her grey dress.

While she was away, Mum and Dad, who was still on compassionate leave, decided they would clean up the house and children. They bought lots of stuff including a bottle of Lysol and a nitty Nora comb. After they had scraped the bath clean, they put all the kids in it and gave them a good scrub. Meanwhile their underwear was boiling in the copper. There was lots of screaming and laughing as clean naked bodies left the bathroom and went running around the house. It was during the bathing that Mum found ring worm on the head of four-year-old Iris.

It was on Sunday, after she had arrived home drunk the night before, that Dora saw the red rings on the bald head of her youngest daughter. There was a massive row with lots of swearing. I learned some really good new words like, poxy, slut and interfering bastards.

I suppose, after the shouting, they must have sorted it all out because we stayed there for almost a month. Dora tried to improve but her weight was against her. Her favourite pastime, apart from scoffing doughnuts and chips, was delousing her children. This she did by sitting in the sun outside the back door and casually picking fleas, nits or lice, from the kid's heads. She pulled the insects down the hair then flicked them under her shoe and crushed them to death. The effort of lifting her leg made her breathe heavy but she did her best.

Sometime in August, we were re-billeted again. This place was in a tall grey-stone house that backed on to the canal. The house had one small room and one bigger room on each floor. We were given the big room on the third floor. The females had the big bed and I had a camp bed that we put up every night so as to make more room during the day. At night, we could hear the canal lapping and gurgling around the small bridge that led to the house, which was a bit upsetting because it made us all think of Eddy. Although we never said.

This house belonged to Beatie and Heeson, a couple of house-proud health freaks, who lived on beans and lettuce and only drank warm water. They were tall, thin and grey, like their house, with features that were so sharp they could cut you in half with a glance. Beatie polished everything and went quite red in the face if a crumb hit the floor before she could catch it. Heeson didn't say much he just gargled a lot with salt water from a jug. They were forever criticising our noise and moaning about the way we were brought up. Beatie dusted our finger marks from the furniture as soon as we moved which made our life very uncomfortable. Somehow with lots of nagging, whispering and keeping our sense of humour by taking the rise out of them we managed to stomach it for a week or so. We would go out as much as we could, often going to visit Eddy's grave, or to have tea with other evacuees.

Things came to a head when Heeson told Mum off for leaving a comb on the mantelpiece. A huge row came about. Me and the girls were in our room playing Ludo, but we had to stop so that we could hear everything. After a lot of shouting I heard Mum tell Heeson to go and fuck himself as she stormed out of the house. I wasn't surprised when, about ten minutes later our bedroom door burst open and she come charging in.

"Johnny, get the case from under the bed," she yelled. "I've had enough of these silly bastards. We're going home. I'd sooner have the doodlebugs around me than that scrawny looking conchie. Put all the clothes in the case, dirty ones and clean ones, everything else put in the carrier bags. It's just after half past five. I've found out there's a train to Euston, leaving Crewe at eight. If we get a move on we can make it."

"But Mum just think about it for a minute," I said. "How can we go home, there's all the rockets, and we can't leave Eddie up here all on his own. Who's gonna look after the grave?

"I'll find someone, Mr. Bailey will do it," she said, tipping clothes out of the drawers on to the bed where Beryl was sitting. "Put that Ludo away Jeanie and look after her while he starts packing. Wear everything you can to save room in the case. Johnny make sure we've got a spare nappy and pair of knickers for her in a carrier bag. Jeanie dress your doll in Beryl's clothes. Keep your big coats handy it'll get cold later on, so you'll need them. I won't be long."

The door banged behind her and I heard her high heels clicking down the polished wooden stairs.

"Looks like we're going home," I said to Jeanie. Then I realised it was September. I ran to the window. Mum was just crossing the walk way bridge and looked up when she heard me call.

"Mummy, Mum," I yelled. "Everyone will be down hopping. How we gonna get down there? How we gonna get to the station? And what about the raids when we get to London?"

"You leave that to me. I'm gonna go and see if old Archie can drive us to Crewe in his cart. We can go straight through London down to Paddock Wood. I want you all ready when I get back. I want to see my Mother," she turned and crossed the bridge.

I had nearly finished packing by the time she returned.

"Archie is gonna be here in about quarter of an hour. Come on kids, lets wire in. We're going home. We gonna see Nanny, Farver and Aunt Kate and Aunt Alice. We can sleep on the train and be at Ploggs Hall by the morning. We can have breakfast in Nanny's hut."

We had finished the packing, had some Heinz tomato soup and sandwiches in the kitchen, and were back in our room ready to leave when there was a knock on the door. Beatrice came in.

"I'm most awfully sorry for the little upset Mrs. Halstead," she said. "Heeson is distraught and we both think that perhaps you ought to stay. After all the eight o/clock is the last train to London and what would you do if you missed it." Mum ignored her. "It isn't just yourself that you ought to think about. As a Mother you ought to be more responsible and get everything organised for a journey like that. You can't just up and leave not over such a slight argument. The Lord knows we have done everything we could for you all. But it has been difficult having three children running loose around the house. Surely you can understand that Mrs Halstead."

"No! I can't." Mum answered politely. "Come on children lets go home."

We collected out luggage and went down stairs to the front door. A wheezing Archie had arrived with his horse and cart and was waiting on the other side of the bridge. By now the news had spread that we were going home so a bit of a crowd had come to see us off.

Daisy Ewer, lifted me on to the back of the cart, gave me a kiss and rasped, "I'm going to look after the grave. You look after your Mummy and be a good boy Johnny."

I told her I would, and she gave me a pack of cards to play with on the train. Mum passed Beryl up to me while Jeanie, carrying our flask and sandwiches in her carrier bag, was lifted on by one of the men.

When the case and another bag was aboard Mum climbed on the front, next to Archie who flicked his whip pulled on the reins and we were on our way. The small crowd started to sing 'Oh Mr. Porter,' as we moved away. We waved, and they waved, a few people followed for a little while and the kids followed for a little bit longer. Slowly we made our way out of Middlewich and began the long journey to Paddock Wood, in Kent.

13 GOING HOME

We arrived at the outskirts of Crewe about two hours later, it was still light, but beginning to get dusk. Archie then confessed he wasn't sure of the way to the station and we couldn't see anyone around to ask. We took the wrong turning and fund ourselves in a street that was blocked off. While we were backing out of it, which wasn't much fun for the horse, Mum saw a passing soldier.

"Oi! Mate, Soldier. Over Here! "she called. "Can you tell us the way to the station?"

"Oh aye, me duck," said the soldier. "But you're the wrong end of town."

"We've got to catch the eight o/clock train, do you think we'll make it?"

"I don't reckon," the soldier said looking at his watch. "It's quarter too just gone. I'll come and show you the way, if your driver will drop me off on his way back."

"Right!" wheezed Archie. "Hop on."

The soldier introduced himself as Harry and with lots of – 'to the left' and 'now right turn's' we arrived at the station at three minutes past eight.

"Not to worry," said Harry. "They never leave on time. You go for the tickets and I'll sort out the kids and the luggage and meet you at the platform where the train goes from."

Mum jumped off the cart and ran into the ticket office, she'd already paid Archie his fare. Harry and I went through an arch, carrying bags and a little girl each. He asked a porter for the London train, who told us it was just going from platform number six. I accidentally dropped the carrier I was holding and had to stop to pick it up while trying to balance Beryl in my arms. Harry ran on with the Jeanie in his arms. I picked up my bag and arrived at platform six just in time to see the train pulling away.

The red light, on the back of the guard's van that was disappearing down the track, seemed to be taking the piss. We were too late! Seven minutes past eight and the bleedin' train had gone. I looked up at Harry with Jeanie in his arms and we both said.

"Sod it."

I stood Beryl down because she was getting heavy now and the four of us all stood there, not knowing what to do until Mum arrived the tickets still in her hand.

"The next train to London? Why that don't leave 'till seven thirty a.m.," said the porter closing the gate behind him.

Archie came trotting up, smelling of horses and out of breath.

"Would thy like me to take thee back to Middlewich, Luv? They'll be no charge, I've got to get home myself."

"No thanks, Archie. If I go back to that pair of loonies, I'll go nuts. I've buried a child and been on the move since I got up here. To tell you the truth, I've had enough. If the German's get us, they get us. I just want to go home and be with my own. I want my mum and my sisters. I'll stay here, if you'll just help me to the waiting room. We'll bed down there for the night, and catch the first train out in the morning."

What a wonderful place to spend the night. Crewe station. It wasn't the last time by any means that I would have a drama at that place, but they would be years later, this was the first.

After Archie and Harry had gone we had some tea and sandwiches. We made friends with some Sailors and a woman from the Air Force who were very kind to us. While other people were waiting for their trains they all took time to say hello. About ten o'clock we decided it was time to make up our bed. For pillows, we used our clothes from the case and covered ourselves over with coats. Mum woke me up so that I could keep guard for an hour while she slept, and the night passed. It was cold and a bit cramped, but it passed.

In the morning we washed our faces under a cold tap that Mum had found and packed the case again. Later we had tea and sausage rolls on the train. We travelled in the middle of the train as this was the safest place. There was an air raid, but I wasn't as frightened as I might have been. We didn't get bombed and arrived safely at Euston. Mum decided, even though we couldn't afford it, that it would be best if we got a taxi to London Bridge. That was a special treat and as we drove over London Bridge we sang the song about it falling down.

We had to wait ages for our slow train to Paddock Wood, but once aboard the journey went quickly because we all fell asleep. Mum woke us when we were pulling into the station, which seemed like a little toy one after the big ones we had been to since yesterday. A porter was standing on the platform to wave his flag and after the train pulled out he came and helped us with our case. Mum left as much as she could in the left luggage place where they gave us a special ticket so that we could get it back later. It was very quiet and very hot when we left the station. There was no transport to take us to Ploggs Hall Farm, so we had to walk.

"Right then," said Mum, "lets step out. It's a bit of a way, but it'll be worth it to see Nanny's face when we get there. She don't know we're coming so imagine the surprise she's going to get, when she sees us. And Aunt Kate with Joycie and Aunt Alice will be there. They left Suffolk after Eddy … It'll be smashing to see them, wont it? Johnny, you carry Beryl for a bit and I'll take Jeanie and the two bags. Come on, step it out!"

We walked out of the town until came to a stile which we climbed over and in single filed followed the path. Mum knew the way because she had been coming 'hopping' since she was a little girl. We walked along the side of two fields then the path turned into a track that led to a farm house, where the only sign of life was a dog barking round the back.

Which made me think of Tony and Neene and I wondered whether they would be hop picking. I got tired quite quickly so Mum and me tried lots of different ways of carrying the girls and the bags. But I got too tired to carry Beryl anymore, so it meant that Jeanie had to walk. It seemed like we had been walking for all our lives when Jeanie just sat down on the grass.

"I'm not walking anymore," she said with a five-year-old's determination. "I'm blooming well fed up."

"Jeanie, get up. We can't stop now," Mum snapped, as she put Beryl down on the ground. "We're nearly there now, Nanny will be waiting for us."

"No, she won't, she don't know we're coming." I said.

"That don't matter, she'll be waiting for us. Don't argue. Johnny, give her another piggy back, it's not far now just down this lane, though the small orchard, over the road and we'll be at the farm."

Mum was such a liar. It was ages! I was practically falling into the ground by the time we crossed the road, climbed up a steep bank land looked down onto the huts of Ploggs Hall Farm.

Below us was a big field with rows of black corrugated tin huts forming a square around a big communal wooden hut. The common was deserted. A smell of burning wood hung in the air and the only sign of life was one or two fires smouldering outside the huts. Mum led us through the hedge to Nanny's hut, with the number 44 painted in white on its black padlocked door. We plonked ourselves on the step. It must have been about five o/clock. I spied the communal water tap and ran to turn it on.

The cold water poured around my face as I put my mouth under it to drink. I washed my hands and made a cup out of them for Beryl to drink from, but no, not her, she insisted putting her face under the water and getting her dress soaked. Jeanie drank from her own hands.

"Right that's enough!" said Mum. "They must still be picking. We're going to find them," she said.

She put her head under the tap.

"Oh Mum! You've got to be joking ain't ya Mum?" I said furious. "We've had enough. I'm not carry those girls another inch. Why can't we just stay here and wait till they come here? It won't hurt if we rest a bit."

She turned away from the tap, wiping her mouth with the back of her hand as water dripped from her black hair. Her eyes were blazing with anger.

"No you can't rest! I don't want to wait. I've waited long enough," she yelled, tears falling from her eyes. "I want to see my Mother. I want to be with my sisters. I want to be with the people I know and who know me, and I want to be with them now. And I'm going to find them and I'm gonna find them now! If I have to search every field from here to bloody Maidstone! So, come on! Leave the bags and get a soddin move on, all of you!"

She snatched up Beryl and started to run out of the common into a nearby lane. Her anger had frightened me but somehow it had put new energy into all of us. I grabbed Jeanie's hand, left the bags and our coats on the step and ran after her.

We crossed the lane into a field that had been picked. There was no sign of people working, just dead bines all wound round still rooted in the earth. We moved down the side track to a wooden bridge and crossed a dry ditch into the next field. This was almost picked clean except for the far corner. We could see the yellow sacking of the bins that were lined up under the bines with pickers working at stripping them of their hops.

"There they are! There they are! Johnny they're up there look. I told you we'd find them, "she screamed, as she turned her head towards me and then back towards the pickers. "Mum! Mum it's me. It's Nelly. Mum.! Kate! Alice. It's me. Look it's me and the kids. Mummy!"

Mum ran away from us towards the crowd still yelling.

They couldn't hear her because we were too far away. But suddenly I wasn't tired anymore. I just wanted to catch up with Mum and get to Nanny. Jeanie must have felt the same because I didn't have to drag her any longer she was running beside me. We were all calling out as we ran.

They heard us.

Groups of people got up and called to other groups who also got up and began to run towards us. I tried to pick out

Nanny or the Aunts, but I couldn't because there were too many of them. It seemed there were hundreds all running and calling our names. It made us want to move all the faster. At last we all met up. It was good. Everyone was crying and shouting and picking us up and cuddling us and there was Nanny and the dogs and Farver and the aunts and some big boys who lifted us up and carried us on their shoulders towards the bins.

It had been a long journey and now we were home; I felt like crying but I couldn't understand why

It was only when we returned to Stepney at the end of September, that I found I had time to miss Eddy. It came as a dreadful realisation that I didn't have him to rely on anymore. He was so much more than my brother. He was my partner, my helper and my best friend. I had a better brain; but he had the personality and the cheek and those qualities in a best friend are very important when you are only eight and a bit sensitive. In bed at night I missed talking over the days doings with him as we fell asleep together and I missed even more when I didn't have him to share some of the jobs I had to do to help Mum. She was always so busy earning money for food and clothes for us so this meant that there was always loads to do. Now all the work fell mostly on me. Jeannie helped a bit, but she was still too young to sort out the ration books and the money let alone decide what to get for dinner or make a Yorkshire pudding. Her turn to do all that would come later. Meantime I had to look after Beryl and be at Mum's beck and call to do things and also to be ready to listen when she wanted to talk things over. I was like her husband. Until Dad came out of the Army

The first time I realised how much I missed Eddy was on the first Saturday morning after we got home from hopping. Mum sent me to get our dinner at the pie and eel shop near Shadwell Station. When I got to the shop it was very busy, so I joined the back of the queue, but when I got to the front, because I was small and the counter was high everyone kept pushing in front of me. That would never have happened if Eddy had been there, he would have said something or waved his hand up in the air at the pie woman behind the counter. I just didn't have the gumption to make myself noticed. After a couple of people had pushed in, I got desperate and clicked my shilling piece on the marble counter and tapped my liquor can against the wood. Despite this I still remained unnoticed and unserved as more people leaned over me and bought their food.

Unknown to me Nanny had arrived at the shop and joined the back of the queue. She noticed what was happening and yelled at me from just inside the door.

"Johnny," she called across the shop. "Don't just stand there, what's the matter with you? Stand up for yourself and be a man. Don't let them push in like that! I've seen three people get served in front of you. They ought to be ashamed of themselves. What's the matter with you people why don't you give the kid a chance?"

This was in front of all the people in the shop. I blushed to my scalp. It was a bit of a shock. Not only was it the first realisation that I no longer had my brother with me to help but it dawned on me that I was a Pratt, a sissy, weak, frightened and a coward and that I should learn to do something about it. After Nanny's outburst everyone was sympathetic towards me, so I got served straight away and rushed home with the pie, mash and liquor. I gave the girls their dinner, washed up, then went down to the lav and had a cry.

After that Nanny seemed to take me over. She took me with her to Mass on Sunday's at St Augustine's with St Philips and encouraged me to join the Sunday school and other social activities at the church. By Christmas I ended up playing an angel in the nativity play. I even tried the Cub scouts. Although I didn't last very long in the troop because I called the Scoutmaster 'a mean old bugger' when he started nagging me because I couldn't tie my knots the right way. Fucking sheep-shank: who wanted to know about that anyway?

Thinking back, that welcome home in the hop-fields and Nanny's influence after Eddy died, had a profound effect on me because from then on hop-picking, or hopping as it was known in the East End, was always a special time right up until the machines took over. It is an activity that no longer exists so I'm going to give you a run down on what it was like.

14 HOPPING

Nanny and the family had been going to Ploggs Hall Farm every year since --- well before I was born. In the olden days she would take everything she needed to set up a temporary home, in her hopping box. This was a large wooden chest on two pram wheels, with handles on each side to guide it. The box would be pushed along the road from Stepney to London Bridge Station where Nanny, Farver, the three sisters and Arthur would board the train to Paddock Wood, in Kent. The box contained; pots and pans, water jugs, special blankets, flat folded ticks and pillow cases, towels, clothes crockery and food. There would also be an oil lamp, plus some chains and hooks to hang the pots over the open fire outside the hut. Even when paraffin and primus stoves came in that was still the way most hoppers cooked and boiled their water for washing.

On arrival at the farm, for the beginning of the season each family would be allocated a hut for their living quarters. The regular hoppers returned to the same one year after year. These huts were made of tin with a sloping roof and a door that was locked by a padlock when the pickers were in the fields. Inside the hut, facing the door, was an area just big enough for a small table and a couple of chairs. The rest of the space was taken up by two beds which were slatted wooden platforms with a narrow gap down the middle.

As the years passed into the fifties and early sixties, when most of the pickers had got better off financially, they arrived in cars or vans. Many of the families would go down on the August Bank Holidays to paper or whitewash their hut walls, ready for the start of picking in late August or early September depending on the weather. They would bring their own sprung beds and real mattresses along with oil stoves to cook on as well as curtains and bits of carpet. By the first day of picking the huts were turned into something resembling holiday chalets.

Nanny often took me with her because as I grew up: not only was it another pair of hands earning money but, as she said, I also came in handy to fetch the water and do the running about.

The first time I went with her on my own, was the year after the war August 1946. I was just over ten. The day before we left I got very excited because we were going to travel down in an illegal lorry. This meant that I had to sleep at Nanny's on Aunt Alice's bed until late in the night when Nanny woke me up to tell me that the lorry had arrived. It stood outside the door in Planet Street and was open at the back with a couple of other families and their stuff already loaded. I was lifted up by Farver and Nanny got on while the driver and the others helped pull the hopping chest and bits of furniture on board. We were covered over by a large tarpaulin sheet that was tied down all round us and ordered to be quiet until we got to the other side of Tower Bridge and into Kent. I found it thrilling even though it a bit frightening. I had no idea who was with us in the lorry or which way we went but I do know that my arse got a good pounding every time we went over a bump. I fell asleep for a lot of the journey and was only woken up when we stopped. Someone whispered it was the police, which was a mistake because it turned out to be only the driver asking if anyone wanted to stop for a jimmy riddle. We arrived at Ploggs Hall just as it was beginning to get light.

I was kept busy because there was a lot of coming and going what with unloading the lorry, fetching water from the communal tap while Nanny lit the fire to make some tea and have a bit of breakfast. She had somehow got six sturdy logs of wood and tied them together to make a pair of tri-pods. On the top of these, placed far enough apart so that they wouldn't catch fire, she placed her iron pole with the hooks on chains to dangle over the hole where the fire was to burn. Once we had eaten it was a case of getting the hut ready to live in.

Our first job was to go to the barn, where the farmer had put bales of straw, so that we could fill our mattress ticks and pillow cases to make our bedding. For the first few days the straw was still quite spiky and stuck into me when I tried to get to sleep, but after a few days it broke down and became quite snug with a comfortable smell. After we had made up the beds, I was sent to gather some fuel for the fire in the form of faggots. These were bundles of twigs tied with string that were put out for the pickers to use to cook their food. I could only carry two at a time, so it meant a few trips before I had managed to build a pile outside our hut.

The huts were numbered, Nanny's was forty-four, the last one in her row and next door to us, at number forty-three lived Auntie Minnie, who was a huge woman who wore thick glasses, mauve frocks and smelled. I couldn't tell you what she smelled off, but smell she did. It was a smell that had its own particular pungency and it was the same every year. Almost as though she never washed.

Sometime during the afternoon Nanny had to go to sign on and be given her 'Tally Card.' This was where the Tally Man would write down the number of bushels we picked when our bin was measured. When she returned from the farm house, we padlocked the hut with the hopping box being used as a table between the newly made beds and went on a trip to Five Oak Green to get some shopping. We took a short cut through the dark hop fields, so that Nanny could check out the size of the hops, before emerging on to the road and walking about a mile into the village. In the small grocery shop Nanny got some food and bought me a sausage roll to eat on the way back.

By the end of the day I was quite knackered as I sat on a stool by the fire, listening to the women's gossip. Most of it was about what had been going on during the past year, who had died, who had had a baby, who had been in the nick, but the most important topic was how much a bushel the farmer was going to pay and the size of the hops. Because the bigger they were the more money we could earn.

The hops grew on what we called bines in rows stretching the length of a field. They were strung up in groups of four. Narrow at the root, tied together at about four-foot-high from there they would thicken with leaves and hops spreading out at the top like the gothic columns in St. Philip's church. When they were ready for picking the bines would be pulled down from the permanent criss-cross of wire that was clipped onto thick wooden poles as it stretched across the field. The hops, which hung in clusters like grapes, would be picked off into large bins. Each family would have their own bin which would be part of a 'set' of twelve with one of the male pickers, called a Pole Puller, in charge.

At regular intervals, mid-morning, dinner time, mid-afternoon and knocking off time, the 'Tally Man' would come accompanied by the Measurer with his bushel basket. The Measurer at Ploggs Hall, was the farmer's son Jackie, who was young and good looking with a very supple back. He measured our pickings by bending into the bin and scooping the hops into his basket until it was full. The Measurer was the man to keep in with, because depending on how hard he threw our hops into his basket, would depend on how much we earned. If he 'rammed them in' as the phrase went, the less they would measure. With a shout of 'One,' for the first bushel, he would lift his basket out of the bin and pour the gathered hops into a wide yellow sack called a poke. This was held open by the Pole Puller, who, after ten bushels would string it tight and leave it on the ground to be carried to the nearest cart track where it would be loaded later.

Hops being light airy-fairy things did not need much pressure on them to be squeezed flat, that is why big ones, usually those at the top of the bine, were always preferable to the smaller wet ones, which laid heavy, at the bottom. When the bin was empty the Tally Man, dressed more like a pox doctors clerk than a farm worker, would enter the number of counted bushels into our tally card and into the book he kept for his own records. This was so that the farmer knew how much to pay us at the end of the season.

When all the 'sets' had been measured, the pokes were piled as high as they would go onto a horse drawn cart and taken to the oasthouse to be dried in the kilns. Once they were on the cart we didn't care how much weight was put on them because by then our work had been counted. Once, at the end of the day, I was allowed to ride on top of the loaded poke wagon. I was told to grip the rope that was strapping the sacks to the cart and not let go, otherwise I would fall from the top of the pokes that were piled high and go crashing down into the mud. It was scary as the cart swayed and jerked its way across the furrowed tracks, but I hung on and felt like a Prince as I drove down the lane past our huts.

In the bad weather the cart tracks around the fields would get all slimy with sodden mud so that the horses and wheels would sink into it. With nothing to grip on to it was terrible to see them straining to pull the full carts, heavy with the rain soaked pokes. Often the cart would get stuck and no matter how much the whip was used on the animals, it became impossible for them to pull it loose. With a lot of verbal abuse towards the carter most of the women would then band together to help the desperate animal by heaving and pushing the cart forward.

There was also a very active social side of hopping.

After a day's work, usually lasting from eight in the morning until around five thirty in the evening, we would return to the common, wash the black hop stains from our hands and Nanny would prepare something to eat. If it wasn't raining I would do the washing up in a bowl on a stool outside the hut, that and other duties done I would spend the evening socialising in the big hut which was provided by the farmer as a church and community centre.

It was right in front of Nanny's and built of wood. There were also two smaller huts that were used as a shop and a first aid post. The main organiser of our social life was Nurse

Whitby, who was rather tall and wore a blue uniform with a navy-blue hat. She was what was known as a 'good woman.' In her shop hut she would provide milk from a big churn, fresh bread, as well as the pies, cakes, sausage rolls and soap. It was a very small shop. Next door to this with a gap between them, just big enough to use for hide and seek, was the nursing hut. This contained a chair, a low camp bed and lots of disinfectant. If there was an accident or an illness, Nurse Whitby, would plaster, bandage or dose people up, until they were able to get to the cottage hospital in Five Oak Green if it was serious.

Her most important prop was a small cart which she would drag to the area that was being picked and at lunch time sell us pickers tea, from a big urn, currant cake, sausage rolls and pies.

At the weekend the Sunday Service was taken, in the big hut, by Father Coldhurst, who had a particularly plumy voice. When I was thirteen he heard me taking the piss out of him during the singing of 'Onward Christian Soldiers,' and without missing a beat, he marched between the wooden benches serving as pews and smacked me round the head before returning to the alter to say his prayers.

The big hut was also used for, dances, games, meeting and concerts. At the end of the season Nurse Whitby would organise a party for all the kids and tables would be laid with sandwiches, jelly and custard. I won the fancy dress competition as Old Mother Riley once; my prize was a Mars Bar.

There was an unwritten tradition that each year we had our 'hopping' sweetheart and so by the time I was twelve I had mine. We met again in nineteen forty-seven we picked up where we had left off from the year before. Except there was a big difference in me being twelve than there had been when I was eleven. At eleven we were just talking about the wireless and the pictures and chasing and playing hide and seek with the other kids. There was the occasional holding of hands and a kiss during postman's knock or forfeits but nothing more than that. Kissing, at that age, seemed a bit stupid. But at twelve kissing made us feel very different.

Now before I go any further, note this carefully, all my partners will certainly be given fictitious names to conceal identities; jobs, situations, locations and times will also be changed. I will not evade the truth of the situations that evolve in my sexual life, but it wouldn't be fair on my partners, of either or indeterminate sex, to name them. So that said: my girlfriend was called Juniper, a red head who was a couple of months older than I was and the same height. Neither of us were virgins, having had just one experience each.

We had both arrived at the farm the previous day and had finished our first day's picking. Her family had their bin two rows up from us. That evening she came to Nanny's hut door to see if I wanted to go out for a walk. The washing up was done, the water had been collected in the pail, so Nanny said I could go but that I had to be back before it got to eight o/clock. We stood in front of the fire for a little while until Juniper said that she fancied a walk through the fields towards Five Oak Green. We still had our Wellington boots on so we walked across the meadow, enjoying the smell of the food and fires as we were greeted by the other hoppers sitting outside their huts. We got to the edge of the common and walked around the road that ran past the farm house talking about how we were getting on at our new schools having just gone to different ones after primary school exams. She had got into a Grammar School, whereas I had gone to Mile End Central, which was just a bit higher than a secondary school. We pushed open the large white gate and closing it behind us, crossed the road and got through a small hole in the hedge of a cornfield belonging to another farmer.

It was the first time we had been out on our own, this year, and Juniper was looking good in her brown flared skirt and cardigan with her hair in plaits. Most girls wore plaits when hop picking because it stopped them catching fleas. We started to look for rabbit warrens among the stubble in the cornfield but didn't find any. We wandered into the next field which was a hopfield waiting to be picked and tramped through the caked mud in the semi darkness beneath the spreading bines. We stopped at the edge of the field and leaned against one of the wooden poles that held up the cross wires and kissed. The kissing gave me a warm sense of belonging and of being grown up. I began experimenting between 'film star kissing' with tight lips and 'French kissing,' with open lips and the occasional tongue. It made me feel very excited.

It seemed the most natural thing in the world after kissing to lie down, on the grass at the edge of the path and do what came naturally. There's not much point in going into the details of what happened because it wasn't particularly exciting and after a few manoeuvres we both got a bit bored and called it a day. Garments were tidied up and we continued our journey to the village.

When we arrived before going into the grocery shop, I asked her if she wanted to have another 'do' on our way home.

"Not tonight," she said. "But I'd like to another time."

So, we shared a glass of lemonade and strolled back to the farm by the road. On the way we found a few blackberries that were ripe enough to eat and some cob nuts that weren't.

The following evening, we did it again. This time was much better. It was in one of the disused huts which was a bit more comfortable and not so rushed. We spent a bit more time kissing and feeling each other. When I got inside her I felt a strange sensation as though I had touched a nerve or something in her body. It made me tingle all over and although it was a bit like an electric shock and should have been painful I liked it. After that, we did it quite regularly and even though I kept trying to find that place where I got the tingle, it never happened again. Well not for a while and then with someone completely different.

At the end of the season we parted until the following year. But by then she had met some boy who played snooker and laughed at me when I called it billiards. So that was the end of us. I didn't care because I was by then courting Brenda, another redhead who came from Walthamstow. She was a well brought up blue eyed girl, but Nanny didn't approve because she was an 'R.C. ' Horror of horrors a Roman Catholic. It didn't put me off and we even met in London.

15 LEFT OF THE LAW

Being under Nanny's wing meant that I spent most of my free time playing in and around Planet Street, with my friends Carol Palmer, Dennis Stag, Mary Simpson and Ellen Grebb. We played lots of street games, but canon was my favourite. This was played with an old baked bean tin can which stood in a chalked circle with two sticks crossed on top of it. We had to knock it over and run to four bases before getting hit with the ball. It was a bit like rounders without the bat. We also used the ball for donkey, which was throwing it at a wall and jumping over it and many other games. Ellen was my special girlfriend at that time and we would talk about love and sing 'I'll be your sweetheart,' to each other. Jeanie became part of this gang and her sweetheart was Dennis.

We would sit in the doorway on the Chapel steps, although it wasn't really a Chapel anymore, just a disused factory. It was there that we played word games like truth, dare, pluck or promise and as we got a bit older, film star kisses. I must have got more confident, because once I was dared to go over to Cohen's, the tobacconist in Watney Street, jump up on the counter and kick all the newspapers off. And I did it! Mrs. Cohen later told Nanny and I got a smack round the ear, but I did it.

The chapel was next door to Old Granny Skelton's house at number eighteen, who was one of the characters of the street and was known by everyone for hating her four daughters in law. She was called Old Granny, as opposed to Nanny. However, there was nothing 'old' about her, except that she always wore long skirts that dated back to the Edwardian era. Other than that, she had the feisty working-class attitude that kept her alive and mainly vigorous until she was ninety-nine. She was what was known in the East End as 'a right Brahma,' meaning a tough, hard-working woman. Farver caught her carrying a half hundredweight sack of coke through her passage and into her back yard. She was then ninety-three years old. Her favourite possession was her fire grate. That is to say - her cooking range. She polished it till it shone and you could almost see your face in it. She would say to the passers-by who greeted her when she was sitting outside her front door in the summer, "You must come in and have a look at my grate."

She went a bit funny towards the end and kept showing me things that she had picked out of her head or skin. Tiny things like one side of a press stud or a bit of coal or an eye from a hook and eye. And once even a small silver three-penny piece. Things that obviously could never appear through her skin but I, like everyone else, humoured her and expressed amazement. I wonder what that was all about? Her husband, Great Grandfather Charlie, died of pneumonia during the war, but her four sons; Charlie, George, Bill and Ted also lived to a good old age.

One of the more flamboyant characters living in Planet Street was a woman known to everyone as 'Aunt Bet Milton.' She made me one of her 'special' kids because I had an innocent face. Bet was a rough, tough, no nonsense woman with four big scars all over one arm. She got the scars when Stan, her safe cracking husband, had thrown a frying pan full of sizzling sausages at her during one of their frequent fights. I was terrified of him but fortunately he wasn't a particularly good safe cracker so spent a lot of his time away doing his porridge.

Aunt Bet was no angel; she swore worse than a stevedore, had a vulgar sense of humour, a filthy wit and had lived on the left of the law for years. She allowed me play truant in her house and gave me food in exchange for helping her with her house work. But my special job was transporting her black-market goods around the streets and alleys to certain addresses during the late evenings. My instructions would be given in the following manner.

"Johnny," she would say. "Come 'ere you carroty headed little bastard, I want you to take this delivery to some dirty old tart in Arbour Square. Keep off the main road and if you pass any blue arsed coppers look like you're on your way to St Michael's for even-fucking-song."

The packet was wrapped in a copy of The Evening News and tied up with a bit of string so as not to look like anything special. I arrived at the delivery point, knocked at a door and a woman, it was usually a woman, answered it. With a quick look, up he street she took me through the passage and into the back kitchen where the smell of Kosher food got right up my nose. She took the parcel and quickly shoved it into a drawer then taking out her purse she gave me, depending on what was in the packet, anything from a shilling to five-bob.

Sometimes I would be taken into the living room and once, in Sidney Street, I was taken into a downstairs bedroom which was all pink just like a film stars. There was a pink lampshade, a pink satin bed spread slung across a pink eiderdown and a set of matching pink glass jars and candlesticks on the dressing table. On the wall, and this is the absolute truth, there was a pink mirror with a carving of a lady in a big wedding frock holding up an umbrella. It was actually cut into the glass! It was while visiting places like these I realised that not everyone was as poor as we were. Some people even had bookcases in their passages.

Once I had been paid and said a quick "Thank you," I would return to Aunt Bet and gave her the money. I was never told what was in the packets but having sniffed one or two, I think it was usually tea, sugar, cheese, cigarettes or any stuff that was still on ration and difficult to get. If it was a large bottle it was usually spirits, and a small one I guessed was a bottle of scent. Sometimes there were very thin light packets and I worked out that these were fully fashioned nylons as I had heard about them from Mum and the women. Even though the war was over, there were still loads of things we couldn't get due to the peace.

Aunt Bet also taught me to shoplift. She was a dab hand at it herself and liked to demonstrate how clever she was to me. She worked her scam like this. Under her loose top coat, she wore one of those dresses that had buttons down the front and underneath that she had on a large pair of, cream coloured passion killer knickers. We would go into a big store, like Wickhams along the Mile End Road or a men's clothing shop like Gardiner's, on the corner of Commercial Road and Whitechapel Road in Aldgate. I would have to pretend to be her son, another acting job. Once in the shop, she would pitch the salesman some tale of how I was prone to bilious attacks and was off sick from school. She would then ask to look at various pairs of socks, pants, shirts, vests, trousers and keep them all spread over the counter. After humming and haring for a while she would ask for something that was on the top shelf like a cap or a scarf and while the shopkeeper was busy up his ladder trying to help her; she would slide as much of his stock as she could grab, through the front of her unbuttoned dress and down into her drawers.

Once she had given me the wink that all was safely stowed, my job was to suddenly come over ill and say that I was going to be sick. At this time, we would hastily leave the shop, to the relief of the salesman and get a bus back to Watney Street. Later she would fence the goods on and I or one of her other helpers would do the usual errands. I suppose she was a female Fagin, but she was always very warm, extremely generous and loads of fun. And the work was exciting too.

Her training stood me in good stead during one of my own shoplifting adventures. I was with my usual gang of Betty Cannock, Dennis Stag, Jeanie and Beryl, who was almost five years old. Our shop of choice was Woolworth's, on the corner of Commercial Street near Aldgate East tube station. Our mission was Christmas presents for our Mum's, Dad's and each other. Our plan was that once we were inside the shop, we all had to go our own ways until we had nicked what we could from things on our list. Once this was done, we were to leave by different exits and meet up on the corner of Gunthorpe Street. I had given strict instructions to Jeanie that she was to walk around the shop and to look after Beryl.

And what is more she was not to take anything herself because I would get all the stuff for her.

We had been in there about a quarter of an hour and I had got, among other things, some 'Evening In Paris' perfume, a transfer book, two pairs of girls socks and two note books and a pencil with a rubber on the end of it. I had stuffed these up the pullover I was wearing under my jacket that I had tucked into the top of my trousers so that the things wouldn't fall out. I knew that I hadn't been seen because it was the Christmas period and all the shop assistants were busy. I was just about to leave but as I got near the exit that leads into Commercial Street I heard someone crying. It was a cry that I recognised.

Following the noise, I saw, round the legs of the grown-up shoppers, that it was my sister Beryl, who was standing beside the penny weighing machine next to the swing doors. I got a shock when I also saw that her hand was being held by a man in a suit. Obviously, the manager! I almost went into a state of panic and my instinct was to run, but aunt Bet's training kept me thinking. I couldn't leave her could I? What would Mum say when I got home without her?

"Oh Beryl? No! Sorry Mum" I imagined myself explaining. "I ain't seen 'er, well not since she was nicked up at Aldgate Woollies. She's probably being hung."

Mum would kill me. And anyway, Beryl didn't know the way home. I don't even know if she knew our address. And where the fucking hell was Jeanie, who was supposed to be looking after her? All this ran through my mind in seconds. I knew there was only one thing to do because Aunt Bet had always told me, 'If the police stop you, brazen it out.' I had to bluff Beryl away from the manager bloke and out into the street before any of the others came up with their nicked goods on them.

"What's the matter Mate?" I asked the man as I moved towards my sister and her captor.

"Is she with you?" he asked. His voice didn't sound too threatening.

"Yeah, she's my sister. She wandered away from me and I've bin looking for her."

"I've just caught her trying to take on of those dolls." He pointed to a display on the counter.

"No, she can't 'ave one of them," I argued. "She ain't got no money."

"I think she was trying to steal it."

I went into a state of shock and it wasn't all acting. I was using the shock I felt as I realised that the things I had nicked were slipping down under my pullover.

"Oh! You naughty little cow!" I glared at Beryl. "You know you're not supposed to steal, the good Lord will punish you and you will go to Hell and burn. Mummy has told you that. Ain't she?"

I took her hand and looked up at the manager.

"I'm really sorry for this Mate," I said. "My Mum will give her such a good larruping when we get home. You leave her to me,"

I could feel the pencil sliding under the belt of my trousers.

"Now come on Janet," I said, as I pushed my stomach out to lessen the gap at the top of my trousers. "You've got come home with me. You are a very, very naughty girl and if you ever do anything like this again I will see to it that Daddy gives you the cane, four times on your bum."

As we started to walk towards the door my heart was pounding with the thought that any minute he might take us to his office and ask me to strip off, or that the things up my jumper would fall out. I dug my fingers into Beryl's hand to make her cry and struggle.

"It's no good trying to get away," I said firmly. "You're going to get a good bashing when I get you home. Thanks very much mister, I'll see to it that she gets told off. Now come on Janet, let me take you home to Mummy and Daddy!"

"Just make sure she doesn't do anything like this again, will you?" said the Manager, smiling a little as he held the door open for us.

We were out of that door and walking down Commercial Street, moving quickly but easily. It meant walking the long way around the block to get to Whitechapel Road. But it gave me a chance to re-arrange my booty and nag Beryl until we met up with the others. I gave Jeanie a wallop and a big telling off for letting Beryl get lost until we got to the chapel steps where we checked over our spoils.

16 WORLD PEACE AND MY LAW

You would think that in nineteen forty-five, when Germany surrendered, and the war was over, it would become a massive moment in my life; but strangely enough it wasn't. I had imagined that when old Adolph was defeated everything would be bleeding marvellous, that the shortages of food, clothing as well as toys and books would end along with the blackouts. In my head I had invented a peace where there would be millions of sweets, chocolates, pineapples, meat, butter, comics, bananas and the street lights would be switched on all night. I dreamed of a fantastic world of colour and plenty. But when the war ended on May seventh, nothing actually changed. I saw on the Gaumont British newsreels and heard on the wireless people singing in Piccadilly circus and crowds cheering Churchill and the King in front of Buckingham Palace. I was just over nine and too young to get involved in any of that, so it didn't mean much at all.

Soon after peace broke out we had a celebration street party. Flags were stretched between the houses in Planet Street. Chairs of all shapes and sizes along with an assortment of tables were brought out of people's houses, covered with old sheets and laid out in a long line down the middle of the road. The women handed out cakes, sausage rolls, sandwiches, pork pies and lemonade. All the kids scoffed themselves fully and the feast was finished off with a bowl of jelly and cold custard. After that the tables were returned into the houses and we had organised games. These were later followed by dancing the Hokey Cokey and a knees-up to records played on a wind-up gramophone. At the end of the party we were given a small bar of Cadburys chocolate to take home with us. Other than that, everything remained the same.

In September Aunt Alice took me down Hopping to stay with Nanny for a couple of weeks. I had noticed that Mum was getting fat and realised that a baby could be on the way, so I wasn't surprised when I was told that Mum had given birth to another sister. However, I was really disappointed that she wasn't the boy I was hoping for. The boy to take the place of Eddy. They called her Christine! Dad thought the sun shone out of her arse because he managed to get demobbed in October instead of having to wait until the end of the year! She became his favourite and was given everything she wanted especially anything that belonged to me! Not a good start to the relationship with my newly returned father.

Our relationship didn't stand much of a chance because for the previous five years I had gradually assumed the role of husband and father. During those years I had learned to help with the running of the family, do some cooking, cope with the ration books, and money, wash and change the babies and had even learned how to mend a fuse without blowing the electric up. I had experienced the death of my best friend and brother, been pushed from pillar to post on evacuation and always with the double threat of either being killed by the German's or of my real Mother appearing out of the blue to take me away.

It was the same for Mum. She had fought her own war and on her own terms. She had survived by instinct as well as hard graft and like most women of her generation had become the leader of her family in a way that had nothing to do with feminism. Even if the women could have afforded a brassier, those girls never have burned it. Instead they would have used their coupons on clothes for their kids. Their tits had been out and proud in their defiance and determination to defeat Hitler. So, in a predominantly female environment where Mum was her own boss Dad's demob meant that there was suddenly her husband to answer to every day.

On the other hand, neither Mum nor I had any conception of what Dad had been through once he had been called up. We knew nothing about Army discipline, the square bashing, the regimentation or sharing living accommodation with other men. What could we know of what it was like being forced into a way of life that was so completely alien from the one he was used to in civvy street. Even though he was never posted abroad, it was a life well away from his wife and children. When the bombing was at its height, it must have been murder for him not being able to communicate with his family. Never knowing whether they had lived or died until he received Mum's latest letter. And once the rockets started falling he didn't even know where we were evacuated to. I can't begin to imagine what it must have been like to receive the news of the death of his baby son.

Once he returned home permanently there was a lot of antagonism between us. I assumed that this was directed at me because I was still alive, and his real son was dead. I am not saying that he actually said anything or even consciously hold it against me, but I felt sure it must have gone through his mind. It certainly went through other people's minds. There were quite a few times when I heard the following remarks in one form or another.

"So sorry to hear about your boy Nell. Funny ain't it? You took a stranger in and you lost your own."

They would say, oblivious to the fact that I was within earshot. Or.

"You're Eddy's was taken but you've still got Johnny. It ain't the same but it's got to be better than nothing."

Consequently, by the time Lance Corporal Edward William Halstead, returned to Civvy Street, in his demob suit and trilby hat, the three of us were ready to engage in the battle for 'Supreme Commander of the Family Halstead.' A battle that raged for the next eight years and got worse as I moved from puberty into adolescence.

When he began ordering me about and telling me what to do all the time, I thought he had a soddin' cheek! Sundays would be the worst because he would be home all day. It was then that he would impose his Victorian and Army disciplines on us. Things like - sticking to a set routine and only speaking when we were spoken to. And saying 'Grace' after we had finished eating before he would allow us to get down from the table.

"Thank God for my good dinner please Dad can I leave the table?"

I sat at the table in defiance or many a Sunday afternoon just to get up his nose. When eventually I thought he had had enough or I was thoroughly bored, I would say my Grace and be allowed to leave the table to play or do some work around the house.

Another thing that used to drive him mad, was when he would make me go to Gussie's for his packet of ten Woodbines. I would argue that I didn't want to go, even though it was less than three minutes' walk away. He would charge at me to clip me round the head, calling me a lazy little sod then chase me down the top stairs to Mrs. Coakley's landing. I would run loudly across the landing so that he would think that I had gone, and I'd then creep back up our stairs and sit on the ragged carpet for about ten minutes and then, instead of going to get his fags, I would have to push it just that little bit harder and pipe up in my squeaky voice.

"I'm still here!"

This would send him nuts, because by that time he would be desperate for a fag. He would call me a fucking bastard or some such, race across the kitchen, out past the coal box and try to get me before I managed to escape. I'd nip back through our pass door slamming it with a crash behind me, dive across the landing, down the bottom stairs and be out into Bigland Street before he could get past the toilet. I would eventually get the Woodbines, return home, take the clip round the head as well as the verbal abuse and try to see it as a victory in an unresolved, on-going skirmish.

He paid me back by not allowing me to listen to the wireless. This meant that I had to sneak into the front room and turn the volume down very low and with my ear almost pushed into the sound box while I revelled in the exploits of 'Dick Barton – Special Agent.' Wondering how Dick, Jock and Snowy would get out of another impossible situation. Even now when I hear The Devils Punch Bowl being played, I am transported back to being that kid on his chair oblivious to everything except the highly polished cabinet with it's cut out fretwork making an impression on my cheek. Later I would do anything to get to listen to 'Journey Into Space.' A privilege that was used as blackmail by both parents to make me do their bidding.

However, despite the above, it wasn't all bad; nothing ever is. There were lots of times over the years, when we sang and had parties and laughed a lot. There was a particularly good trip to Southend which took place on the Easter Bank Holiday Monday. We had been bought new clothes for the occasion. I had a tweed suit with short trousers and the two elder girls had white blouses and kilts. Chrissie was in the pushchair with Mum and dad in their Sunday best. We had a photo taken outside 51A with Dads Kodak camera, then we walked round to Commercial Road and got the bus to Fenchurch Street Station where along with loads of other holiday makers, we caught the train to Southend.

Southend, was the best day out ever because it had a beach that was very muddy and packed full of people. We walked along the sea front and had cockles on a small plate and wanted to go on every ride that went up and down or round and round.

Eventually after a lot of pleading we were taken into the big amusement park called the Kursal which was a permanent

Fun Fair site. Once through the turnstiles we entered into a long hall with game stalls on either side before we got to the rides. Walking through the hall we were already being encouraged to start spending the little money we had. It was three-pence a go so we had to choose carefully. We could play Roll the Penny, which Mum loved, and hoop-la and coconut shies, and shooting things and knocking down a load of tins with a mop head, Dad was very good at those. One that was very difficult was trying to get a ball into a bucket that was lying on its side. Mum and I were useless at that and a shilling was spent before we realised there was no point in trying to win the poxy chalk statue of a girl holding a sun shade.

The only thing we won was when Dad went on the rifle range and shot enough points to win a painted Alsatian Dog standing on four grey steps. We all cheered, and Jeanie carried it for about ten minutes until she got bored. That ornament stood on the corner table in the front room for years. It was eventually knocked to the ground and smashed to smithereens after being hit by a flying piss soaked napkin, during a family fight.

Having passed through the hall we went into the open air. In the park area it had a ghost train, a crazy house, roundabouts and loads of rides. We went on some of them and they cost sixpence each. Chrissie and Beryl went on the roundabouts while Jeanie and I went on the chair-o-planes. Dad went in a big round wooden building and watched the riders on the Wall of Death. We stood outside in the sun, listening to the noise of the motor bikes revving up and going round and round and smelling the petrol fumes. I was desperate to go on the Scenic Railway, but Mum was terrified that I might fall out, so I never got on it. We all went on the Caterpillar ride, which was a roundabout with a big cover, like the skin of a giant caterpillar, that went over our heads as it went up and down spinning on its tracks. A lot of people, mainly young men and boys, would gather at a certain spot where there was a great gust of wind blowing between the rails. This would blow the girls skirts up and sometimes over their heads. The men-folk would whistle and yell out, but all they saw was stockings and suspenders and a bit of lacy knicker. That is if the girls didn't push her skirt down quick enough. I couldn't see the sense of it myself. But that was before I discovered Lucille. So, there were some happy times but mostly it was sporadic bouts of arguments and anger.

It was soon after the end of the war Mum had heard, from Louis Patmore and others, that they were taking names of kids whose parents had been killed during the war and that the child would be given an American Foster Mother in America. The foster mother would send the kid parcels to keep their spirits up. under the slogan,' Adopt an orphan of the war.' It was something to do with Meredith and Drew the Biscuit makers, who had their offices in Cable Street.

"Now you get down there and get your name on the list, "she said when I got home from school. "You never know where it might lead. You could end up going to America, Dolly Crutch told me when, she read my tea leaves, that you would go to America one day. I think this is what it could be about."

Dolly Crutch was the one-legged fortune teller who lived near Arbour Square.

"But Mum," I argued. "I ain't an orphan! I'm just fostered. And my parents weren't shot or bombed in the war. Me mother may still be alive, and no one knew who my father was, so I can hardly be classed as a war orphan can I?"

"They're not to know that, you silly sod. Get down there and get your name on the list. Say I'm your foster mother and I've been looking after you all these years, since you parents got bombed and killed during the Blitz. They ain't gonna check up are they. Anyway, if they say 'no,' what have we got to lose. Go on take a walk down Cable Street."

"But Mum..." I tried to argue.

"You can take Chrissie for a ride in the push chair. Find Meredith and Drew's office; it's not far from Glamis Road, facing the New Park, you know where that is.

"But Mum..." I tried again.

"When you get in there, tell 'em your name is John Ross and say that you're an Orphan of the War. Tell 'em you got bombed out in Hemming Street and I took you in. You can make something up. If they want to know any more tell 'em to get in touch with me. And don't forget, if they ask my name I'm not Nellie, I am Helen Elizabeth Rose Halstead."

Experience told me that there was no sense in arguing with her after that. So, I put Chrissie in the pram and went to Cable Street. I found the office quite easily as I had passed it on my way to the New Park quite often.

It was a brown brick building and I climbed up the four steps, bouncing the baby in the push chair behind me. I heaved open a heavy glass and brass door by pushing it with my back. The two girls, behind a counter, watched as I struggled to get through before it swung back and pushed me out. I shouted through the closing door as the pram began to pull me back down the steps.

"I'm an orphan of the war, called Johnny Ross and I've come to get an American Foster mother."

One of the women came from behind her counter and across a small foyer. She swung back the door and grabbed the pram handle, pulled us inside and took my hand. It was obvious that they were not getting too many orphans of the war, because they seemed overjoyed to see me.

"Oh, look Iris, he's an orphan and come down here all on his own. What smashing red hair. Come on Johnny, I'll take you in to see Mrs. Hudson. Iris will keep an eye on your baby." Iris came out and look the pram and I was taken down a bit of a passage, shown into a smaller office and introduced.

"This is Johnny Ross," said the woman. "He tells me he's an orphan he's just arrived with a baby in a pram outside."

"Thank you, Beatrice. Sit him on the chair. Hello Johnny, my name is Mrs. Hudson."

Mrs. Hudson, was a large woman overflowing with sympathy and dressed in a cheerful spotted brown dress trimmed with white braid. Her voice dripped with tragedy and compassion at the end of every breathy sentence.

"Now tell me all about yourself. I will see whether we can help you to find a good American foster parent. Where are you living now? Have you got a Mummy and Daddy at present?"

I answered all her questions with what Mum had told me to say: plus embellishments. She sighed and 'oooh'd and aaah'd' and said she would come to see me at home.

The following day Mrs. Hudson arrived at 51A and by the time Mum had finished telling her our story, plus bolder embellishments, she was practically prostrate with compassion and we were filling in the necessary forms to apply for an American mother. Before she left, I was given a couple of sheets of paper to write a letter to an anonymous woman as if she was my foster mother already.

That night Mum and I pieced together a suitably dramatic letter which I took down to Mrs Hudson after school the next day. She who read it with brimming eyes and told me that she would forward it on to America and that I must not fret or worry because she was convinced that she could get an outcome. I forgot all about it until six weeks later, there was an outcome. The outcome turned out to be a lady, who lived in New York.

The lady was called Viola Walbridge and along with a nicely written letter she enclosed a black and white photo of herself standing in front of a big iron gate. She is dressed in a black two-piece suit with a white jabot, looking like Bette Davis in 'Now Voyager,' she looks rather pretty and carrying a handbag. Across the bottom, in real ink, she had written the words 'From your loving Mother.'

We corresponded three times a year and I was only ever allowed to write to her through the organisation. I never knew her actual address, nevertheless I will always remember her and often wonder what happened to the letters she wrote to me, telling me about New York and plays and films she had seen. Always urging me to grow up a good boy.

When I wrote to her, I would tell her about the church and the camping holidays and what was going on with the family and my school stuff. Sometimes if I was a bit tired or keeping out of the way of Dad, Mum would write them for me in a hand similar to mine and I would sign it at the end. Viola must have noticed but she never remarked on it when she wrote back. She did send me terrific parcels on my birthday and Christmas.

To us kids the parcels were amazing. Mainly because they came with different American stamps on the outside and with the most unusual contents. The contents included, striped sweat shirts, called sloppy Joe's, trousers with a zip's instead of buttons on the flies, shirts made of synthetic materials in bright colours that were nothing like the grey and dull colours we were used to in England. There were also magical boxes of sweets called Candies, along with books and comics and tins of nuts that opened, not with a tin-opener but, by pulling a round bit of metal on the lid.

Daddy always instead that I share everything with the girls. I thought that was a bit much because I was the orphan and had to write the letters, whereas the girls had their proper parents and Jeanie looked silly in the yellow brown and green sloppy Joe. Once there was some stuff called Turkish Delight, which was pink and lemon soft stuff with white powder over it and I absolutely loved it. Oh yes, and a tinned toffee pudding which almost caused a family tragedy.

It was on Sunday and Mum decided that we were going to have the American toffee pudding with custard after we had finished our sausage toad, greens and potatoes. It was put on top of the gas stove in the corner of the kitchen to heat up while we were finishing our dinner.

When the custard was ready, and it was time for the pudding, Dad took the saucepan of boiling water, containing the tin, off the stove and got the opener to pierce the lid. He came back to the table and took the tin, wrapped in a tea towel, out of the saucepan. As he put the point of the opener into the tin a stream of scalding hot toffee spurted out and up in the air. We all screamed and ducked out of the way. I threw myself across Beryl who was sitting next to me. Mum threw herself across Chrissie and Dad turned the tea towel across the top of the tin causing the rest of the toffee to spurt over the table as we all yelled and screamed. It all happened and was over in just a few seconds.

Dad got burned hands and Mum was burned on her arms, which was much better than burns on to the baby's face. The rest of us were o.k. but very shocked. I burst into tears with the thought of what it could have done to Chrissie who was sitting in her high chair right in the direct line of spurt as it were. At first everyone thought I had been scalded with the toffee and got concerned. But when they found out it was my over-active imagination, I was told to pull myself together and grow up. We never did get to taste that toffee pudding and Viola never sent another one, even though I never told her what had happened.

17 AT SCHOOL IN LOVE WITH MARY

It was well into nineteen forty-six and Mr. Atlee, who was trying to get things back to normal, made education an important part of the regeneration. Bigland Street School was reopened, because most of the kids were back from their various evacuations in Britain and abroad and the schools were starting to fill up again. This was good news for me because the school was on the other corner facing our house, which meant that I got to lie in bed longer in the mornings.

Immediately the school opened Mum managed to get a job as a cleaner and Nanny became one of the dinner maids. It was Nan who stuck up for me when I had difficulty eating my dinner, during my first term. I got blamed for causing the trouble even though it was the schools fault; because they gave me creamed potatoes that had horrible hard little lumps in them and looked like white rats' turds. The more I thought about it as I tried to eat it, the more I couldn't swallow. There was also a stupid rule that we couldn't take our plate to be scraped off until it was empty.

I sat at the dinner table and managed to get through my mince and beans, but I just knew that I was never going to be able to eat the potato without being sick. I waited till most of the kids had gone and then eased myself away from the table as slowly as I could and went to the bin at the end of the dinner counter, to scrape the terrible tasting stuff off. I was almost there when eagle eyed Miss Edwards, the dinner superintendent, saw me.

"What are you doing Johnny, I hope you are not going to put those lovely potatoes in the bin?"

I nodded.

"No, you are not, young man. You are going to return to your seat and you are going to eat them. There is no excuse for wasting good wholesome food while the country struggles to get back onto its feet."

"But it makes me sick, Miss. It tastes like warm soapy water and there's lumps in it and they make me feel bilious."

She grabbed me by the shoulder and marched me back to an empty table that was much nearer to the dinner counter, so she could see me. Nanny saw this happening and came over.

"What's going on Enid?" she asked.

"He wants to throw away that lovely creamed potato, Sarah. And look he's hardly touched it...."

"I ate the beans and mince," I interrupted. "Nan, there's hard white lumps in it and it really does make me want to be sick. Honest."

"Perhaps we will let him off this time," said Nanny, adding a little white lie. "He's prone to bilious attacks."

"No! I'm sorry Sarah, I can't make fish of one and fowl of the other it wouldn't be fair on the other children. And he should eat all his food, he's far too skinny as it is. You ought to be grateful for a lovely dinner like that Johnny."

"I'm not grateful because it's awful and I am not going to eat it. If you think it is so good and you don't want it wasted, you can bleeding eat it."

I realised I had gone too far with the swearing when Nanny poised her lips and Edwards gave a sharp intake of breath and stormed out of the hall.

"Oh Johnny," Nanny said. "You've done it now, why don't you eat it up like a good boy."

"Because it tastes like shit Nan and it makes me want to vomit." I explained.

Nanny shook her head and moved away, muttering to me quietly.

"You've done it now. I can't help you. Here comes Mrs. Murray."

Mrs. Murray, the head mistress, came to me with Miss Edwards trailing behind her. She then told me all of what I had already said, to Miss Edwards along with a brief outline of what had been going on. Which was a bit pointless because all of that I already knew, Mrs. Murray then bent over me and insisted I finish my dinner and stop causing a fuss so that the dining room could be cleared and ready for the afternoon lessons in the hall.

"But I hate it and it's cold and makes me sick, Miss Murray. It really, really makes me want to be sick."

"Well we can't throw good food, away can we? There are loads of hungry people in the world who would be only too happy to eat that lovely creamed potato. So, come on Johnny set a good example and finish it just for them."

"Fuck 'em," was my reply. I had had enough. "If they want it, then let them come and get it. In fact, it you think it is so good why don't you bloody eat it."

It was a silly mistake. It was even sillier to push the plate across the table towards her, because it hit her dress and all the watery creamed potato went over her skirt.

Everyone went nuts. Before I knew what was happening, I was dragged to Mrs. Murray's office and caned twice on my bony little arse.

After school Mum was told and Dad gave me a good ticking off. Nanny was really upset because she didn't know where to put her face. On the end of her neck seemed the right place to me. But I held my tongue.

I had another run in with Mrs. Murray ten days later. Me and Harry Maitland. He had started taking the piss our of a new kid that had come to the school called Michael Daniels, because he was skinny and wore glasses. Michael and I had started up a bit of a friendship because he liked Dick Barton and was Jewish, and although I was a Christian I didn't blame him for crucifying Our Lord.

Harry was a tricky bit of good and had already got a reputation for being a good fighter and a bit of a bully. Michael and I were just minding our own business in the playground when he came running by and happened to collide with Michael.

"Oi! You wanna watch where you're standing," he shouted at us as he ran on his way.

"You wanna look out for other people, you fat pig." I shouted back.

He carried on running but in a semi-circle which brought him back to us two. He stopped in front of me and put his fists up.

"D'ya wanna fight?" He demanded to know?

"You should be more careful, "I said. "You could have smashed Daniels's glasses."

"It's alright," said Daniels.

"No, it's not, he's a bleeding bully," I said.

Smack. Right in the chest. Maitland had started the fight without my permission. I threw a right at him and he dodged out of the way, I must say he was light on his feet. He came back at me and hit me in the face, which stung a bit. I aimed a blow at him and it landed on his shoulder as a crowd of boys began to gather round us.

We had got into a wrestling hold with hands and legs going fifty to the dozen before we fell onto the gravel of the playground surface. We had no time to land many blows on each other before Mr. Bridges, who was on playground duty, appeared above us and heaved us up from the floor before wrenching us apart. He took us straight to Mrs. Murray.

We both got a thwack of the ruler on each hand in her office, delivered by Mr. Bridges who warned us that if there was any more fighting, we would be for the chop! There was no more fighting, I never had another fight during my whole school years. Harry and I never became friends but kept a respectful distance between us. The following week Michael Daniels left our school, because he lived in Stepney Way, on the other side of Commercial Road and it was too far for him to come.

From that moment my form teacher Miss Caddish, or Cake-Dish as we called her behind her back, was warned that she ought to keep a special eye on me as I was a trouble maker. This gave her a good excuse to give me the ruler across my slim calves whenever she got the slightest provocation. Which wasn't that often because I was mostly a shy, sensitive boy. Although somehow, she would find an excuse to thwack me. So, by the time my last primary term came, it was a great relief to leave that frumpy old cow and move up into Mr. Green's class.

Mr. Green was great fun and apart from making his lessons interesting and lively, he even tried to get me to make my voice deeper. Which meant that I had to keep saying 'Sixteen men on a dead man's chest,' from somewhere deep down in my belly. I did have a very high voice, which was apparent when I sang the part of the page in Good King Wenceslas at the Christmas concert. My first public appearance. I loved it. I felt very at home in front of an audience and had a singing voice that hit all the right notes. Standing up in front of the school was where I felt I really belonged.

It was in the new year that I moved into Mr. Green's class who took us for English and History and I believe that it was his lessons that made me want to learn something. Another reason why I liked him was because, after being in his class a couple of weeks, he let me sit next to my sweetheart, Mary Simpson.

I really loved Mary with all my heart and often told her so. As soon as school was over, and I could get out from 51A. We would roam around the bombed ruins together. There were loads of badly blasted buildings that hadn't been pulled down or cleared away. Especially the old shops in Watney Street Market. We had a secret kissing place in a bombed-out fish shop that stank of rancid cooking oil, charcoal and rotting fish. It had been badly burned in a raid years ago and was boarded up. We managed to crawl through the gap under the wooden battens, into a narrow area that was dark, secretive and away from the world of grown-ups. Despite the stench we would often go back there to play kissing and cuddling. These ruins of burned wood and falling bricks were the play grounds given to us by the bombs of the Luftwaffe.

Our favourite place was the tall baker's ovens on the Winterton Street bomb site as it was called. The whole of Winterton Street had been completely wiped out by the

Nazi's, because in it, there were the two huge round air ducts that let the air get down to the Metropolitan line that ran underneath it. This was the line that had carried arms and supplies to the Docks. The Gerry's were desperate to knock it out by landing a bomb down one or both of the shafts. Fortunately, they never actually managed to put one into either of them. But the top of Watney Market and the whole Winterton Street got blown to nothing. It was strange because Planet Street, on the other side from the Market, had only one bomb. It fell on Mrs. Arnica's place and the whole family were killed outright.

So Winterton Street was flat apart from the two round towers and the tall ovens, that was all that was left of the pie shop. It was in one of the ovens, where I found the rarest of treasures, a soft toilet roll. Nanny was disgusted with me for keeping it, because it was all crumpled and dusty but I hung on to it. I used it sparingly, as I had been taught, with a bit to wipe, a bit to polish and a bit to dust.

Our favourite game in the ovens, was climbing the rungs, set inside the walls and where they used to slide in trays of pies to cook. We would climb to the top and look out of the iron doors. These spaces would become a pirate ship, or a church that was on fire, or a mountain in the jungle, or even a spitfire that we had to abandon. Mary would be on the ground I would be waving my last goodbye to her as I took off for Germany to destroy the Nazi's. Once she was a princess in a castle and I had to climb up to rescue her. When I did that she gave me a film star kiss, as we hung over the rusty doors. When I rescued her from the concentration camps she rewarded me by letting me have my first 'do.' It wasn't much, just a feel of one of her small breasts, but it turned out to be a rehearsal for Lucille later in the year.

It was because of Mary, that I did what I did to the table cloth, which Mum never forgot or forgave. Alright, what I did was unusual in as much as I've never heard of anyone else doing anything like it, but is that any reason why Mum should still be going on about it years later? Especially when I take a new friend round to see her or if there's a family gathering with new people to embarrass me in front of.

I have to admit it was a lovely cloth. It was a yard and a half square of pure white Damask with a four inch royal blue border all round. Mum had bought it with saved three penny bits and borrowed clothing coupons towards the celebrations of the peace. It represented a little bit of luxury and covered the rickety old table in the corner of the our front room. I violated it because I was passionately in love.

Mary was six weeks older than I was and the prettiest girl in the school. Her hair was loose and frizzy because her mother didn't approve of plaits, despite the ever-present threat of nits and fleas. She had freckles and a red mouth and wore home-made frocks in lemon and pink. Everyone in Stepney knew we were going to get married even Mr. Green, who at the end of our exams, gave us his blessing and presented Mary with a velveteen clutch bag in orange to match my ginger hair.

It was our last day together at Bigland Street Primary. Mary was going to Rains School and I was going to Myrdle Street Middle, so we were going to be separated for ever. To make matters worse, on that day, she was going away for two weeks with the Country Holiday Fund Scheme. This was a charity that organised holidays for underprivileged Cockney kids. I had to stay home because I was not underprivileged enough to go for free and Dad couldn't afford the amount that it cost if you were not completely underprivileged.

Mary was so excited by the thought of going away, that if I hadn't loved her as much as did I would have hit her. I had been round her house the previous night and had been shown her borrowed attaché case, her new Bakelite soap dish and flannel, but worst of all was her new tennis bat. It had a shiny cream handle with writing on it and real cat gut strings. I did feel sorry for her because being a girl she kept calling it a racquet. I put her straight and told her that the racquet was the bit of wood with the wire springs that held the bat in its place so that it wouldn't get buckled. I thought it was important for her to know things like that otherwise when she walked on to the tennis pitch she could easily show herself up.

At dead on four o/clock the bell rang for home time and we rushed out of the school gate for the last time. I kissed her and said.

"I'll be round your street in less than a quarter of an hour. O.K.?"

"O.K." she said. "But don't be late because my Mum won't wait. If you don't manage to get there, meet me outside the Palaseum before the coach leaves."

"I'll be there don't worry," I said as we parted, and I nipped along the pavement to our house. I went through the ever-open door and rushed up both flights of stairs, yelling as I went. "Mum it's me. I'm home. Can I go out?",

"No," was her reply, as I dashed into the front room. "I'm gonna need you here. And don't you dare think of running down those stairs."

She had read my mind, because I had seen piles of navy-blue dresses with white spots on them, draped all over the furniture and knew that I would have to work. The dresses had to be finished. Aunt Kate and Aunt Alice were already working; their fingers busy with needles sewing on hooks and eyes, press studs and tacking in shoulder pads. They were too busy even to take any notice of me. Mum gripped my wrist with her hand that had been made strong from years of pushing a hot iron up and down the board. She pulled me into the centre of the room away from the door.

"Mossy Goldberg wants these frocks done by tomorrow morning," she explained, as she pulled me into the room. "So, we'll be working most of the night. Now listen, the three girls are round at Nanny's. What I want you to do is get the shopping, collect them when you've done it and then do the tea by the time Daddy gets home. He'll take over then, but he's on a long-distance drive so it might not be to till after seven. The ration books are on the sideboard and there's some money in my purse"

Having given me her orders she let go of my arm and returned to her chair by the door to work on a frock.

"Mum!" I said firmly. "I'll do all that later but now I've got to go to see Mary before she…"

"Johnny, don't argue with me Son. I know you, once you get out I won't see you gain for the rest of the night."

"No, Mum. Honest," I pleaded. "She's going on the coach with the country …"

"The more you argue Johnny, the longer it'll take," said Aunt Kate, sticking her nose in where it wasn't wanted.

Aunt Alice nodded in agreement as she hummed along to the record, spinning on the portable gramophone. I got the feeling that they were ganging up on me and I wasn't going to have it. I was grown up now. I had just left primary school! I walked to the end of the sideboard and turned to face the three of them.

"I'm not gonna do it. If I can't go to see Mary off, then I'm not …"

A wooden coat hanger flew past my head, just missing me and the Alsatian china dog on the small table. Fortunately, Mummy's aim had never been of the best.

"Johnny be a good boy," said Alice, who never liked confrontation and had grown up terrified of her sister's temper.

"Mind your own bleedin' business," I said, surprising myself in being so saucy to my favourite Aunt.

Mum was out of the chair and across the room in an instant, aiming a blow at my head. I protected myself with my elbow.

She grabbed my arm and dragged me over to one of the oak dining chair belonging to the suite. She swept a pile of frocks off it with her other hand and threw me on to it.

"You'll sit there till you come to your senses and learn to do what your Mother tells you," she said as she returned to her chair by the door. Where she sat like one of those women at the foot of the guillotine.

All four of us were very quiet. The record finished and there was just that scratching sound that the needle made on the bit at the end till the motor ran down. A train passed along the Fenchurch Street Line, at the bottom of the street. The ornamental dog, on the Damask cloth, did a tiny dance to the vibrations as the house gently shook.

Time was passing. Mary would be waiting. What could I do?

As I sat there, I imagined Mary getting into her white blouse and new brown shorts. She would be waiting for me to knock. If I didn't see her now I wouldn't see her for two weeks. Two whole weeks! If I didn't turn up she would think I didn't love her. And I did.

"If you're going to sit there like some gormless idiot dreaming away, you might as well thread some needles for us," said Mum. "Alice pass him the saucer and a reel of cotton."

I often helped with the needle threading because Nanny said my young eyes were better than theirs. As I took a needle from the saucer, I thought of a line of attack.

"Mu-um … I want to do a wee," I lied. Working out that if I got down to the lav I could quickly nip out and round to Mary's.

"Do me a favour Johnny! Do you think I am some sort of dozy Pratt who was born yesterday? You are not going nowhere, my boy, not 'till you've sorted those ration books and money."

"But Mum, I have to. I'm nearly doing it," I insisted.

"Cork it up then," she said. "Alice turn that record over,"

In silence Aunt Alice got up and wound the handle on the gramophone, turned the record over, released the brake and put the sound box on the spinning plastic. The Andrews Sisters sang about Apple Blossoms. The work continued and so did Alice's humming. The record finished followed by more silence. I was aware, as I threaded another needle with navy blue cotton, that time was racing by. Mary would have left her house to get to the coach. I could still get to see her if I rushed straight up to Commercial Road. Drastic measures were needed. I began to wriggle on the chair.

"Mum, I'm gonna do it, if you don't let me go."

"Kate, put the Ink Spots on," was all Mum said.

I watched squirming as Aunt Kate went through the whole procedure of making the Ink Spots sing 'Whispering Grass.' The women 'la-lahd', along sometimes singing bits they knew or liked. All of them deliberately ignoring me. I was fuming with anger, worry and frustration. I knew I had to do something and I had to do it now. So, I did.

I calmly got up, went to the other end of the sideboard towards the gramophone, took the arm off the record and stopped it spinning. There was silence. I turned to face the three sisters who were staring at me, astounded by my arrogant cheek. I looked towards the door and spoke firmly and clearly to my Mother.

"I wanna do a wee and if you don't let me go down to the lavatory to do it, I will do it up your new table cloth."

Their three mouths dropped open like three goldfishes in a cartoon film. Aunt Alice spoke first.

"He's a little liar Nell and he's ruined that song now. Don't you let him out of your sight"

"Don't worry I won't. I'm not falling for any of his lying little larks," Mother replied.

I realised that they were calling my bluff, but I was determined not fold easily. It wasn't just about Mary any more, it was now about a man's honour. How dare they call me a liar?

"Right then. Don't blame me," I said as I walked towards the table in the corner.

I was wearing my short tweed trousers, so I didn't have to undo any fly buttons I just pulled my little winkle out from under my left leg hole. I turned sideways so that they could all see me, and I prepared to pee. The main part of my preparation was a silent prayer that something would come out. Unfortunately, nothing happened. I looked away from my winkle towards the women, my sharp chin jutting out.

The three of them had stopped sewing and were staring at me as they sat among the spotted dresses, like three witches in a navy-blue snow storm. Their expressions showed their conviction that I was lying, and nothing would come out. I realised that unless I expressed some liquid I would be vanquished.

There was a pause. I raised my eyebrows, relaxed my body and waited.

A warm, satisfying stream of piddle came out, in a slight arch and fell onto the Damask cloth. Not on the top of the table near the Alsatian because I was too small to reach up that far. No, the liquid fell on the bit with the royal blue border that was hanging down. I must confess it was not a long pee, but it was long enough to make the point. I had spoken the truth and they were wrong. I hope they realised that they had been wrong as they numbly watched me.

The moment was broken by Nellie finding her voice. Not her usual raucous shout, but a voice that was quiet, comfortingly unbelieving and tinged with a little sorrow.

"Girls, he's pissing up me table cloth."

As I finished and tucked myself back up the leg of my trouser her anger broke. She lunged across the room towards me. I ducked under her arm and knocked the dresses off the armchair as I dived across the room. I had just reached the door when the ornamental dog smashed into pieces above my head. Her aim was still bad. I rushed out of the room past the coal-box and flew down the stairs. I slammed the glass door behind me. This cut down the sound of fury I could hear from upstairs and it wasn't pleasant.

My legs, going fifty to the dozen, got me to the Palaseum in time to see the coach pulling away towards the Blackwall Tunnel. There was no sign of Mary, but the kids in the back who were still waving to their mum's must have told her I was there because suddenly there she was, waving and blowing kisses to me out of the rear window. I jumped up and down and waved both my arms until the coach was out of sight leaving me filled with the ache of a lover who had gone far away.

I returned home late that night when I paid, in no uncertain terms, for my actions.

As it turned out it was all for nothing. When Mary came home, all brown and smothered in wasp stings, she didn't love me anymore. She told me she now loved an older boy of twelve and half. It turned out he played tennis and knew the difference between a bat and a racquet. I was heartbroken for over two days. But I forgot all about her and met Lucille, when I went hopping at the end of August.

Mum, on the other hand, never forgot or forgave me, especially when there are new opportunities to embarrass me.

18 SECONDARY SCHOOL AND ITCHIE

Nineteen forty-seven was the year of the big frost. For me this meant wheeling the pram round to the greengrocers at the bottom of Watney Street Market, and spending a long time queuing for coal, gathering wood from the bomb sites for the fires and getting dressed in front of the gas oven in the kitchen. I had to make a big sacrifice when we were desperate for wood by giving my bedside table for kindling. The bedside table had been a vain attempt to copy the luxury of what I had seen in the posh houses that I had 'delivered' to for Aunt Bet. It was in fact just an orange box stood on end with the middle partition acting as a lower shelf and covered in an old piece of cloth. Behind this I kept my special possessions. It was a little oasis of privacy in the flat and my sacrifice was rewarded when in the spring I found another one when wood wasn't such a luxury

The summer holidays came and went as holidays did in those days and before we knew it, we were off to Kent for the hop-picking at the end of August. Dad had been laid off from his job, so he came with us and got a job as a pole puller for the season. Unfortunately, he got something wrong with his eye, so we stayed on at Ploggs Hall Farm, for the apple picking. This was because wouldn't have been able to get a proper job with only one eye. This meant that it was October when I eventually started big school at Mile End Central, known as Myrdle Street Middle.

I was feeling very shy and insecure as I left 51a, with my shining new satchel slung over my shoulder, to go to start my new life. Instead of just crossing the road to school; I now had a long walk which took me along Tait Street, passed Aunt Alice's at No. 40, Aunt Kate's at 15, and across the bomb site, into Cannon Street. Stopping to look at the camera's in the window of the Pawn shop, I then continued up to the traffic lights at the junction with Commercial Road. Over the crossing, I turned left at the laundry and took the first on the right, into Myrdle Street. It was an historical route because if you now check this route in the A to Z of London, you will find that most of these streets are no longer there.

As I passed through the gate the playground was full of boys and girls all involved in their own activities. I had no idea of where to go until I found a teacher in charge who directed me to go to the headmaster's office. He was called Mr. Ward, and he informed me that because I had missed so much of the term I had been put in the 'C' stream with a form teacher called Mr. Powell and I was to report to his class on the first floor.

I was eased into the school's system by Michael Daniels. He was the boy who I had met briefly when Bigland Street first opened. He was a quiet, likeable Jewish boy with black hair, horn rimmed glasses and thin ankles. He was the youngest of four, two brothers and a sister Mavis, who all lived in Stepney Way with their Mother. She often gave him smoked salmon and cream cheese bagels which he shared with me at school. He was also quite intelligent, so I don't know what he was doing in the 'C' class. We became firm friends; not just because of the food, but because we had a lot in common. We both liked the cinema, radio and reading. Plus, as in all lasting friendships, there was something indefinable that drew us together and has kept us friends for decades. He kept his eye out for me when I first started, and told me where things were. It was him that explained double sessions to me which meant that on Friday we had to start and finish school early so that the Jewish kids could go home early to do Shabbos. Which was something to do with their God.

I remained insecure and worked hard during that short first term in an effort to become accepted and keep up with the lessons. My low profile continued until the Christmas Concert, which took place in the hall and was put on by the older pupils and some of the teachers.

Because we were first years, we saw the morning show along with the second years. The other years would be seeing it in the afternoon. It was lots of fun. That is apart from Mr. Black, the music teacher, singing 'Drink to me only, with thine eyes.' He pulled such terrible faces trying to make the words sound posh that Michael and I nearly pissed ourselves as we tried to stop laughing. I had particularly enjoyed a Punch and Judy show performed by Doris Benjamin, one of the girls in the third year, and two of the boys doing a sketch where they pretended to be pigeons. It was during the dinner break that we heard that Doris had broken her arm and had been rushed to the London Hospital, where she was having it set. To this day I don't know what possessed me, but I volunteered to take over her act.

Mrs. Abrahams, the teacher in charge, couldn't believe that I knew most the words only having seen it once but agreed to let me do it. She gave me the script, the puppets and the props and I threw myself into it so much that by the time afternoon concert started I knew it would be alright. Actually, it was only about five minutes long, and having been introduced to the audience as the saviour of the show, I had nothing too loose. I relaxed and enjoyed myself making them laugh a lot more than Doris had done. Due to a bit of ad-libbing when I dropped the baby doll. So, I became a hero for a day. After that experience everyone knew who I was, so I managed to settle down and enjoy being the centre of attention. This since became the pattern of my life i.e. arrive at a new job or place. Be quiet, shy and insecure to start with then relax and show off large.

The following term Michael and I, were transferred into the B stream with Mr. Delmont as our form master. He had a big ginger moustache, heavily built and was a much sterner teacher than Mr. Powell because he had served in Africa,

We still saw Mr. Powell, known to us witty kids as Bucket, when he came to our class to teach us maths as it was called, and it was during one of his sessions that a dreadful incident occurred, which although I was blamed for it and sent to see Mr. Ward, it was definitely not and I repeat NOT my fault!

It happened after R.I. - Religious Instruction which was the last but one lesson of the day, R.I. was given by Miss. Goodman, a tiny woman with an old face, who stood rather squat in her green knitted suit and polished brogue shoes. The theme of her lesson was one guaranteed not to offend any sect, 'brotherly love.' However, by the time the end of lesson bell rang, in her effort to avoid offence to the girls, the boys, the Blacks, the Jews, the Catholics, the Protestants and the Atheists, she had made it so boring I could have willingly murdered her and all of her bloody brothers.

She closed her bible and with her two-penny bun face cracking into a creamy smile, she looked up and down each row of seats and whispered in a conspiratorial way.

"As Mr. Powell has not yet arrived and I have another class to take I will have to leave you alone for a while. Now, I am going to put you all on your honour not to disturb Mr. Jackson's class next door. I accept your promise that you will remain as silent as mice. I go now. Good afternoon 'One B',"

"Good afternoon Miss. Goodman," we whispered back, as she turned the other cheek and left the room.

We all watched with relief as she shut the door and passed along the glass partition of corridor and out of vision. Our class room was surrounded by glass apart from the brick wall behind our desks. In front of us, from floor to ceiling, was a glass partition made of lots of small windows in wooden frames. This partition separated us from the classroom where Mr. Jackson was giving his double geography lesson to 'One A.'

One B, consisted of twenty-six mixed silent mice sitting in desks six rows across and five rows down. I sat four in three down behind Brenda Rember, whose parents were known for their sense of humour. I take the time to explain all this so that you can picture the class room and understand that despite what happened; I was in no way to blame.

A bit of time went by after Saint Goodman had left but there was still no sign of Mr. Powell. Naturally some murmuring and fidgeting started. I took no notice because I was trying to work out whether I could buy the 'Beano,' see Danny Kay in 'The Secret Life of Walter Mitty,' at the Troxy and still have enough for the bus fare home, out of the money I had earned taking the bag wash for Mrs. Coakley and Aunt Kate that morning, on my way to school. This was my way of making maths useful.

In the middle of my calculations I suddenly felt something sting the back of my neck and I knew straight away that it was NOT a wasp. My ginger head flicked round just in time to see David Kaminski turn away and pretend to be staring at Maureen Nesty's breasts. I looked down at the floor boards and lying there, to the right of my desk, was a paper pellet dead and spent.

"O.K. Kaminski," I thought to myself. "Your number is up!"

Daniels, who I now called 'Itchie,' on account of me once calling him Mitch and Brenda Rember getting it wrong, was sitting next to me but across the aisle. He heard me give a bit of a gasp when I was stung by the pellet and looked over to see what I would do.

My eyes locked into Itchie's and I flicked them towards the floor. He knew instinctively what I wanted him to do, so he leaned out of his desk towards mine and picked up the pellet.

This of course camouflaged me from Kaminski who I knew, would be looking at me with his spare eye.

I opened my desk just wide enough to get my hand in. This allowed me to collect my rubber band plus some ready-made pellets. I was actually removing the weapons as Itchie swung upright, back into his desk and put the spent pellet into his chipped inkwell. Good teamwork or what?

I slipped the elastic bank over my thumb and forefinger, armed it with a pellet and as I pulled it back, turned quick as a searchlight finding a Messerschmitt and fired it at Kaminski. It flew down the classroom and missed him. But it did score a hit.

Unfortunately, it was a direct hit on the liver lips of Big Alfie Smith. Immediately Alfie reached out, grabbed his ink rubber and slung it at me. I turned and lurched to my left, so it went past me and hit Brenda Rember on the head. Right between her mouse coloured plaits tied with the red ribbons. As the rubber bounced off of her head, Brenda must have thought she had been attacked by Essey Wilson, because without any declaration of war she leant over and smashed the bewildered Essey in the face. By this time, I had had another pellet from Kaminski and deciding to do something about it,

I slid out of my desk and took my tennis ball out of my jacket pocket. I had just drawn my arm back to throw it, when I was jogged by Essey and Brenda Rember who were now wrestling on the floor. The ball jerked backwards out of my hand and bounced towards the front of the class. I turned to go after it but fell over the wrestling girls. From the floor I saw Dennis Andrews who fancied himself as a Tommy

Lawton, nip out from his desk and kick the ball towards the side partition. It hit the door, rebounded and would have smashed one of the windows if it hadn't hit Caroline O'Connor, who had to sit in the first row because she needed special care. It gave her a good thwack on the head. But she didn't cry, she just climbed on top of her desk and started to sing 'I'm gonna buy a paper doll that I can call my own.'

As I struggled to free myself from the writhing girls, I noticed that by now the whole class was at it. Shouting and moving around and throwing stationary. I managed to scramble up and with my head down was going towards the ball, which had rebounded off of Caroline's temple and was bouncing towards the door again. I was moving quickly towards the door when it sprung open, hitting the ball and sending it, I don't know where, as Miss Diamond came charging in her red skirt flailing around her ample thighs. I did actually see her thighs coming towards me but there was nothing I could to stop my momentum. That is until her stomach moving into the class and my head moving out of the class – collided.

We fell to the floor turning our bodies to get away from each other as we dropped. Unfortunately, we both turned the same way, so that as she landed on her back, I found myself on top of her with my face buried in the red sea of her utility skirt. It was very embarrassing. And it got worse. She started to scream and banged her legs up and down on the floor as she tried to kick me off of her wriggling body.

Anyway, as luck would have it, Mr. Levine, our French teacher wearing a limp pin-striped demob suit, happened to be passing. I suppose hearing Miss Diamond screaming and seeing me buried in her lower area, he must have thought the worst.

He tore into the room.

"You dirty little tyke!" he yelled, in his perfect French accent. "Remove yourself from that woman.!"

He then stepped over the pair of us, grabbed me by my jacket collar and yanked me up in the air. I was still small for my age. He threw me against one of the front desks, which slid back straight into Bernice Goldstein.

Let me tell you about Bernice Goldstein. I need say no more than that she was a large child and so highly strung that she was known to everyone in the school as - the barrage balloon. She just went do-lally and started screaming and throwing all her books at Mr. Levine. He threw up his arms to protect his face and backed straight into Miss Diamond who was rising from the floor, clutching her stomach. Before you could say Ted Ray, down she went again gnashing her teeth and going hysterical. Only this time Mr. Levine was on top of her, flailing around like a live eel on Harvey's fish stall in the Market!

As for me? Well I was really annoyed by now as you can imagine what with the pain in my back from hitting the desk and losing my ball. I lost my temper. I saw a double compass among the scattered contents of Bernice's desk. I instinctively grabbed it and just as Mr. Levine, was bending over Miss Diamond, I rammed the point right into his arse. Between the lines on his pin stripe trousers.

As the steel pierced into him, Mr. Levine jerked forwards and put his head through one of the windows in the glass partition. Mr. Jackson's double geography lesson was thereby disturbed as the whole of 'One A' turned to see the French teacher's head through the glass partition looking for all the world as though he was on the block waiting for the dropping of the guillotine blade.

Mr. Jackson bellowed that he was coming in to deal with us!

Back in our room: Miss Diamond had stopped gnashing her teeth as a slow deep whine issued from the back of her throat. She had risen, for the third time, looking as if she was in some nightmare. She looked behind her at Mr. Levine's twitching body, then at us, then back to him. With her whine getting ever louder, she bent towards Mr. Levine and wrenched the compass out of his bum as her whine turned into a scream that sounded like Johnny Weissmuller in the Tarzan films. As her scream faded into a sob, she stood up and with great force slung the compass towards the blackboard, where it embedded itself right up the bit where you screw in the pencil. She fell to her knees sobbing and wailing as she tried to free the Frenchman.

By now the classroom was in chaos. Kaminski, the real cause of it all, was in the same desk as Maureen Nesty, who was trying to put her fingers up his nose. Brenda Rember had Essey Wilson at her mercy and was gnawing on her forearm. Itchie Daniels, while trying to calm Bernice, had been hit by a hard-back copy of Jane Eyre and Caroline O'Connor, had changed her song to 'Knees Up Mother Brown,' and was dancing.

The rest was indescribable.

Back at the partition, Abigail Kimberly whose mother was a nurse, was urging Miss Diamond to take the pieces of glass out of the window before she dragged Mr. Levine back into the room otherwise she might rip open his jugular vein. While in the 'One A' classroom some girl was dabbing at his face with a grubby handkerchief.

Mr. Jackson appeared at our open door, only to have his head knocked back as his glasses fell to the floor and smashed. He had been hit by a copy of 'Basic Algebra' that Itchie had thrown at Bernice and missed. Jackson not seeing very well, came into the room, grabbed hold of me by the shoulder and slung me out into the corridor.

"Ross! Go at once and report to Mr. Ward!" he yelled, slamming the door shut between us. Cutting me off from the noise and commotion in my class.

I stood there astounded. I mean, it wasn't my fault. I didn't see why I should get the blame, but under the circumstances it seemed best not to return to protest. I decided to do as I was told.

I walked slowly down to Mr. Ward's office, trying to sort out in my mind a reasonable explanation, as to why what had happed, had happened. It all seemed a big muddle in my head. I arrived at his office, which was situated at the end of the passage on the second floor and knocked on the door.

"Come in!"

I turned the handle but found it hard to push the door open because it had one of those iron things at the top that kept pushing me back as though it was trying to keep me out. I struggled against it and fell into the room as the door clumped slowly shut behind me. A pause, as the headmaster resolutely refused to look up.

"Yes?" rasped Mr. Ward, eventually. His red rimmed, watery blue eyes glaring at me from behind his cluttered desk.

"Mr, Jackson told me to report to you sir. There's been a bit of trouble in 'One B', but it wasn't my fault, I don't ……"

"Well it is your fault now," he interrupted and looked at his watch. "Fifteen hundred and fifty-one minutes on Tuesday 17th February, in the year of our Lord, nineteen hundred and forty-eight. Sit the other side of my door on the seat provided and I will see you at four thirty. Go!"

I sensed there was no point in arguing. I fought to drag the door open again and by the time I got to the stool provided it had clicked shut. There followed a long silence that was only interrupted by bells. First the bells of an ambulance followed by the bell for going home time.

Lots of kids ran down the staircase giggling and going right past me. Soon after this Mr. Jackson arrived. He glared at me, knocked on the door and was called in. I could hear voices raised but couldn't hear anything of what they were saying even though I popped my ear to the keyhole. But those big brass handles were awkward to get around. Mr. Jackson, was ushered out by a white faced Mr. Ward, who said to me through gritted teeth.

"Four-thirty, Boy!"

He disappeared back into his domain.

It didn't bode well. Gradually the school became silent and all I could hear was my own breathing, until the silence was disturbed.

"Psst!"

I looked along the corridor. Empty.

"Psst!"

I looked at the staircase and there right at the bottom of the wall reflected in the rust coloured tiles was the head of Itchie Daniels. Our eyes met, and he beckoned me towards him. I tip-toed over.

"Are you alright John?" he asked, his eyes grave behind the horn-rims.

"Yeah, I'm swell," I lied. "What happened after I left?"

"Well, Miss Diamond was still sobbin' when they took her home and Mr. Levine has been rushed to the London Hospital."

"Yeah, I guessed as much when I heard the ambulance. But listen, Itch, can you do me a favour?"

"Course I can," he looked very brave. "What d'ya want?"

"Me Mum's doing some Hoffman pressing at Nossek and Nathan's," I had to give him all the details. "Can you pop round to Cavel Street and tell her that I'm being kept in and that there will be no one to look after the girls when they get home?"

I looked down at him kneeling on the stone steps, his brain ticking over.

"Tell you what," he said almost immediately. "I'll look after them 'till you get home then your Mum and Dad needn't know that you're being kept in."

"Oh great! Thanks, Itchie," I whispered. "Give them a condensed milk sandwich till I get home. Here's the key, in case Mrs. Coakley's shut the door."

He took the key. I watched him scurry down the stairs without a sound before I crept back to the stool to await my fate.

My fate, at precisely the time stated by Mr. Ward, turned out to be a big telling off. Which was bad, and I thought that was going to be it. But no. It was followed by three whacks on each hand and the threat of expulsion if anything like this happened again. I nodded and left the room.

When I left the school, with both hands very sore, it was late which meant a desperate run home to arrive before anyone missed me. I raced up the stairs to the kitchen. Itchie was more than pleased to see me. He had done his best, but being the youngest in his family he wasn't used to bringing up kids. The two girls had played him up and were smothered in condensed milk, sugar and there were bits of bread all over the table.

He left straight away to get back home, and I cleaned up the girls before Mum returned from work. She was picking Chrissie up from Nanny's, so she would stop for a gossip and a cup of tea and that would give me time to have them all nice and clean by the time she arrived, as though nothing at all had gone wrong.

19 TAKING UP THE CHURCH AND ACTING

Apart from School the other big influence on my East End life was the church. This interest was very much encouraged by Nanny, who was an ardent church goer once a week and a staunch Anglican. From the time I was just over ten years old, every Sunday I would get washed and dressed in my best clothes, go around to Nanny's and we would walk to St. Phillip's church, in Newark Street round the back of Philpot Street. It was really called St. Augustine's with St. Philip's on account that St. Augustine's had been bombed and was now only a shell with no roof. But it was always referred to as St. Philips.

We would arrive in time for the eleven o'clock Mass, and sit in the front row next to Mrs. Whitehead, who was Beryl's Godmother. The Mass, was taken by the vicar Father Archer and was a high Anglican service with hymns, bells, incense and some of the responses in Latin. The alter would be decorated with candles, flowers and gold braid on different coloured cloths, depending on what was happening in the church calendar.

After the service the grown-ups would have a bit of a chin wag outside until they had said enough, and we would go to Mrs. Whitehead's flat, in Parfett Street Buildings. It was on the ground floor at the back, through a dark passage with very little light coming in the window. Once inside we would have tea and biscuits and more chat. The Whitehead family were great friends of Nanny's and had mixed closely with all the Skelton's over the years. I enjoyed all this, as long as I could get home in time to hear Family Favourites on the light programme. This ritual and continued well into my teens by which time Beryl had joined us.

Looking back, my involvement with the Church was a Godsend, (no pun intended), in my life and had a huge influence on the way it panned out. It is difficult to pin point any one thing but the social side of it was certainly a help in getting over my insecurity of being an orphan. It got me away from the hard slog of home and provided an interest outside of school. It also put me in touch with older, wiser people who encouraged me to become aware of a world that presented opportunities and to focus on different things other than those I was used to.

By the Summer of nineteen forty-eight I had become a member of the boys group and we were asked if we wanted to go camping, It would be for a week, living under canvas, at a place called St. Mary Axe near Maldon in Essex. We would be supervised by some adults from the church. Dad and Mum agreed that I could go, especially as it was going to cost hardly anything. I was looking forward to it, because it was the first time I would have ever been away without a member of the family. But on the day I was due to go, I woke up with a terrible feeling of dread. I thought that by the time the week was over, the whole family might have moved away and when I got home I would have no one. It was a horrible feeling and as I was packing my small case with my few belongings, I thought that I would have to cancel the trip. But I realised that I couldn't do that mainly because Dad had paid the money and I was too worried about saying I was too scared to go. So, I went. Nanny came to see me off and as I got on the coach, I smiled and prayed that they would all still be there when I returned.

The coach dropped us ten boys plus our three minders off in the village where we had our photo done with the Deacon, who hid at the back. We were then led up a hill where we passed lots of cows and sheep. We went through a gate to our field that already had two small tents erected and a one-story brick cookhouse. This also had two rooms for the men to sleep in. I shared one of the tents with three other boys which was a change from being around all those girls at home. I made a special friend of one of the boys called Peter, which was like having Eddy back again but not quite as good.

Actually, the whole camping thing was just like being down hopping except there were only boys and men around and we didn't have to work. Instead of picking hops we played football, cricket and rounders and went on rambles and walks. We also had races and competitions with small prizes. We lived and cooked mostly in the open air and had to fetch and carry water in big things called dixies which I found too heavy for me to handle on my own, so Peter and I did it together. I got a little homesick for the first couple of days but with all the activities and games it soon disappeared. When I got back to Stepney, the family, much to my relief, were all still there. It turned out to be a good experience and was the beginning of me getting a bit more confidence in myself.

As far as St Phillip's was concerned the camping holiday had proved such a success that they did it again the following year. Only this time girls were allowed to come as well. They didn't sleep in tents but in a thing called a dormitory in the village. At this time, I was in love with Kitty, who was a year older than me but the age difference didn't matter to us. Because she and her two elder brothers were going, I went again. Kitty and I had already decided to marry when I left school. in fact, we had even picked out our furniture from the window of Wickhams department store in the Mile End Road.

I was much happier the second year. I even managed to carry the dixies of water and chop the logs, and wasn't as afraid of the cows as I had been the previous year. This year we had one large tent in which all the boys slept on individual paillasses. On the second night us smaller boys, were invited to watch the big boys playing with their dick's. They were holding a competition to see who could shoot the farthest and hit the tent pole. Harry won and we all cheered. The others kept on going even though the game was over. I couldn't see the point myself. When Peter and I tried it after breakfast on the following day, we both got bored so gave it up.

One evening, later in the week, some of the older lads encouraged me and Peter to climb through a tiny window so that we could nick some Wagon wheel biscuits and other stuff from the cookhouse. The food was missed, and the grown-ups found out that it was us when the wrappers were found in the tent. They held an inquiry and we were all questioned individually. Peter and I confessed, as there was no point in denying it. Three of the older boys also admitted being involved and were sent home in disgrace.

Kitty's brother Tommy was one of the boys who got sent home and his family gave up the church after that. Our relationship dwindled when her Mother took a dislike of me after I had gone into their front room, thinking that Kitty was on her own and shouted as I went through the door.

"All right you old mare get your tits out I'm coming to get ya!"

As we came face to face in the doorway we both got a huge surprise. After which Bancroft Road suddenly seemed too big a distance to walk.

While I was down hopping that year, I decided that I loved Betty, which was handy, because she also went to St. Phillips and lived a lot nearer to me than Kitty had done. Betty was only five months older than me and although she was over a foot taller, we were both sensible about it and agreed not to let her height stand in our way.

I continued to get more involved at the church. I think I was drawn to the ritual and the theatricality of the services. I became a server on the altar and found that I liked dressing up in the black cassock and white surplice. Being a server, meant serving the priest who was saying the Mass, it entailed ringing the bells as the Host was raised and passing the bottles for the mixing of the wine and water. I found the genuflecting, crossing oneself and being part of something that had been going on for hundreds of years gave me a sense of belonging. Even though it meant getting up very early for the weekday service when I had to serve at a seven o/clock mass. This was hard especially if I had been doing a bit of 'business' for Aunt Bet the night before and had been late getting to bed.

Without doubt the best things about being involved with the church was the social side of it; most of which took place in a small hall across the road next door to the vicarage. I thoroughly enjoyed the Beetle and Whist Drives, where I played cards and threw dice with the grown-ups and the winner got a small prize. They occasionally showed films about religious subjects and on very special occasions a comedy with Laurel and Hardy or Johnny Weissmuller as Tarzan and what was an added bonus was that we didn't have to pay anything at all. They held dances in the hall and that's where I learned to waltz and quick step to records played on a big electric gramophone. Christmas was a very special time because there would be a big party, with a tree and lights and special sandwiches and the inevitable jelly and custard. And it didn't really matter that we would always be given a religious present. There were also the Boy's Club, mothers' meetings and the Scouts, although I only went to them twice, due to the already mentioned knot trouble. But the most important club to me was the Drama Group.

The group was called the Leadenhall Players, which was a collection of grown up actors who had formed a group to do a play in the crypt twice a year. There would be three performances and the congregation of St. Phillips were urged, from the pulpit and with notices in the church porch, to support it. The first time I saw them was on a Saturday night. I was taken by Nanny and Mrs. Whitehead, to see their opening production. It was magical; a real play.

It was called, something with 'Veil,' in the title and it started with the excitement of going into the crypt, Nanny having handed in our tickets to Miss Head who was collecting them at the door. We got a piece of paper called a programme which told us the names of the people in it and where it was taking place and when half time would be.

I sat next to Nanny near the front so that I could see better and not have to look around or over bigger people's heads. Not too far in front of me was a pair of dark green curtains that had lights in front of them casting magical shadows on the material., It all felt very special and became fantastic when the lights were switched off and the curtains parted.

The crypt was transformed into a world of light, painted faces, intrigue and drama. It was like Saturday Night Theatre on the Home Service only in colour and 3D. It was absolutely marvellous! I lived in the play as it continued under the lights and was shocked when the interval came, and we had to stop for a cup of tea and a couple of Peek Freans shortcakes. When we had hung around for a bit and the second half started it was even better. Especially when someone got shot with a real gun. But he didn't die because at the end he stood in a row with all the others as they smiled and bowed to us as we clapped them. I clapped the hardest because I thought they were fantastically terrific and swell. I wished I could do a loud whistle through my fingers like some other boys. But I couldn't, so I did a limp breathy one through pursed lips. I absolutely hated it when the curtains closed for the last time and I had to go back in the Stepney Streets.

I could hardly contain myself until I got to school on the Monday and told Itchie every detail. He had seen a real play, before he was eleven, and had always been really smug about it. Saying things like,

"Oh yeah, I like going to the pictures they're real good. But don't get me wrong, it don't beat seeing a proper play in a proper real theatre" or "I enjoyed that film but I really like a live play best. Don't you John?"

Smug or what? And no matter how many times I told him that I would have also seen a real play if I hadn't got the measles when I was in Devon, it didn't score over him. But now I could actually sense what he had been going on about.

The following Sunday after church, the secretary of the group Hilda Lee, came up to me in the porch, while I was dipping my finger in the holy water to make the sign of the cross before leaving. She told me that the Leadenhall Players might be needing a young boy in their next play and Father Archer had suggested me. So, would I be interested?

"Fucking Hell Would I!"

Was what I felt like yelling. But I was still in church, so I just said. "Yes Miss, I would be interested. Thank you."

"You will have to get permission from your parents. If they say 'yes', then inform Father Archer. And if we do decide to produce the play we are thinking of we will let you know."

On the way to Mrs. Whitehead's I talked it over with Nanny. She said it was a good idea. "After all, it might make a man of you."

Would she ever stop try to make me a man?

As soon as I got to the top of the stairs at home, even before going to the wireless, I rushed to ask Mum and Dad if I could do a play. They said 'yes,' and they also said that it would be good for me, but it wasn't to go to my head and I was not to neglect helping out at home. Dad warned that I wasn't to get too excited in case they changed their mind or found someone better, because he was sure, there were a lot of boys who could do it.

But they didn't change their mind and the following Sunday I was asked to play Albert, a page boy servant, in a play called 'The Sport of Kings' by Ian Hay. Mrs. Lee, told me that they would send me a script and asked for my address. Other than school, I had never, ever been asked for my address before. I told her very carefully and so that she would not let the script go astray, I emphasised that the 'E' after Stepney, comma, one. E.1. which stood for East One. I watched her write it down in a diary that had its own little pencil stuck down the side. Everything was so glamorous.

On Tuesday, an envelope arrived addressed to John Ross and it contained the script. I had never seen anything so wonderful. It was a dark blue French's Acting Edition. No. 106. Inside it had pictures of what the stage would look like and in one of them a picture of some of the actors, including the boy who had played my part, when it was first produced in 1924 at the Savoy Theatre. It had cost four shillings, but there was a letter in it, saying that I did not have to pay for the script and that I had to attend rehearsals for a reading on Thursday evening at 7.30 in the crypt. It was just the most magnificent feeling. I was going to do real acting. Not just working puppets or doing my own show in the yard for the other kids at a penny a ticket. This was gonna be on a stage with real actors and lights and curtains.

Daddy giving me the benefit of his experience when he came home from work that night.

"Don't just read your own part. Read the whole story."

It was of course very good advice and I was surprised that he had taken an interest in what I was doing, me being such a thorn in his side.

I read the story. It was a domestic comedy and took place in a very posh house called Newstead Grange. In fact, it was so posh the house had its own library, which was the stage set, with French windows and lots of chairs and a big settee called a Chesterfield. I know this because it was on the furniture list at the back, with the picture of the original Albert, which I outlined in ink. I also put down the numbers of the fourteen pages I appeared in and underlined my part with a ruler and in real ink.

I was more excited than nervous at the first rehearsal. when we all sat around a table and read the three acts. The gown up actors were all so stunning and were very helpful to me especially the women. I was petted and looked after and spoilt rotten, which made a terrific change from being the one who was always having to take responsibility and being told what to do at home. George Lee, who was producing this play told me that I had to come to rehearsals when I was 'called.' You didn't say, "I'm goin' to work." Instead you said, "I've bin called." I was also told that even though they were grown up I was to use their first names and not call them Aunt, or Mr. or Miss, as I was used to. This was really being a man and grown up So pick the bones out of that Nanny.

However, the play took a long time to rehearse so it was months before we actually got to do it for an audience. Not that I minded because the rehearsals were brilliant.

That night before the first performance we had to have a dress rehearsal. This was the last rehearsal during which we had to put on our costumes and pretend there were more people watching us than just George. I was told that we had to carry on without stopping, no matter what happened. That night I was given my green suit with brass buttons down the chest. Hilda put grease paint on my face that had numbers called five and nine. Then she spat in something and brushed stuff on my eyebrows and lashes, to make them stand out and look good. Finally, she put a red dot of make-up, on the inside of my eyes to make them sparkle over the footlights. When this was done she powdered all over my face so that I wouldn't sweat. The smell of Leichner make up continues to transport me backstage to that church hall, even after forty odd years of slapping it on. After being 'made-up' I had to sit still and concentrate until it was time to stand by for my entrance.

I loved the dress rehearsal, but it wasn't a patch on the performances. While I was performing I felt that I really was

Albert, and that I lived in that house with those people and I wanted to live there forever. I had a great feeling of being me and that this was where I belonged. It was like I had come home from a long journey. It was the best feeling I had ever had. I thoroughly enjoyed it all. I even liked it when I was just sitting back stage listening to the other actors and waiting for my 'cue.'

I also enjoyed, though surprisingly no quite as much, all the praise I got. 'I was a natural. I was marvellous. I was very good. I was wonderful and had real talent.' Can anyone wonder that I was suddenly aware of what I wanted to do in life. I had an identity. I was someone. I was the centre of attention. I was happy.

But it only lasted three days! On Saturday night the magic ended. The curtains came together after we had taken our bows and I stood still, feeling a little bewildered. Everyone moved away backstage to get changed and I followed them. The other cast members thanked me and gave me some chocolates and said that I would have a part again the next time they needed a young man. I got changed and put my green page boy suit on the table to be collected and sent back to the place where it had been borrowed from. I helped to clear up some of the stuff, but the grown-ups said I could go to meet my parents.

Mum and Dad had come to see me, even though Mum was heavily pregnant again. Dad even wore his trilby hat. As we walked down Philpot Street they told me that they were very proud of me and God knows where that sort of talent came from, but I mustn't let it go to my head. I didn't say much because I was feeling very deflated. It was strange, because I would have thought I would have felt over the moon. But no. I had the depressing feeling that a fantastic time had passed and gone.

Eventually I heard that the Leadenhall Players' next production was to be Arnold Ridley's play 'The Ghost Train.' And, although there were no parts in it for boys, they would produce what they called a curtain raiser. They chose a short one act play called 'In the Cellar,' by Gertrude Jennings, and this meant that I and my girlfriend Betty, could be in it. It was to be done in September at St. Phillips, and it would also be put on at Clerkenwell in the city, on sixth and seventh of October nineteen fifty. I would also be doing a play at school, so this would be my first double booking and my first tour. Yippee!!!

20 NEW BABY AND NEW BARREL

Although the war was well over things weren't getting much better. There wasn't the bombing but there was still rationing and shortages and very little chance of getting a proper house to live in. Mum, Dad and us four kids, were still living in the condemned flat. The three sisters had one bedroom and Mum and Dad had the other. Because I was now too big to sleep with the girls in the corner room, I slept in the kitchen on a chair bed. This was a wooden armchair that unfolded and was turned into a narrow single bed by spreading three cushions along it to make a mattress. It was alright to start with, but as the cushions got worn down with sitting and sleeping I developed a permanent bruise on both my bony hips.

At a quarter past six in the morning on October the fourteenth, nineteen forty-nine when Daddy woke me up, to go to serve for the seven o/clock Mass, both parents were already up. I was told to knock at Nanny's on my way to church because it looked like the baby was coming. Another baby! Which we were all hoping would be the boy to take Eddy's place.

After I had given Nanny and Farver the news about Mum, I walked up to Commercial Road and into Philpot Street on my way to St Philips. My eyes began to sting a little as I thought of Eddy and how old he would be now and what he might be like. During the service I did a little prayer of my own to say I hoped his soul would be saved and that the new baby would be a boy just like him.

I rushed home after the service only to find baby Joanie lying in her cot in Mummy's room. I had my fourth sister. Once I saw her, I didn't mind that she wasn't a boy because she was beautiful. I did mind that it was going to make life even harder and more sacrifices would have to be made. Things were never going to get any easier. I was already trained to, "Save a bit for the baby," or " Don't eat that, give it to Chrissie." As well as "There's other people to think of other than yourself you know!"

Mr. Attlee was doing his best and even took sweets off ration but there was such a rush on them, they were back on again before you could say gobstopper. You couldn't get a Mars bar for love nor money no matter how many coupons you had. Clothes had come off ration as well but that didn't mean much to us kids. Nestlé, Cadbury, Trebor, and pear drops were what we wanted. All that we got was Nibbits which were black, foul tasting, cough sweets that weren't on ration but were coated in sugar with a strong taste of liquorice menthol.

I forget to tell you this, but while all the previous chapter was going on, Mile End Central had moved to a new school, called Robert Monte Fiore. Known to us as Robert Monty Fury. This had happened just after the Olympics. It was a bit further to walk every day, across the Whitechapel Waste and into Valence Road, but it was worth it.

The actual school building had been renovated and decorated so it was in a much better condition that Myrdle St. It was also larger, airier and better equipped. It had ropes in the gym and Bunsen burners in the science room. There were proper carpenter's benches, with built on vice's, in the woodwork room, and another room just for Art with a sink to wash our brushes and palates. However, the best feature of all, without a shadow of doubt as far as I was concerned, was a large hall with a real stage that had beige curtains. Also, and very luckily, Miss Fagg, a glamorous figure who wore new look skirts and had tinted hair, joined the staff as a Drama Teacher. It seemed they thought a bit of art and some drama would be good for us.

A few kids from school had been to see 'The Sport of Kings' and word got about that I was a bit of a performer. Miss Abrahams took much more of an interest in me and I was even asked to read in front of the class. That Christmas, encouraged by my new status as a school star, I composed and sang a speciality number (as they were known in the trade,) to sing in the school concert. It was freely adapted from a popular song of the time called, "A You're Adorable." The kids loved it because I used the names of most of the teachers and my new lyrics put them in light, amusing and occasionally lustful situations. However, the staff were far from pleased and I was threatened with expulsion if anything like that happened again. The main problem seemed to stem from the fact that I had called the teachers, just Abrahams, Diamond and Delmont, instead of using the prefix Miss, Mrs. or Mr. I was not allowed to perform at the afternoon show. But that didn't stop me from doing lots of private requests all over the playgrounds.

"Silly old sods," I commented to the audience during my 'underground performances.' "If I'd 'ave called them Miss or Mister, the bleeding thing wouldn't have rhymed. Or fitted in with the music." I'd never heard of the word Scanned.

Miss Fagg told me that she did not approve of my disrespect of the teachers when I did my song; but it was well performed. We only had her for a couple of lessons a week, but it was always just hunky-dory. She treated us like people and taught us that it could be fun to be creative in our own right and make up things in our own words. Improvisation she called it. We played at becoming characters from a book or made someone up in our heads. We had to pretend that we were actually those people and find a way of walking and talking and thinking like them. She taught us to imitate each other and observe the people around us at school or in church or down the market. We would be put into a situation and have to carry on as though it was absolutely real. I just loved it all.

Miss Fagg, was asked to put on a play for the end of the summer term and had chosen, "The Rising Of The Moon" by Lady Gregory a one act Irish play. The cast consisted of only four men. I did my best reading hoping that I would be given a part, no matter how small. There were lots of changing the parts around and some of the boys hardly bothered. Especially Barry who had boils on his bum and couldn't sit down. This upset some of the girls, when we read it in class who just had to listened with false smiles and gritted teeth. But quite frankly, like Rhett Butler, I didn't give a damn.

At playtime, after we had read The Rising of the Moon, Brenda Rember droned on about how silly it was to do a play with only four boys in it.

"Men," I corrected her. "Three Police MEN and one ragged MAN."

Itchie, ever the helpful one, looked at her seriously from behind his glasses and suggested.

"You could design the costumes if you are so upset. You keep saying you want to be a dress designer when you leave school."

"I can't design dresses if there aren't any women in the play. Can I?" She snapped back.

"The three Irish policemen will have to have hats, perhaps you could design them," was my suggestion to shut her up. "And as the fugitive, well you could design my costume for my disguise. But no bloody dresses."

"Wait a minute," said Itchie. "Who said you're gonna play the fugitive?"

"Well, it's obvious ain't it," I explained. "He's got to be two people, the ragged man and then the fugitive when he unmasks himself to the Sergeant. I'm best at being different. You ought to play the Sergeant, it needs someone a bit simple.

Itchie then used bad language at me.

Just before we broke up for Christmas, Miss Fagg decided that in the interests of balance, four of the girls would be able to do a scene from "The Merchant of Venice," by William Shakespeare. Our play was cast with me as the ragged man who turns out to be someone on the run and Itchie with Danny Kaminski as Irish Police officers in the Garda, who were looking for me. Paddy Donahue was also a policeman, but he didn't have many lines because although he had a good Irish accent, he was a rotten actor. After the second reading to the class when we read the parts as we had been cast, Itchie informed me that he had twelve lines more than I did. I retaliated with the fact that, it wasn't the size but what you did with it that counted. An expression I had heard in the market.

The play would be extra mural which meant that after school, until it was put on, we would meet, twice a week, in the art room with Miss Fagg and Brenda Rember who would help with the costumes. Our first concern was the set. It said it the script;

Set: - Side of a Quay in a seaside town. Some posts and chains. A large barrel. Moonlight. Enter three policemen.

The woodwork class would make the posts and chains that would be standing on the dockside. Miss Fagg suggested a couple of brown stained orange boxes and an old car tyre painted white, to represent a lifebelt. Abigail Kimber would draw the wanted posters while hats and clothes would be designed and gathered together by Brenda.

The major problem turned out to be the barrel.

Without thinking too much I said that with my contacts in the market I would be able to get one, consequently I looked a real pratt when all my contacts came up with nothing. Manny at the Mason's Arms Pub, was the only offer I had managed to get, but his barrel was far too small. We needed a barrel that had to be big enough for me to get inside. We searched and searched, asked and enquired all over the area. Despite a few offers nothing came near to what we wanted.

Three weeks before the play was due to go on, things were getting a bit desperate. One light summers evening, I was round Itchie's house going over our lines when I had to confess my lack of luck, as far as barrels were concerned.

"Well Johnny," he said in a patronising tone. "You will just have to get one from somewhere."

"If we can't get a big enough barrel, I'll just have to hide in a box," I argued.

"Look," he continued in a maddening way." "A box won't do it. I mean as I've got the biggest part in the play, I know that the whole success of the show will depend on us having the proper sized barrel. You know I am right."

I could have smashed his soddin' face in. We continued practising our lines and every time the barrel was mentioned whether in the words or in the directions, he stopped and gave a deep sigh followed by a small 'Tut' and a slight shake of his head.

The pissing barrel was mentioned about five hundred times in ten pages and in the end, I could stand it no longer.

"Let's get some chips." I suggested, with the emotional control that made me the best actor in the school.

"Alright," he said getting up from the couch. "There's not much point in carrying on without a barrel. Is there?"

Bastard!

It was a bit of a walk to Goldstein's fish shop which was not far from Monty Fury. On the way we passed the Rivoli Cinema, which was showing 'The Snake Pit,' an 'H' certificate, so we weren't allowed to see it. Nevertheless, we went automatically to the side door just in case the push bar was jammed, and we could dodge in. It wasn't open, so we passed on without undue comment and arrived at the chip shop.

Bernie Goldstein was behind the counter as usual. He was a huge bad-tempered man with a red face and wore a white crease stained coat. He was always eating oranges, although where he got them from God only knows. While he was dishing up the chips into their newspaper wrapping and I was scraping the sawdust into patterns with my foot, I looked along the counter to see his daughter Ruby, resting in an old armchair outside the open back door. I just happened to look past her and saw standing against the back wall of the yard, a barrel.

No! Not A barrel. THE barrel!

It was exactly what we needed. Not too large, not to small, just big enough for me to hide in, with a barrel shape that would look swell on our set. It was all I could do not to give a shout of triumph. But I didn't. I knew that it would be pointless asking Bernie, or even Ruby, for a loan of the barrel, because like all shopkeepers who live near schools, they had an inherent hatred of children and anything to do with education.

The chips were now in the Evening Standard and while we were smothering them with salt and vinegar, I kicked Itchie's skinny ankle and nodded towards Ruby Goldstein, sprawled across her armchair as she waited for the 'after cinema' rush to start.

"Look in the yard. Gy the wall," I whispered, without moving my lips. Just like Humphrey Bogart in 'Casablanca.' "Gy the wall look there's the garrel."

Itchie always quick on the uptake, looked beyond Ruby, clocked the barrel and turned back to me.

"Useless." He pronounced.

"Hey! Vot are you two up too?" Bernie demanded loudly. "Ruby sit up straight and stop showing your legs like that. Come on you two, you've got your chips now out you go, out vith the pair of you!"

We left instantly. Standing outside, shovelling vinegar and printers ink sodden chips into our mouths, we started to argue.

"What the bleeding hell do you mean, useless," I asked.

"Obvious."

"Like obvious, how?"

"Like it's too big."

"Like it is just exactly the right size for me to hide in with room to spare," I pursued.

"Also, it is too filthy. I bet it stinks of fish."

"We can clean it" I said my voice getting louder as we moved away from the shop.

We crossed back over the Whitechapel Road towards the London Hospital.

"And anyway," Itchie concluded his argument. "Bernie would never in a million zillion years let us borrow it. Or lend it to the school. He hates the school and everyone in it."

I refused to give up.

"We could ask someone else to borrow it for us. A grown up or someone like that."

"Oh yeah! Well who are you gonna ask and what excuse are they gonna have to come up with to say why they want the blooming stinking barrel in the first place?"

"Don't you worry, Itchie Daniels," I predicted. "I'll think of something,"

Good to my word, within a week I had found the solution.

"We're going to nick it," I told the cast during playtime. "Well, not really to nick it forever. Just borrow it for a fortnight. We borrow it, scrub it for the show and return it to Bernie all cleaned up after the show has finished."

There was lots of opposition to start with. Kaminski and Itchie, both being Jewish like Bernie, put up a lot of resistance, but 'For the Good Of The Show,' was a wonderful persuasion and won them over. Paddy, on the other hand, had a great deal of opposition. He was a catholic and although he wasn't practising he thought he would go to hell if he helped us to steal. He took a great deal of persuading but finally agreed when I convinced him that God would be merciful because he knew we needed Paddy for his strength. Abigail and Brenda Rember, didn't need any persuading. They had got wind of what we were up to and insisted that they be part of it. Abigail wasn't allowed out after seven in case her mother had to do a night nurse duty, so we would just have Brenda.

Itchie, Kaminski and me, did a daylight reconnoitre. That was a word I had picked up from Gregory Peck in 'Twelve o/clock High,' at the Palaseum. We discovered that one of the bombed out empty houses in Montague Street, not far from our school, backed on to the yard of Goldstein's shop. In order to get into the yard of the bombed house we had to, get through a hole in the front of the house, cross the disused front room by balancing across the joists over what was the ceiling of the cellar and climb through what used to be the window and out into the back yard. Once there, a loose lavatory door would be put up against the wall which would enable two of us to climb up it and drop into Goldstein's yard. As soon as we were in there we would lift the barrel over the wall, roll it down the door to the other two. They would then roll it into the house, across the joists, towards the hole in the wall. Where it would stay, out of sight, until the following morning when we could roll it to school before all the other kids arrived. It was a perfect plan.

I was convinced it would work. Well maybe not as easily as that, but in principle it would work.

The borrowing of the barrel could only take place on a Sunday night. This was when the fish shop was shut, and most people were either in the cinema's, the pub's or at home listening to Variety Bandbox.

On the actual Sunday night, I had to make a special appearance as a server at evensong because some Bishop was coming down and they wanted me to be there because my ginger hair looked nice on the altar. All the time I was doing holy things I was thinking about the robbery. After the service we had to hang around for a bit and meet the Bishop and be praised and blessed. So, it was later than I thought by the time I left St, Philips and scooted across Whitechapel Road towards our bombed house.

I nipped through the hole and quickly balanced across the joists. Fortunately, there was a bit of a moon because I hadn't thought to bring a torch. Anyway, it would have been too dangerous. I arrived in the yard which looked deserted because the other four were hiding, squashed behind the angled toilet door, in case it wasn't me they had heard coming. I checked that Paddy Donahue had got his mother's washing line and that Brenda Rember had got her skipping rope which we needed to pull the barrel up with.

Itchie and Paddy held the door while I climbed up it ready to drop into the Goldstein's yard. I rolled quickly over the wall so that my silhouette would not be visible against the sky, so many people in escape films had given the game away like that.

The yard was quiet and stunk of fish from the piles of boxes around. I made my way to the barrel got hold of the top and pulled. Nothing happened. I stood on a box and looked inside, it was empty. It must have been all the mud and dirt round the bottom that was preventing it from rolling over. I went to the side and threw my skeletal body against it. It moved and I overbalanced.

"Shit," I exclaimed, and just managed to stop myself falling onto the filthy floor.

"Shush. Shut up!" Whispered Kaminski who was now down in the yard with me.

Together we managed to tip the barrel onto its side and some stinking water came running out. You could tell that it had been a fish barrel by the stench and all the fish scales that were still stuck to the inside. We rolled it to where the other three were peering over the wall.

My plan was that now the ropes would be lowered and threaded through the bung hole of the barrel and out through the top. This would enable those three to pull and us two to push, the barrel up the wall and roll it down the door on other side.

"The bung hole." I whispered to Kaminski, as the rope came slithering down the wall, the skipping rope handle first to give it weight.

We felt around the barrel and looked all over it but there was no bung hole. I couldn't believe it. This thing wasn't made like a barrel in a pub. This sodding thing was for holding fucking fish and didn't need a poxy bung hole. I became a little desperate. The desperateness led to an idea.

"We'll make a stair case," I ordered, once I had let the others know of our plight. "Lay a row of boxes, then another row on top and then another, 'till we can roll the barrel up and lift it over the wall. Paddy get down here. We are going to need your strength."

Paddy, Kaminski and I did this a quickly as we could, but it was not quite high enough, so we had to make a huge effort on both sides to lift and push it over the wall. Once over it was fine because they just had to guide it down the lavatory door. Paddy climbed back to help on the other side.

"We had better cover our tracks," Kaminski suggested. This meant putting the fish boxes back around the yard. While we were doing this the barrel was wheeled across the joists. Itchie and Paddy returned and helped us climb up the skipping rope and line to get over the wall. Once over we lowered the lavatory door quick across the joists and hid the barrel under a smelly old carpet just inside the hole in the wall. It was getting quite late by now, so we made a solemn vow of secrecy, accompanied by another one to meet at 8.45 in the morning, to smuggle the barrel into the art room. We then went our separate ways.

It was well after ten when I got home and needless to say Mum and Dad had been worried out of their lives about where I had been,. They me a good yelling at and a hard clip round the ear. The punishment was not only for being late but for arriving home from church, in my Sunday best, stinking to high Heaven of fish and covered in brown muck and silver scales. My suit was thrown into a carrier bag to be washed later and I was made to have a good all over wash and scrub in the sink, right down to my vest and pants. I went to bed tearful.

I got up late for school the next morning, never mind being late for the barrel meeting. I got into class and made my excuses to Mr. Delmont, who was in the middle of the rainfall levels in Egypt, and sat down. As I looked around the room, I was given very obvious winks and looks by Itchie, Kaminski, Paddy, Brenda Rember and even Abigail to reassure me that all was well, and the barrel was safely in the art room. Talk about give the game away!

At playtime I lied to Miss Fagg that I had managed to borrow a barrel at last and we all took her to see it. There was a class still going on in the Art Room, so she could only see it through the door window. She told us that she was thrilled, and it would make the set look 'just perfect.' This gave us all a glow of pride.

After School we went to the art room and began the pongee work of cleaning the barrel. Miss Betts, in the staff room over lunch, had already complained to Miss Fagg that it was stinking the whole room out. It took hours to get rid of the smell and make it ready for the stage. We used soda, soap, vinegar, carbolic and even made Abigail Kimber, who got some strong disinfectant from her mother, get right inside to scrape the bottom. Well she was the smallest and was only really doing the posters. When it was finished, and we put it on the stage with the other bits of the set Miss Fagg was absolutely thrilled.

"I am absolutely thrilled." She said. "The barrel gives the set real depth. Well done everybody. I am very proud of you all, especially you John."

"The others helped a lot," I replied modestly, adding quickly in case she asked how. "You know, cleaning it up and fings."

It was a busy term and almost before we knew it the dress rehearsal was happening. The set looked absolutely wizard, with ropes from the gym draped around 'the water's edge,' balancing on the blue painted poles made in woodwork class. I didn't like the 'WANTED' picture of me that Abigail had drawn. But she was right when she said that when it was stuck on the barrel and from a distance it would look great.

Brenda Rember had made three very good hats out of cardboard and painted them bright blue. They looked a bit bright, but at least they fitted. I don't think they bore any resemblance to the real Garda uniform, but as a girl from East End she knew nothing of research. My disguise was very realistic because we got most of it from the second-hand clothes stall in Watney Market. It consisted of an old raincoat, a pair of brown trousers tied up with string, some worn out boots of my own, a torn shirt and a battered old pork pie hat; all for five pence ha'penny.

The Rising of the Moon, was the first half of the show, and second half was the trail scene from 'The Merchant of Venice.' We were giving two performances. The morning performance would be for the top half of the school and in the afternoon, we would do it again for the lower years.

The first performance commenced just after playtime and it was a triumph. We were given cheers at the end. Over dinnertime everyone was saying that we were really like proper Irish people and that we should be on the stage. The barrel came in for a lot of attention too. We members of the cast, ate our sausage roll and mash sitting together with subtle bits of make-up still visible, so that people would know we were the actors. Itchie was getting a lot of praise but I didn't mind because everybody said I was the best. The Shakespeare girls had also done very well, especially Barbara Rolf as Portia. I had watched her from the wings and thought she was marvellous when she was gonna tear out Shylock's heart.

By the time we got to the afternoon show we were full of ourselves. Despite that, the play was going very well because Miss Fagg had warned us that we must concentrate much harder the second time. The audience were really held and when it came to the song that was the signal, in the play, for the boat to come and pick me up. The hall was dead quiet. Itchie and me were alone on stage and I started to sing. The first verse very quiet. You could hear a pin drop. I began the second verse, and then - BANG! WOLLOP! The hall doors crashed open hitting the walls as a man came storming down the centre aisle.

It caused a sensation I don't mind telling you. Even I was a bit shocked. All heads turned away from the stage to see who had come in.

It was Bernie Goldstein. His white coat flapping behind him as he rushed towards the stage.

"I vont my barrel. There it is. They told me it vas here and there it is for all the vorld to see. Stop this play. I vont my barrel!"

He was halfway down the hall by the time Mr. Delmont had wiggled through a row and stopped him while Miss Fagg made her way down the centre isle to keep him from getting to the stage. The first and second years all began talking and giggling while the few teachers, who were not skiving in the staffroom having a Woodbine, tried to regain control of the situation. On stage Itchie had gone quite white, under the heavy five, nine and carmine two and was edging towards the exit up left. I ran and grabbed him.

"Stand yer ground and bluff it out. The show must go on. Carry on with the play."

I, under the duress of the situation, went back a page and started my longest speech again. As it turned out this wasn't such a bad thing because no one was listening anyway. By the time we had got to the bit where we were interrupted, things had been sorted out. Bernie Goldstein had been removed from the hall and was threatening to bring the police. Miss

Fagg had managed to give me and Itchie a reassuring look while Miss Betts had collected the boy from 2.C., whose nose was bleeding, taken to the staff room.

Itchie, although badly shaken, was a real trouper and we continued to the end of the play fully in line with the professional slogan. Unfortunately, once we had finished there was no more show to go on. We took our bows to strong applause while Mr. Ward watched us though his watery eyes with pursed lips. The curtain was pulled across so that we could strike our set and the girls set up theirs.

The barrel, in its pristine condition, was returned to the fish shop and us boys were given a couple on each hand from Mr. Ward. The physical abuse was accompanied by a verbal warning of suspension.

To me the whole experience was an early lesson in, 'getting your art right can often be painful.'

Seeing or doing a play was something special to me, because there was no proper theatre near us in Stepney. Those that had been around were all bombed out or waiting to be pulled down. People had to go 'up West' to see a show and that was out of the question for a working-class family like ours. A show 'up the other end' was only enjoyed by a very few grown-up people and usually as a special treat for a very special occasion.

21 RADIO, FILMS AND GAMES

My winter evenings were spent mostly indoors, at the church groups, running 'errands' for Aunt Bet, working on the dresses, doing the shopping, cleaning, cooking or doing homework. For pleasure I passed the time: by putting together jig saw puzzles, playing cards with Mum and the girls or cutting things out and sticking them in scrap books. I painted water colours from a black lidded paint box that I got as a birthday present from aunt Margie and wrote stories or plays in an old exercise book. But best of all the thing I absolutely adored, beyond measure was - the wireless.

Just after Joanie was born, Dad got a new radio set on the never-never. It was a highly polished cabinet with three knobs at the bottom and gold mesh behind the fretwork, masking the speaker. I worshipped the Light Programme and, to a lesser degree, the Home Service where the news was a bit of a nuisance. Everything on the Light programme was magnificently tickety-boo. Workers playtime twice a day to sing along to when there was no school. I.T.M.A. Ray's A Laugh, and later Take It From Here, with Joy, Dick and Jimmy. Family Favourites at Sunday lunchtime with Jean Metcalf in Britain, flirting over the airways with Cliff Mitchelmore in Germany. They would play the latest records and I would learn the songs after only one, or at the most, two hearings. On Sundays night, there would be the genius of Frankie Howerd on Variety Bandbox pursuing his 'feud' with Derek Roy, as well as big guest stars. Sometimes they even came over from America to be on this hit show.

There were also the drama serials; Dick Barton, The Daring Dexter's, Journey into Space. And later The Archers. I would sneak into the front room to listen to 'The Man in Black,' my ear glued to the speaker. I would be twice scared. First by the play and second in case Dad would suddenly come in and catch me listening. He hated me 'wasting my time listening to all that shit.'

Those wonderful radio actors of the time, Griselda Harvey, Gladys Young, Valentine Dyall. Not forgetting Paul Temple and his various cases. Steve his wife with her 'good old intuition,' played by Marjorie Westbury. I still have my mind's image of her; a tall slim blond, impeccably dressed in a black tight skirt and jacket with a diamond broach on her left lapel a black hat and veil, excellent legs in sheer stockings placed in high heeled black patent shoes. It wasn't even diminished when I actually met her years later. She was charming and lovely, but she did not match up to my image. Who could? The radio was where I could escape into my own imaginative world and create my own sense of perfect pictures.

Along with the radio there was also the Picture Palaces. Palatial building with exotic names. The Palaseum, the Rivoli, the Poplar, but most of all The Troxy. That really was a palace, an Aladdin's cave of delights. It was a vast cinema, with art-deco walls covered by metal scrolls that had lights on them hidden behind coloured glass screens. From the foyer a wide thick carpeted staircase swept up to the circle which was gold and red like a real Palace in an M.G.M. film. In front of the screen was a huge white electric organ that rose up out of the stage with lights flashing and being played at a fantastic volume.

Mum and Dad went through a period when they went to the Troxy pictures every Friday night. If I had been good and worked hard all the week I was given the honour of going with them. Aunt Kate stayed at 51a looking after Joycie and our girls. I would be enthralled by Patricia Roc, Stewart Granger, Jean Kent, Sally Gray, James Mason and the queen of them all Margaret Lockwood. There were also the American stars, Judy Garland, Mickey Rooney, Bogart, Gable, Gregory Peck, Mrs. Miniver and Ronald Coleman. Oh, so many stars who took us away from our grey drab surroundings into a world of magic, mystery, music and mirth. How's that for alliteration?

One film, 'The Wicked Lady' and the incident that accompanied it, always makes me go red with embarrassment whenever I hear the name. It came about like this: As part of our last lesson on a Friday afternoon Mr. Green, would let us do 'tell a picture.' This meant that one or two members of the class, who had been to the cinema earlier in the week, could go to the front and tell us the story of the film they had seen. One week Terry Lawler told us all the story of 'The Wicked Lady.' It starred Margaret Lockwood, and was the film everyone was talking about. Terry's version was so full of melodrama and excitement that I could hardly wait to get to the Troxy that night.

I was on my utmost best behaviour all evening which must have worked because the three of us got the number fifteen bus to the cinema soon after seven. There was a long queue round the building, but because we had got there early enough we just about managed to get a ticket. The problem occurred once we got inside. The one and sixes in the circle were bulging with bodies. We had to stand for a while during the first film, until Mum and Dad got two seats together. There wasn't one for me, so the Usherette suggested that I sit on the steps at the end of the row until a seat became available. Which it did, just as the main film was starting after the organ and the news. The usherette, in the dark but flashing her torch, moved me to my seat between Mum and Dad.

It was a wonderful story about highway men with Margaret having to dress up as a man to get to kiss James Mason and something to do with Patricia Roc who was the good girl. I got utterly wound up in the story and started whispering to Mum what was going to happen next, having heard it from Terry Lawler. I could hardly contain my excitement when Felix Aylmer, who found out what Lockwood was up to had to be silenced by her. I knew what was coming and I told Dad not to worry because in a minute she was going to murder him by suffocating him by putting a pillow over his face.

It was only when the lights went up I discovered that I'd been telling the plot to complete strangers. They were very amused about it when Mum and Dad came down the aisle to collect me and told them all about it. Was I embarrassed or what?

The 'pictures,' along with Guy Fawkes Night, were an occasional source of income. When there was a musical showing at the lesser cinema 'The Palaseum.' I never 'worked' the Troxy or the Poplar because it wasn't financially viable: what with the bus fares there and back. At the 'Palo,' I would often manage to dodge in by the side door, when someone was coming out. I would sit through two showings and learn the tunes, and words of the best songs. I would practice and work out a routine the following day ready to busk the queues outside with the songs from the film. For the rest of the week, sometimes I even used Jeanie, Dennis or Itchie as a partner. When she wasn't being featured with me, Jeanie would go around with the collecting box. It was a bit cheeky and occasionally we were told to 'Eff Off' by the manager. Especially if we had recently been caught dodging in. That was my first professional work, in as much as I got paid about four pence a night.

In the Summer the evenings were spent playing street games. At that time very few people had cars, so the middle of the road was our playground. If it was a smooth asphalt surface, we could roller skate on it. The tarmac became my rink when I got my first pair of cheap roller skates and I would imagine that I was this great ice skater who could leap over barrels and beat everybody in the world at speed skating. Eventually I did become quite skilled and could 'spin' quite fast with arms flailing to give me speed and do 'the flying swan,' with arms outstretched and one leg stuck out behind me. After lots of practice and a few slight injuries I learned to 'jump over' two apple boxes on top of each other.

We would also ride around the side streets on scooters that were home made from two planks of wood, taken from a bombed house, with two screw eyes and a thick bolt to hold them together. The bottom plank had two ball bearing wheels at each end to give it balance and move ability. Carts were put together with fruit boxes and abandoned pram wheels. There were of course the obvious road games such as football and cricket with the stumps drawn on a wall. Other ball games like 'Donkey,' jumping over the ball when it bounced back from the wall with someone behind catching it or 'Pig ion the middle' etc. were also very popular, and had many variations.

Of all the ball games, "Canon' was my favourite which was a game played by two teams. An empty baked bean tin with two crossed sticks on top was put in the middle of a chalked circle in the road. From behind a line a couple of yards away, a ball was bounced by the defending team who had to knock it over in three tries. When this was achieved the defenders had to try to stand the can back in the circle again, with the sticks crossed on top of it, before they were hit by the ball and counted out by the attacking team. The team with the most Cannon's at the end of a specified time were the winners. Rounders was another road game, but we had to make sure to hit the ball downwards for fear of smashing peoples' windows. The four bases were the corners of houses on a crossroads. If it was a nice evening or a Sunday afternoon, the grown-up sitting outside on the pavement enjoying the air, might even join in our games too.

There were also kerb games too. Games of swinging around a lamp post, five stones or 'Gobs,' as it was known to us and knock down ginger. This was played by knocking at someone's front door and running away to watch their faces when they opened it and no one was there. In the streets where two doors were close together it was an added excitement to tie both door handles together with a skipping rope so that tugging and pulling would ensue inside the passages. Then if anyone was brave enough they would untie the rope, with obvious results inside the passages. If you get my meaning.

I also did 'Johnny's Penny Shows' for which I wrote a short play, usually a ghost story. played all the parts and found the costumes and props. I charged a penny for kids to watch. The tickets were quite classy because I made them from my John Bull printing set. "John Ross in The Ghost on The Landing." Was one of my titles. This venture didn't last long due to the demand for new material. I managed to do four different shows, two of which were based around stories I had read in books from the children's section of the library in Cable Street.

22 THE NIGHT WATCHMAN

The journey to the Library included passing a coal yard. They have all disappeared now, like the miners that supplied them. So, for readers who don't know: a coal yard was a local name for the place where coal and coke were stored and sold. High sided tip-up lorries would deliver and slide the fuel into small mountains around the yard. Later it would be shovelled into hundredweight or half hundredweight sacks, put on the backs of open lorries, or on horses and carts and delivered to the homes of those who had ordered it. Sometimes the coalmen, if there was a warm spell, would stop and yell out "Coal for sale." When there was a fuel shortage they didn't deliver, the lorries stayed stagnant in the yards and the customers had to collect their own. This was done by queuing with prams, push chairs, home-made carts or tin baths or anything that would carry the amount of rationed fuel; we would wheel it home to warm our houses.

Passing the yard quite often on the way to the park or library and being ginger as well as a friendly sort of lad, I had got to know quite a few of the men who worked there. I would always look in as I was passing to see if anyone I knew was about. I knew it was a good thing to keep friendly because when the next fuel shortage came, they would remember me and perhaps allow me a little more than they should.

So, it was the library, in an indirect way, that awoke something secretive in me. So Just like they do on TV, I hereby give a warning of adult content and language. If you don't want to read it turn to the next chapter. If you do and are offended, well you have only yourself to blame.

I was 'growing up and beginning to feel my feet' as Mum often remarked when I got a bit above myself. It was a Saturday afternoon in October and I had been to exchange my two books for the week. It was still light as I passed the yard after coming out of the library and I saw that Ben, the night watchman, was dragging the two big iron gates together, in preparation to pad-locking them for the weekend. He was a tall, good looking, man with a couple of kids. We had spoken a few times before, so I knew that he had been in the Army, where he had served in Africa fighting Rommel, some Nazi git.

"Hello, Uncle Ben. You getting ready to go home to Aunt Rene?" I asked, trying to be grown up and sociable.

"No, not yet, going to have a bit of a brew up," he said, raising his blond head. "Wanna come in and join me? You look cold, Johnny."

Now that was an invitation I didn't get every day. A brew-up with a real, grown-up watchman.

"Yeah. Alright," I said, as I walked into the yard. "I've done the shoppin' so I ain't got nothing to do till I go to the Whist Drive round the Church after tea.

I put my two books on a pile of coke as we both pushed the big gates shut and locked them. While Ben shut a small door at the side for us to get out later, I collected my books, and we strolled up the yard, between the piles of fuel and dusty lorry's. At the end of the yard we went into a small warm brick building that was the office and rest room for the drivers.

There was a bench across the left-hand wall, facing a long high desk that a man would have to stand up at. Behind the desk and running the length of it, was a window looking out into the yard and at the other end from the door was a lino covered card-table with a primus stove and tea making stuff, on it.

"You get the water John, and I'll get the stove going. Tap's outside to the left." said Ben, passing me the soot covered kettle.

I went back into the yard and found the tap that was just outside the toilet at the end of the office block. I put just enough water in for a couple of cups and returned to where the primus was hissing out a blue flame.

"Good man," said Ben. "You get the mugs milk and sugared. I've put the tea in the pot so make the tea if the water boils. I've got to go for a pony. The brown enamel one is mine, you have the ordinary one."

He went out and I watched him pass along the window. Alone in the office, I did as he told me. I looked around at the books and papers on the desk, which was at the height of my chin, and lifted up the heavy flap-top and looked inside.

There were date stamps, rubber bands, tobacco tins and lots of books and papers, nothing to get too excited about. I turned away and found a copy of the Daily Mirror on the bench. I sat looking at the pictures. It wasn't very long before the kettle started to boil. I waited 'till the whistle sounded, poured the water into the teapot and turned down the primus. The smell of the tea, the stove, coke and coal made it all feel very cosy.

"John! Johnny! Can you hear me, mate?" It was Ben calling from outside.

I went to the door and called back.

"Yeah Uncle Ben. What d'ya want?"

"There's no paper in here, being us a couple of sheets of the Mirror down will ya?"

"Yeah. O.K. Hang on," I said, as I removed two pages from the newspaper.

I left the office and walked to the lavatory.

"Here's the paper Uncle Ben." I said, as I knocked on the door ready to slide it under the gap at the bottom.

But before I could do that the door opened and Ben was standing there, his shirt pulled up above his waist, his trousers and pants round his ankles. The whole lower part of his body was naked. I could see everything! Especially everything. Everything was big and erect and on a level with my chest.

He was a tall man. I blushed, feeling my face going all hot and red.

"It's alright," Ben reassured me. "Don't be embarrassed. I've been in the Army mate, lots of men have seen my cock. We've all got one. Have you made the tea?'

I swallowed trying to cover my feeling of embarrassment and shock. I turned away saying.

"Yeah. It's in the pot, I'll pour it out."

I hurried back into the office shaking. I was feeling such strange things.

The cups rattled as I poured the tea on to the sugar and milk. I could feel myself burning with the sense of shame, excitement and bewilderment along with a strong sense of guilt. I knew I desperately wanted to hold his thing and I felt terrible and mortified and yet so thrilled I could hardly breathe.

Then I got a strange feeling of a hard-on. I put the teapot down and felt myself. No, I didn't have a hard-on, but it felt as though I did. It was like I was ready for a wank but with a limp dick. A feeling I had never experienced in my life before. This was so much more than what I had felt with Mary or Lucille in the hop fields.

I was jerked away from my thoughts by the sound of the chain being pulled and the outside tap running. Ben passed along the window. He was coming in. Fuckin' hell! What was I going to do? What would he think of me? He will think I am some sort of queer and tell my family and the church and everyone in the yard and everyone at school and everyone I know. Shit! Fuck.

"That tea smells good," said Ben as he came into the office. "There's a couple of biscuits in the tin up on that shelf if you want one. I keep them out of the way so that those bastard drivers, don't nick 'em."

I couldn't believe it. He was acting like nothing had happened. I had just seen him naked and he had seen me look at his thing and now he was in here as though it was the most normal thing in the world.

"Yeah, er... thanks Ben," I said, forgetting to call him uncle. "We ain't got none at home."

"Right then, get the tin down."

He lifted me up and stood me on the desk so that I could reach the tin on the shelf. I brought it down and opened it. There were three digestives in it.

"Sit up there on the counter, I'll hand you your tea," he said, as he took the tin. "We'll have one each and share the other one."

"Thanks," I said beginning to feel a bit easier.

We both sipped our tea and I dunked my biscuit. Ben leaned on the counter and put his tin mug the other side of me so that he had to lean across to pick it up. I could smell his body as well as the coal dust on his shirt and jerkin, mingling with a smell of lorry oil that I recognised from my Dad's clothes.

"What's the books you've got?" he asked.

"Oh, just a couple of adventure stories."

"Anything to do with girls in 'em?"

"Dunno. I ain't read 'em yet."

"Have you done it with a girl yet?"

I just went hot all over again. Here was a grown up asking me if I had had a do! What should I say? What if he told my Mum and Dad? I hesitated, and he sensed my reluctance to give anything away.

"I suppose you have started other things," he continued. "You know like wanking and coming your muck. Have you managed to shoot your load yet?"

There was a silence. I thought I would explode.

"It's alright, you can tell me, I'm your mate. I won't say anything. Do you wank off? I bet you do inside those pants of yours."

At that point he put his hand on my private area and noticed the zip on the American trousers I had got from Viola.

"It feels as though you do. But what's this zip? Why ain't you got buttons like the rest of us?"

I explained about being an orphan and getting the stuff from America and how they had zippers on their trousers and not fly buttons. All the time I was explaining this I could feel his hot hand just resting on my fly. He moved it slightly which sent a shock wave that went right through to my body and I felt myself getting a hard on. I was so mortified.

"I suppose it must be easier to undo that than all the buttons on my fly. I mean one little tug and it's all open," he said, and gave my zip a playful tug that opened my fly. "Blimey that was quick. It goes up and down so easily don't it."

He started zipping it up and down. Talking all the while and then his hand was inside feeling me.

"That's a nice cock you've got there Johnny. D'ya mind if I pull your trousers down and get a better look? Let me lift you down."

I offered no resistance in fact I really wanted to be lifted off of the desk and my trousers taken down. As he lowered me, he slid my body against his and I could feel his hot body rub against me. It was the most amazing sensation. I was so scared, so excited, so amazed and so willing. I felt that nothing else in the world mattered except this moment between me and Ben. I stood on the floor in front of him. He undid his own fly and what came out was on a level with my chest. He took my jacket off, eased my pullover over my head, slid my braces from my shoulders then my trousers and pants down all, more or less, in one movement. I felt the cooler air rush around my lower half. My own dick was sticking out hard and proud, but it looked very small against Ben's, which in comparison, was enormous.

"Would you like to hold it? asked Ben. "Go on, rub it up and down, like you would if you were wanking your own knob."

The words he used. I never thought I would hear them spoken by a grown up. These words were only whispered and giggles about among us boys in the playground. Just the way he was talking was filling me with anticipation.

I reached over and grasped it. It was uncircumcised and there was some liquid coming out of the hole at the tip.

"What's that stuff? I asked alarmed.

"It's nothing, it's just pre-cum, just rub it around the top and especially underneath with your finger. I'd like that. That feels good. Now rub the foreskin back and forth over the knob. Oh yes, that's right Johnny, that's very good."

Then he bent down and taking my head in his hands he kissed me. He put his tongue right into my mouth, not like I had done with Lucille and other girls, but with hard throbbing thrusting movements. I pulled away because I couldn't get my breath and was suffocating. I looked towards the window and he saw my look.

"Don't get worried no one can see in. There's only a brick wall opposite, we're well away from the world here so relax. I am not going to say anything to anyone. And you're not. Are you? Are you enjoying it? Do you want to stop? We can stop if you like? I want to carry on. Let me help you come your muck."

I didn't know what 'coming my muck' meant.

But I found out pretty soon. And it was grand, it was swell, it was wonderful, beautiful and fuckin' fantastic!!

I didn't feel like it any more after I had come my own muck, but Ben said it was only polite to always finish off the other bloke. So I did. I was amazed at what muck I made come out of him and I felt pretty good when it was over. We cleaned ourselves up with the Daily Mirror. After we had got our clothes on and finished our tea, I picked up my library books and Ben walked me down the yard, to see me out.

"If you liked it, there's always more where that came from. Come round again when I'm on nights and the yard is empty and we can do it again if you want to."

I didn't want to. It had been amazing, but I didn't want to do it again. So I thanked him and walked away feeling like I had really grown up. Now I was a man. I had come my muck and I had talked dirty with a gown up. However, as I walked away, I didn't feel that I ever wanted to do it again.

Strangely enough though, after a couple of days, I felt that I wouldn't mind doing it again. So, whenever I had the inclination and the time I often re-visited the coal yard.

23 THINKING ABOUT A TRADE

It was after the Ben incident that I began to get sick of being asked, "What do you want to be when you leve school?" Stupid question!.

Deep down in my gut I knew that what I really wanted to be, was an actor, to become someone else on the stage and to get paid for it. But there was no way I could have admitted that, to those questioners. They would have fainted away in shock.

Of course, I knew it was madness. I hadn't got the first idea what being a proper actor was about. I had never seen a real play, on a real stage. My only experience of watching a professional show was 'Soldiers in Skirts,' at the Queens Theatre in Poplar. It was a review, where they performed sketches, songs and dances. There was a massive surprise at the end when the girls took off their wigs and revealed that they were all blokes.

The 'work' subject eventually came up at school when Miss Fagg, told me that she would like to talk to my parents about me going to study at a drama college. She thought I had a real talent and showed great promise.

I was terribly excited but somehow managed to hold the news in until the family had settled down after tea that night hat I managed to broach the subject.
"Miss Fagg, has told me to ask you if you would go up the school to see her," I informed them, as Jeanie carried the dirty plates to the sink.

"Oh No! What have you done now?" Mum asked.

"He's a bloody pest," said Dad.

"I ain't done nothing," I quickly cut in. "She thinks I ought to go to college and do acting so I can go to go into films. Once I've bin there I can sing as well as to do plays on the stage and on the radio like Valentine Dyall."

As the words were leaving my lips, I knew it was a mistake.

"What the fuck are you talking about?" said Dad. "Going to a college? You do enough acting around here without going to a soddin' college to learn how to do it!"

"Besides," said Mum. "People like us don't go on the stage. It's work, home and bed for us. And anyway, we can't have you wasting your time up at a college Johnny. We need you to get working. You're the eldest and with the four girls growing up, we're going to need your money coming in."

"You can forget all about doin' all that stage stuff for a livin'," Dad's final word was. "It will do you much more good to grow up and find a proper job."

The point was that other than acting, I hadn't got a clue what I wanted to do when I grew up. I wasn't even sure that I wanted to grow up. It smacked too much of responsibility and I had had enough of that in my life so far. If anything, I wanted a childhood. Something I had been deprived of due to that old bastard Hitler.

As my war with Dad got worse, I spent most of my spare time time across the street with Aunt Alice and Uncle Ernie, who lived at number 40. They were going through a hard time because they had two young sons now. Ernie Boy who had been difficult, until they found out that he was deaf and Baby John. A chubby boy with soft brown hair and huge dark eyes that stayed bright, even when he had trouble breathing. If Uncle Ernie was away driving, I would go over and spend the evening keeping Aunt Alice and her boys company They were the youngest of the generation above me and we had a good strong bond between us.

That night, I mentioned to them what had been said about going to drama college and they agreed with Mum and Dad. I had to face my responsibilites and help the family
Later, the same evening, after the boys had gone to bed, we were sitting round the fire, when the conversation came back to what I could work at. After a lot of chin-wagging, we came to the conclusion that I wasn't strong enough to unload and carry heavy things, so lorry driving was out. I didn't have enough money to start my own stall in the market so that was out. And all the jobs in shops were taken by women. We

never even considered office work or anything like that, it just wasn't in our way of life.

A strong possibility was, that factory work might suit me. I had worked in the dress and coat factories, where I had learned how to operate a Singer sewing machine, use a steam iron, and do basting and finishing, as well as pack and fold coats and dresses, so maybe I could go into the rag trade. Alice felt sure I could get a job in a proper factory and learn to use an Hoffman pressing machine, which was usually a man's job in the clothing trade. I really didn't want to do all that. As far as I was concerned, it wasn't a proper job because I done all that as a kid.

Bored by it all and for a quiet life, whenever I was asked, I learned to say, 'I'm gonna be an Engineer.'

I hadn't got a clue what I meant by 'Engineer.' But it was one of those things I had heard people describe as a good trade. Dad had been in the Royal Engineers, so I must have imagined it would be reasonable thing to do. Once I was asked by some clever dick, "Where are you thinking of applying?" I just replied "Charrington's Brewery." This generalised response was usually enough to shut the patronising prats up, after all, they had only asked to appear interested and I had evaded telling them what I really wanted to say, so everyone was satisfied.

The following week, Alice, Ernie and me were sitting in their living room talking about films, when we were interrupted by baby John. He started really struggling to get his breath and began to cough and cry as his breathing got really bed. So I stayed with Ernie Boy while Alice and Ernie rushed him to the London Hospital. The Doctor gave him some stuff and put him on steam. This meant that two large kettles were kept boiling around his bed and the steam from their spouts was fed towards his head to aid his breathing. During his stay, which was just over a week, the steam had somehow been allowed to severely scald the left side of his face and head.

Poor little sod. He must have really suffered, but because he had been drugged, it was quite a while before anyone had noticed. When he came home he looked like someing out of the film, 'House of Wax.' At the end, when the museum is burning, and all the dummies are melting.

Uncle Ernie tried to sue the hospital, but was persuaded by some big-wig solicitor, that there would be no point in wasting his time and his money, because the medical professionals all stuck together to avoid any scandal.

It was around that time that I decided to become a solicitor. After all they earned good money and they didn't have to lift things. When I mentioned it to Mr. Delmont, he said that I would have to go to University, which was even worse than having to go to college. Or so Itchie Daniels told me.

I was telling this to Alice and Ernie, when Baby John had another bad turn. They did what they could for him but the Doctors couldn't save him. So at just under three years old, this lovely little baby died.

I was over at number 40 the night before the funeral. It wasn't a good night. The small white coffin was in the front room with the green wooden shutters closed and we were all upset. Uncle Ernie asked me if I would like to go in to see

Baby John. I had never seen a dead body before so I must have looked a bit scared.

"He wont hurt you Johnny, he looks so lovely, come and say goodbye to him." Ernie said looking at me with his deep blue eyes brimming. I felt that he wanted me to go with him because it was an excuse for him to go in and see his son again.

He took me into the front room to see his baby in the coffin resting on the table. And I saw him just gently tweak the soft brown curl across his child's forehead to hide the, still raw looking, scars from the scalding and the blue veins standing out. It made me think of Eddy and I was glad I had not seen him in his coffin. I don't think I liked it. I stayed until Uncle Ernie, put his arms round my shoulders.

"Ok. Johnny, let's leave him now," he said in a chocking voice. "Night, night son."

24 THE DRIVING LESSON

It was a quiet Sunday afternoon in October. Mum, the girls and me were indoors playing 'Banker' on the kitchen table, where instead of money our stakes were buttons. I shared them out equally from the Oxo tin for us to bet with. We put buttons one of the face down, piles of cut cards that we fancied. When they were turned up the highest card won and whoever was Banker had to pay out or rake in the losses. No skill was involved it was all down to luck. Mum, being a bit of a gambler loved this game. We were having a great time even though Chrissie kept trying to grab the cards and nick our buttons.
Dad was sitting on the chair bed, reading the News of the World when, out of the blue, he put the paper down and stood up.

"Right now, listen to me Johnny," he said. "Because you are now fourteen, I think it's time that you learned to drive!"

Us four card players turned towards him as though he was an imbecile. Feeling a little scared I reminded him that I didn't have a licence, that I didn't think I wanted to learn to drive yet, that I didn't think that I could do it and anyway, I was too young to be given a licence. But as usual he refused to listen to me.

"Don't be such a prat. You don't need a licence you are under age. Of course, you can do it. You've seen me do it enough times it should come easy to you," was his argument for pursuing his argument.

"But Dad," I said my eyes widening. "I've never even thought about driving!"

"Don't worry about that. You'll soon get the hang of it. Come on put those cards away and let's go downstairs. I'll be your teacher and give you your first lesson now. It's Sunday afternoon so there won't be much traffic about."

Before I know what was happening, Mum and the girls got very excited, the cards and the buttons were pushed aside and the whole family trouped down the stairs. Mum was carrying baby Jo, and as we crossed the landing she started telling Mrs. Coakley all about me having a driving lesson. We poured out of the front door into Bigland Street. There our little black Austin A.40 was parked nicely against the curb facing the arches.

"Okay," said Dad. "Here are the keys. Now get in and start her up."

"What on me own?"

"Oh no! I'm not going to let a born fool like you loose on your own with my car, am I?" He said, sarcastically. "No, I'll be in the other seat telling you what to do. Go on, get in."

A few people who were just hanging about in the street came to watch, joining Mum and the girls on the pavement, while

Mrs. Coakley and Ruby leaned out of the first-floor window. It felt like the whole of Stepney was staring at me as I got into the car, slammed the door shut and tried to find the hole where I thought the key ought to go into.

The door across from me opened and Dad threw himself into the passenger seat, slamming it shut behind him.

"Come on then, don't hang about. Get the soddin thing started. What are you waiting for? Put the fuckin' key in the ignition and pull the choke out."

I didn't have a clue where the ignition was, let alone what the choke was. He leaned over me, grabbed my hand and forced it down the steering column until I found the key hole.

'That's it, push it in. Now pull the choke out, that's that button over there." He said pointing to the row of buttons along the dashboard.

I pulled out the choke and four of his dog-ends fell out of the ashtray. I pushed it back quick and jerked on the button next to it. He thwacked me on the wrist with a rabbit punch.

"Not that far out, ya silly sod. Just a bit. It's already bin warmed up to-day you'll flood the fucking thing."

I eased the choke slightly back in.

"That's it," he said, encouragingly. "Now turn her over, put your hands on the wheel: with your right foot on the clutch and your left on the break and don't take it off till you feel the bight."

"What?"

He repeated it a bit louder.

"What?"

He repeated it even louder with gestures, and bent down to move my legs, dragging them towards the pedals.

"Yer bleedin' legs ain't long enough. Get out!" He said as he turned off the engine.

I heaved a sigh of relief as I opened the door and got out into the middle of the road. I started to walk towards the kerb.

"Oi! Don't piss off. I'm just adjusting the seat for you. That's it. Now get back in and start to drive. I've told you what to do."

Very reluctantly I returned to my seat and found that my boots could just about reach the pedals if I pointed my toes.

"Now keep your hands on the wheel. Next push the clutch pedal down with your left foot and I'll put her in gear, but not until you have turned on the engine. Keep your right foot on the break 'till I tell you to ease it up."

With so much to think about the added problem of not knowing my right from my left just compounded the panic I was feeling. Knowing right from left is still a problem, it's a form of dyslexia.

I pushed the right foot down.

"No! Not the right, you silly Bastard, the left! The left! You've got to ease the clutch. Fucking Hell. You're supposed to be intelligent ain't ya? Turn the poxy engine on you great Nance!"

I did that. Then I pushed the left foot down.

"Take your foot of the break," said the instructor, as he put the car into first gear. "Ease up the clutch and turn her out of the kerb into the road."

The car shuddered and stalled.

"Bastard," I said.

'Fuckin' useless," said my Dad.

We repeated the whole procedure twice more before I managed to move her away from the kerb. My successful manoeuvre was greeted by cheers and jeers from the onlookers.

"Right, go across Tait Street and down towards the arches, to Chapman Street and when you get to the bottom turn left and we'll go round the block back up Morris Street. Push the clutch down and I'll put her into second. Now clutch and third. Put your foot down a bit harder on the accelerator. No! No! Keep steering on this side of the road and stop looking at your feet you're nearly up the soddin' kerb. Turn the fucking wheel."

He helped me by pushing on the wheel as we moved back to the right side of the road and proceeded down Bigland Street. I desperately tried to sort out which was left as well as keeping my mind on the clutch, the accelerator, reaching the peddles, holding the wheel and all the other things I was supposed to be doing. I had hardly got over my panic by the time we got to the bottom of the street and I turned the wheel left towards the Watney Street Market. As I did, I inadvertently increased the pressure on the accelerator, this sudden burst of speed took me faster around the corner than we were both expecting, and I mounted the kerb heading for the brick wall of the Strieberg's house, on the corner.

"Turn the wheel! Turn the fucking wheel!" said Dad, as he grabbed for the steering wheel and kicked my foot off the accelerator before pulling hard on the handbrake. We stopped about three inches from the wall.

"Get out yer silly fucking sod,' he ordered. "I'll take her round the block and see you at home.

There ended the first lesson. I did not take another until twenty years later.

25 TO GO OR TO STAY?

Six years after we had moved in we were still living at 51A. A father, a mother, four girls under twelve and a fourteen-year-old boy, sharing three rooms and kitchen on the top floor of a house that had been condemned even before we arrived.

On October the fifteenth, the day after Joanie became one year old, Dad received a letter stating that we were now officially overcrowded in our accommodation and asking him to make an appointment to see someone at the council offices. It went on to tell us that we were eligible to be re-housed on one of the new estates Mr. Attlee had been putting up. It went on to say that he could view a four-bedroom house on the Harold Hill Estate just outside Romford in Essex. This would be a house not just a pre-fab like Uncle Arthur and aunt Margie rented in East Ham.

Mum, lost no time in telling everyone she met all about the offer and they all had an opinion as to whether we should look at the Romford house, or not bother and hope for a new place in the East End. Some suggested that we ought to hang out for a new flat in the buildings they were soon going to build Stepney, others thought that we should hang on and hope for one of the big converted houses they were renovating in Bow. Louis Patmore warned, that if we didn't accept this offer we might lose our chance and be put back until another baby was born. I thought it would be good to go because of the extra space. Mum and Dad would have their own room, the girls would have a bedroom for two, and I, being the only boy, would get a room of my own.

After a lot of debating between family friends and passing strangers, it was eventually decided they we nothing to lose so why not just go to have a look at the place.

Mum filled the form accepting the viewing. After a couple of days another letter arrived. It told Dad to be at 9 Dulverton Road, at Harold Hill, at 12.30 p.m. on the following Saturday. He would be met by the housing officer from the Romford Council, who would have great pleasure in showing him around the property.

Mum immediately decided that it would be good for me to have a look around the place and that Dad could use his van to drive the three of us there. After breakfast on the Saturday morning, Nanny came around to stay with the girls while we three drove out towards Essex. We had a good journey until we got to Romford. It was a market town and on the main road through it were stalls and animal pens along both sides. This meant that the actual throughway was clogged with cars, lorries, busses, green lines and everything on two or four wheels. It took ages to get through which I didn't mind because there was loads to look at out of the van window. Dad was effing and blinding something chronic all the time.

Once we were through the town, we drove past a lot of big posh houses until we got to Gallows Corner. Unfortunately, there were no gallows, just a huge roundabout with a pub called The Plough, standing behind the signpost that pointed to the Harold Hill Estate. We came off the roundabout and drove along Straight Road before turning right into the newly built Farringdon Avenue, with fields and farm land on either side of it. There were no pavements. Mum checked the instructions that had been sent with the letter as we drove passed a row of eight shops, over a hill and turned left into Dulverton Road.

It was hardly a road at all. More like a track in the middle of mounds of clay. There were two blocks of semi-detached houses on the left, and three on the right. We worked out which would be number nine and pulled up. Mum got out first and helped me down on to a clinker pathway. We saw some bloke, in a striped navy-blue suit, waving at us as he leaned against a new wooden gate-post outside the furthest of a semi-detached house. It looked very big. Dad came around the front of the van without bothering to lock the door and we three trouped towards the suit.

Mum and Dad introduced themselves and showed the man the letter they had from the Council. I noticed that there were loads of iron windows in the front of the house and a large bit of garden with a side door in it. The grown-ups were going down the path and Mr. Suit, now known as Mr. Parker, was opening the front door. I followed them in for our first look at Number 9.

The contrast to 51a was astounding. First thing I noticed, as we went into the hall, was the smell of distemper and paint because the walls, doors, skirting boards and picture rails had all recently been done up in cream and beige. The whole of the floor was covered in dark thick rubber tiles. The uncarpeted stairs were on the right and on the left there was a good sized room that looked out onto the front garden. Straight ahead of us was the kitchen so we made our way there.

It was bright and airy and had a sink with hot and cold taps in the middle of a long draining board under the window. I went straight away to the hot tap and turned it on, but it came out cold. I heard Mr Parker saying that there was no gas laid on, so everything would be electric. I checked out the built-in kitchen cupboards from the ground to the ceiling. I opened the back door which lead to a small porch area where there was a toilet and a coal cellar. It was fantastic lav of our own and a view of the back garden piled up with mud and rubble at the side. The whole thing looked really swell. I was trying to remember every detail so that I would be able to tell Jeanie and Beryl all about it when I got back home. Wishing with all my might that Eddy was still alive to see it.

I was called back into the house as we were invited to go into what Mr. Parker referred to as, the lounge.

"This tile surround," said Mr. Parker proudly as he led us into the room. "Has a boiler behind it for heating the water when you have a fire so that you can save money on your immersion heater."

He pointed to a tiled fireplace on the wall that backed on to the kitchen. The lounge also had a pair of iron French doors that opened out to even a bigger back garden. I couldn't believe it, it was huge. It was like having our own private park. He unlocked the French windows and we looked out at the bricks, wood and mud piled on the other side of a narrow concrete path.

"Nice bit of garden there." Said Dad.

"They are going to build a school on the other side of that fence." Said Mr. Parker locking the doors. "Would you like to view the upstairs rooms now?"

We trouped back out of the lounge and as we passed the downstairs front room, Mr. Parker commented that that was the fourth bedroom. The other three were upstairs.

"Three more upstairs! Fuckin' ell!" I thought to myself, "It's a palace."

At the top of the staircase was a storage cupboard built next to an airing cupboard with an immersion heater it in. Facing this was a small box-room, obviously for me. I was thrilled to notice that it had a built-in wardrobe already waiting for my overcoat. Along from that was the room looking out over the front and behind that, to the right at the end of a small passage was another looking out over the back. But best of all was the bathroom. It had its own sink which like the bath was pure white with chrome taps in hot and cold in front of a frosted window.

Mum and Dad stayed talking to Mr. Parker while I went back through the rooms. I was opening all wardrobes and seeing hanging rails and shelves and top cupboards. All the rooms had windows with handles to open them, instead of rotting wood sashes. It was just like being in a film.

The house had to have time to 'dry out' according to Mr. Parker, so we would have to make our minds up and be prepared to move in after the end of term by the 20th of December, which would mean we could be in for Christmas.

In the van on the way home there was lots of talk about the pros and cons of taking the house. Mum was against it but Dad was all for it and I certainly was. A room of my own meant that I might get a proper bed, at last!

The arguments that raged over the next few days.

Mum had a problem with how were we going to furnish the new house?

"It's almost three times the size of the space we've already got!"
"I'll go down to Five Oak Green," Dad said "And pick up some of the iron beds from the hop huts, they would do 'till we could get something better. After all, we've got the dining room suite and some kitchen chairs and a table."

I liked this idea because I still didn't even have a bed of my own just the chair bed in the kitchen. I was still rubbing margarine on the bruises that I got from the thin cushions. There was just the big bed for the girls and Dad's bedroom suit and a spare dressing table that had no mirror.

Mum argued that there was also the problem of the floor, because no way did we have enough mats to cover upstairs and down.

Dad said it didn't matter because the tiles made it o.k.

Mum said she hated the tiles and wanted them all covered up if not with carpets then with lino or cheap floor covering.

She also thought the house was too cold and the only heating would be the fire place in the back room. At home at least, we had a fireplace in every room. Even if we couldn't always afford coke to burn in them.

Dad said we could buy electric fires and a paraffin convector heater if we needed more.

I suppose it was a foregone conclusion that the right decision would be made. We would move to Harold Hill.

As soon as it was decided I became intensely aware of the huge difference the move would make to our lives. I would have to leave Robert Monte Fury and start a new school. Where was that school? Mr. Parker had said that there were none yet built on the estate, so we would have to go to a school at Harold Wood wherever that was. and what about Church and the drama group and not seeing Betty and Itchie and how would Jeanie cope when she had to leave Dennis Stag. We would be leaving all our friends and relations along with the support we got from the wider family network; to go into an unknown place with strangers. How would Dad get to work and where would Mum work?

The fifteenth of December 1951, was my last day in the East End and my last day at school. I was in my last year and was the school's star actor and even though I was a 'saucy little bastard,' according to Nanny and the aunts, I was well liked. An attribute which allowed me to get away with a lot of stuff without being punished. When I said goodbye Bernice Goldstein and Abigail Kimber they both cried, but they often cried so that didn't mean much. Brenda Rember was very upset because for once she didn't have anything to say. Itchie Daniels immediately began making plans to come down to see us, so that was going to be swell.

I also managed to say good bye to most of the teachers: Miss Fagg told me that I must pursue the acting at my next school as she expected great things from me. Miss Abrahams warned me to keep up with my English as it would always stand me in good stead. Our arithmetic teacher Mr. Powell, still known as Bucket, nodded, twitched and looked relieved that I was leaving as did Monsieur Levine who wished me a very nasal 'Bon chance.' At the end of my final lesson Mr. Delmont, our form teacher, got the whole class to wish me and Solly Greenberg, who was moving to Welwyn Garden City, 'Good Luck.' That was the end of me and Monty Fury.

I walked out with Itchie and felt the cold December air as we crossed the playground and went through the gate into Valence Road. This being my last night in the East End, he was coming home to have tea with me and the family. We crossed the Mile End Road and walked as fast as we could up Cannon Street. The shop lights were on because it was already getting dark.

Arriving at our ever-open door Itchie and I climbed the two flights of stairs to reach the top landing where the centre passage was filled with tea chests.

"Mum, I'm home." I called loudly not knowing which of the three rooms she might be in.

"Johnny, is that you?" she called out, as if it could be anyone else! "Now don't hang about there's a lot to do. I'm putting all the kids' clothes in one chest and in that small case in here. You had better get the tea on. Daddy won't be home till after seven and we have got to have a early night because you've all got to get up early in the morning."

"But Mum, I've got to go to the club to say goodbye to everyone. What do you want me to do for tea?"

"Do a nice sausage stew. I've got some onions and potato's in a bag behind the door and there's some sausages I got from Carter's in the dipper."

I stood at the top of the stairs wondering whether I should escape now. On quick reflection I decided against it and raised my eyes in a gesture of resignation to Itchie.

"Can Itchie stay to tea Mum?"

"He can stay as long as he… Oh hello Itchie," she said as she came out of the girls' bedroom her black hair sticking out from under her turban. "You can stay as long as you don't hold us up and keep out of the way. In fact, you might even come in handy if we need another pair of hands."

Itchie looked at her through his horn rims and promised he wouldn't get in the way.

Mum went into her bedroom, Itchie and I went into the kitchen. Joanie was sitting in her high-chair eating a condensed milk sandwich with the crusts cut off. I went over and kissed her.

"Hello Jo, what d'ya know? I said.

This always made her laugh and I was rewarded with a gurgle as she struggled to say my name.

"I'll do the potato's if you like," said Itchie as he removed the brown paper carrier bag from behind the door.

" Swell," I replied as I got the sausages from the drop down flap in our kitchen cabinet.

While we were preparing the food, Jeanie came in from school and started to interfere. We got into a bit of an argument over whether we should have boiled rice with the sausage stew. Voices were raised and in no time Mum appeared to tell us off before Mrs. Coakley started banging on her ceiling to shut us up. That was something we wouldn't be getting at Harold Hill.

By the time tea was ready Beryl and Chrissie had joined us. Mum dished out the stewed sausages rice and onions from one pot the mash from another pot and baked beans from a third. The seven of us sat bunched up round the kitchen table and ate. Dad's dinner was put on a plate with another over the top to be 'on steam' until he got home from work.

After we had finished eating Jeanie and Beryl had to wash up. We only had a cold tap, so they put the kettle on the gas stove to boil the water. Chrissie played with Joanie while Me, Mum and Itchie went into the living room to sort out what stuff of mine had to be packed.

I never had a space of my own in the kitchen, so my stuff was stored in one side of the carved oak sideboard of the dining room suite. Clothes were on the top shelf and personal stuff in the drawers underneath.

There actually wasn't much. Another pair of long trousers, three pairs of grey socks two shirts, three pairs of underpants and a couple of pullovers. There were also a couple of worn out sloppy Joe's that I loved. They were too small for me, but I didn't want to let them go. They reminded me of Viola Walbridge and the Orphans of the War scheme. Viola had been very kind to me and these were the only things I had left of all her presents.

In the bottom drawer was my prized collection of film star pictures. Itchie and I had written to millions of stars in America and J Arthur Ranks in Pinewood, with a hope of getting a signed photo back. I now had over fifty. Including two big one's ten by eight. One was of Bette Davis he other of Gregory Peck, both personally autographed in ink, not like most of the others, which were just printed on. We would lick our fingers to rub the signature and if the ink moved we knew they had signed it themselves. All these along with my school books, comics, paint box and drawing book were put into a special attaché case which had been allocated to me. It wasn't in very good condition and had a broken catch, that took a lot of persuading to lock but it was my own and I treasured it. Living in a family of seven meant that anything private was very precious to my teenage self. Especially because as the eldest I was expected to sacrifice most things to and for the younger ones.

At last, having done all my packing and helped as much as I could, Mum said that I could now go to say goodbye to my mates. Itchie and I had just got to the top of the stairs when Dad's thick wavy hair appeared at the side of the coal box as he came up around the bend.

"Where the fuck do you think you're going?" came his paternal greeting.

"I'm going round Itchie's to say goodbye to his Mum before we leave tomorrow."

"Nell," he shouted to Mum as he reached the top of the stairs. "Has this little git done all his work or is he trying to dodge out without you knowing?"

"No, it's alright Edd, he's all packed." Mum yelled back. "He's just going round the streets saying goodbye to everyone."

"Hello Itchie," Dad said, as Itchie started going downstairs. "And as for you, flyboy, don't you be home late. We've got to be up early. There's a lot to do tomorrow."

With that he clipped me round the head as he went into the kitchen. I followed Itchie and heard Mum call out.

"Yer dinner's on steam Edd. Turn out the light under the pot."

Once outside, Itchie and I went straight to his house in Stepney Way. It was getting late, so I only had time to say a short goodbye to his family before running towards St. Phillip's for the whist drive.

I walked into the Church Hall which was full of the warmth of Christmas. This was the last meeting until the New Year, so a fir tree stood in the corner with twenty big light bulbs in purple and blue on it and there was a smell of mince pies in the air. Tables were laid out for a whist drive and the urn was hot for tea.

My girlfriend Betty saw me and came quickly towards me. She was now only a few inches taller than I was, so I didn't have to stand on tip toe to kiss her. We made a good contrast as our heads joined. Her blond hair and blue eyes mixing in with my carrot top and brown eyes. The grown-ups watched us as we broke apart and went to the counter to get our cup of tea and biscuit. It was a very happy evening. We danced, sang, played whist and I was glad when I came second and didn't have to win the stuffed owl that was the first prize. I didn't need it. I would have real owls in Harold Hill, because it was the country and there would be trees for them to live in.

Around half past nine, when the club was over, I walked Betty home to Cavel Street. We said our last kiss goodbye on her doorstep. Although it wasn't really our final goodbye because I would be see her when I came back to stay with Aunt Alice and she and Itchie had promised that they would come down to see me. We had found out that they could get a Green Line Bus half-fare return for under a shilling.

When we had done enough kissing, I left her and walked up to Watney Market hoping that I wouldn't be too late to meet my other girlfriend. Thankfully, when I got to Andersons the bakers, Katrina was waiting for me. She looked extremely pretty tonight. We said 'Hello' to each other and walked towards the doorway at the back of the shop, where the smell of the baking bread was hanging around in the cold night air just like we were. We pushed ourselves into the corner of the doorway and began to kiss and touch each other. I felt the usual stirring as Kat undid my flies. I put my hands under her coat and blue cardigan and began to stroke her. I knew she liked that. While this was going on we were kissing each other with full 'film star kisses.' That meant tongues and everything. Recently I had really started to enjoy it, perhaps it was the way she did it. After a while I had to take my mouth off of hers to tell her I was finished.

"Are you alright?" I asked. Uncle Ben had always told me to return the compliment

"Yeah, I'm alright," she said. "That's the last time ain't it? I suppose you'll find some other gel to do it for you, when you get to your new posh house."

"I dunno," I replied. "But I fuckin' hope so. Come on Kat, we'd better go. Shall I walk you to the flat's?"

"Yeah," she said.

At the bottom of her stairwell we were having our last big romantic scene, like George Raft saying goodbye to that blond tart whose hair hung over one eye in the Blue Dahlia, when I realised that the pubs were turning out and I would get a wallop round the ear for being out so late. We had a last quick kiss before I ran home dodging the Friday night drunks only to get a clip round the ear from Dad, who told me to get to bed so I would be ready for the move in the morning.

I fell asleep worrying about starting at another school, because despite all the showing off, I was still that insecure orphan who had found a bombed-out toilet to hide in just in case my real mother came back. Not that I thought much about that now. It had been over six years since we had heard from her and it seemed obvious that she had died or disappeared in the war. Whatever had happened she would never find me. My foster parents were my real mum and dad now and we were moving away.

It's strange but I never, ever thought about my real father.

Saturday the sixteenth of December was frantic from the time I got shouted awake at eight in the London morning, until the time I went to bed after ten in the Essex night. I was ordered about all day and it got on my bleeding nerves.

After our porridge the first job that had to be done was to take the beds apart and fold all the bedclothes into boxes. I was in the girls room squashing the pink eiderdown from their bed into a sack, when I saw the blood stains all over it. I took me back to the time, over two years ago, when I was still sleeping in their bed and Dad had been standing on it cleaning the window behind the bed-head. He slipped because while he was doing it he put his arm through the glass and slashed his wrist. The blood had spurted all over us and the eiderdown and while he stood on the bed holding his arm. He yelled at Mum, who was in the passage, to run across the street to get Uncle Ernie. When Ernie arrived, we were all in the kitchen and watched him make a thing called a tourniquet with a necktie twisted around a desert spoon. He took Dad to the London Hospital where they stitched him up before he bled to death. Dad hated hospitals so much that he never went back to have his stitches out, he just took 'em out his self. SMASH! I suddenly felt a crack on the head and Dad was telling me to stop bloody dreaming and get a move on, as we didn't have all fucking day.

I was on the go all the time, packing, folding, unscrewing and taking apart anything that had to be done. It wasn't just me, the whole family were at it, including the aunts and uncles when they had time to pop in.

After dinner, even though it was very cold and beginning to get dark, the sash windows were removed from Mum and Dad's bedroom so that the wardrobe, tallboy, settee and larger furniture could be lowed through the gap and down the side of the house on to the pavement. It was the reverse side of what had happened when we moved in.

It brought back memories of the time me and Eddy had been running up and down with stuff when we were little. I was now fourteen years old and he had drowned six years ago yet I still missed him. It worried me that we had never even had the time or the money to go back to Middlewich to visit his grave. It would sometimes make me sad that he had been all on his own up there since we left him in nineteen forty-four. There was never much time to think about him. There was always too much to do. Or maybe it was to painful to remember him.

It was nearly three o/clock when the lorry, borrowed from Harris's where Dad was working, pulled up outside. One of

Dad's mates, Terry Lyons, was driving it. There was loads of stuff on the kerb and in the downstairs passage, including a sack of coal dug out from the coal box. Me, Jeanie and Beryl were busy carrying the smaller boxes and lighter stuff down to the street until the lorry was fully loaded and Terry pulled away. He was leaving ahead of us, but we hoped to overtake him on the journey.

Mum left the front door key with Mrs. Coakley and the whole family piled into the black Austin. Dad was at the wheel and Mum was also in the front with Joanie on her lap. The other three girls and I were on the back seat. Once Dad started her up we got completely over excited and wound the windows down to shout goodbyes to the friends and neighbours who had been coming and going most of the day. Now at last they could wave us off and wish us good luck. Dad drove round to Planet Street so that we could say goodbye to Nanny and Farver then up into Commercial Road and were on our way.

As Dad turned the car into Sidney Street and then into the Mile End Road, it was dark and felt like it might snow. But it didn't dampen our spirits.

"Nine Dulverton, here we come," we chanted as we drove along.

But we soon got bored with that and didn't argue when were told to shut up and settle down. It was a long journey and we must save our energy for when we got there. I sat in the back and as we drove through Bow, I thought of the many dramas and changes that had happened since we had left the flat there nine years earlier.

"Well at least it won't be that bad in Harold Hill," I thought to myself.

How wrong can ya get?

26 A NEW LIFE

It was dark and had started to snow when we turned into Dulverton Road. It wasn't nice heavy snow but that light annoying stuff that floats down, doesn't settle just gets everyone annoyed and makes everything damp. The family clambered out of the car and ran along the clinker path towards Numer 9. Dad had just opened the front door, when the lorry arrived with Terry tooting the hooter and smiling and shouting as he leant out of the cab window.

There was no time to think about organisation. It was a case of first getting the little ones sorted.; meaning that we put Chrissy and Joanie in the kitchen where they could be warmed by the new electric cooker and watched over by Beryl. All the lights on and we started to move the stuff off of the lorry and into the house as quickly as we could. There were no friends and neighbours to help us here; just us. Dad and Terry worked like Trojan's carrying the heavy stuff.

Mum Jeanie and I carried what we could of our belonging, through the gate down the path and into the new house and then rushed back for more. We put the boxes of whatever we were carrying in the downstairs front room or carried it through into the kitchen. The heavy stuff like wardrobe, dressing tables, sideboard, dining tables, settee and armchairs were carried in and put straight into the room where they were going to be used. While they were doing all that, Jeanie and me started putting the beds together while Beryl was sorting out the crockery in the Kitchen; all the time being hampered by Chrissie who was desperate to help.

While all this activity was happening all the lights suddenly went out and we were left in complete darkness. Dark that is apart from the street light coming thorugh the front door and window. The girls started screaming and the grown ups yelling from the vairious rooms they were stranded in.

The big important question on everyone's lips was : 'Where's the fucking meter?'

After a couple of minutes with everyone looking everywhere, including the coal bunker and the upstairs toilet, the meter was eventually found behind the front door in a cupboad all by itself. Mum had her usual collection of pennies only to find out that the new meter took only shillings. Which was very practical when everything in the house was powered by electric. Neither Mum nor Dad had a shilling piece but fortunately Terry found one in his dungerees and volunteered that. We had just the one!

As soon as Terry's coin had been dropped, with a tinny clunk, into the empty box the lights flashed back on. While enjoying the relief it was agreed that one shilliing wasn't going to last very long.

"Johnny," said Mum. "Take tis half a crown plus a sixpence and go up to the row of shops we had passed and get three more shillings. They should last us for the rest of the night and the morning."

Jeanie was given the newly found torch and told to go out into the garden to find some wood so that we could light a fire to get some warmth. While we were doing this, the grown ups would continue bringing in the last of the stuff from the lorry and start getting the house liveable.

I argued that the shops might not still be open. Pointing out that it wasn't like back home where Gussie's or Katz stayed open until late or 'till they felt like closing. These were proper shops all standing in a row. I was told to shut up, piss off and not to come back without some shillings. So I pissed off along the dark paths up to the road at the top of our street. There were only a few street lights as yet, so I relied on the lights coming from the few occupied houses to find my way up and over a hill to what turned out to be the Cambourne Avenue shops.

The shop on the corner was a tobacconist and stationers. There were a few kids hanging around outside and I prayed they wouldn't start on me or anything like that. They didn't didn't cause any trouble but they eyed me up suspiciously as a stranger. The woman behind the counter was very friendly and even more so when I explained that we were just moving in and the shilling had gone. She made lots of sympathetic noises and gave me the coins I needed. When I got back to home the last two tea chests were being wheeled into the house. As I passed number seven I noticed that there were no lights on. Obviously no one was living there yet.

Inside number nine ,Jeanie had experienced great difficulty in getting the fire going. The wood was very damp so she had been platting and burning strips of newspaper that had been wrapped around the crockery, as she tried to get the wood dry enough to catch and burn. Before I coud help her, I was ordered to make the tea before Terry left to drive back to London. We didn't have an electric kettle but our tin kettle was eventually boiling on the top plate of the new cooker that stunk to high Heaven.

Cups and milk and sugar was found and we all took a break to enjoy our tea and wave Terry back to Poplar.

The rest of the night passed in a blur of making beds, hanging curtains, unpacking what we needed immediately, making more tea and going with Jeanie back to 'the shops.' to get some fish and chips. It seemed strange saying 'The shops,' instead of 'Gussie's,' or 'Bernie's,' or just 'The Market.' The first indiction that we were loosing the sense of community we had experienced all our lives in the East End. We were now living among strangers.

On Sunday morning I woke up in the back room which to us was known as the front room, because it was the best room. The best room was always called the 'front room' in the family and because we didn't use the words 'lounge or parlour.'

I has spent the night on the utility put-u-up that I was using as a bed. It had wooden polished arms and the rest of it was covered in pale green cloth. When the back was pulled up and the seat folded out, it turned into a small double bed which was arguably just a little better than sleeping on my chair bed or the floor.

I was aching and feeling cold when I opened my eyes and saw that I was surrounded by a jumble of furniture and boxes, with the December sunlight coming through the panes of dirty glass, in the French doors, I could see the piles of mud and rubble that was our back garden. The room stank of dampness coming from the drying wood that had been left on the tiled hearth.

I stayed in bed listening to Mum and Dad in the kitchen doing breakfast until hunger overtook my lethargy. I rolled off the settee and placed my pale thin legs onto the cold dark Marley tiles as I dragged my trousers up over my underpants. I was pulling my shirt over my head as I went into the kitchen in my bare feet.

"I fucking hate electric," Mum was saying to the cooker. "This toast is taking ages. On the gas it would have been done by now."

"Yeah, well it ain't on the gas is it?" said Dad, leaning against the draining board and blowing his cigarette smoke out of the open window. "So, you'll just have to wait wont you?"

"What ya got that window open for?" I asked. "It's freezing in here."

"To let the smell of the paint out," said Dad. "Don't just stand there open a tin of beans. It's on the table."

"Alright give us a chance. Where's the opener?"

"Ask her. She's supposed to have packed it."

"Don't start again Edd," said Mum. "Johnny go in the small room and have a look. Somewhere in there there's a box with Saxa salt written on the side. I think it's in there with the baby's nappies and that green glass dish. If it's not in there fuck knows where it is."

"It is in there," I said. "I remember I put it there yesterday. I'll get it. Can I put the radio on?"

"No," said Dad. "You'll wake the girls up. I wanna bit of peace before they all start going mad. And put your fucking socks on."

I didn't think it was worth arguing so I put my socks and shoes on. I successfully opened the beans and stirred them into a small saucepan on the smelly cooker. The toast was done and buttered, so we sat down to our first meal in the new house: beans on toast. Despite not having the radio on the girls were up before we had finished and were given their corn flakes.

We were all feeling the cold, so Dad smashed up one of the wooden tea chests and managed to light a fire in the front room. The other rooms were cold and uncarpeted. We did more unpacking to keep warm. Boxes were emptied, and their contents carried around the house to where they would be needed.

I was given the small bedroom upstairs as my own. It didn't have a bed only a wardrobe with a rail to hang my jacket and overcoat on. It also had a cupboard at the top where I would keep special things like my film star photos and books. It was decided that I would still sleep on the chair-bed that I had slept on, in the kitchen at home. Until Dad could drive down to Kent and get one of the old hopping beds for me and another one for the girls. I carried the chair-bed upstairs and it was while I was putting the cushions on the struts I realised that this was now my home. Tait Street was a place in the past.

Just before dinner time I took Beryl for a walk up to the shops to get Dad's Woodbines, the 'News of the World' and some more shillings. Meanwhile Mum was roasting a leg of lamb for dinner. By the time we got back, her hatred for the electric cooker had developed into an aggressive intensity. Being new it was pungent and made the food taste very strange. Mum, who was never the best cook in the world, made no bones about how much she loathed her new appliance.

"I fucking hate that poxy thing!' She declared to the whole of the new estate. "I'd sooner cook on the fire in the front room! That put up with this load of shit!"

After dinner we sat round the table to have a bit of time to review the situation. The floor boards, in the upstairs bedrooms still white with brick dust and paint spots had only one tiny bit of mat in each room. That and the un-curtained windows, plus double the space we were used to, made us extremely aware of just how much money we needed to get the house in a livable state. As for the garden, well, we had nothing to work that with, not a spade, a hoe, bucket or watering can. All that would have to be thought about if and when we could afford it.

The Big question was, where was the money going to come from? Dad was the only one working to keep two grown-ups and five kids to be fed and clothed. Mum had managed to get a bit of outdoor work in Stepney but down here with there was no prospect of outdoor work. The estate was still being built and it would be a few years before any factories could be erected to provide work for the emigrating people of London. That was the situation that continued for a long time.

On Monday after the weekend, Dad had to go to work back in London. I was up and looking out of my bedroom window as he drove the Austin away in the early morning dark leaving Mum and us kids to carry on getting the house in order.

Mum found fault with everything to do with the new house. Apart from the cold and the mud outside there was all that was wrong on in inside: that included, among lots of other things: the lack of gas, the cracks in the beige walls where the brickwork settled and mostly and more vociferously, black tiles on the floor. I did agree with her about the tiles. Why the council didn't make them in a more cheerful colour I'll never understand. Mum was missing the patterned lino that she always took a pride in keeping shiny. She also hated the lack of a market and people to talk to. There was no one next door at number seven and number eleven was the other side of the road across Cricklaide Avenue. Mum constantly moaned that she just wanted to piss off back home to her family and friends.

"It's no good you moaning Mum," said Jeanie. "This is where we live now so we've just got to make the best of it." That was her advice as she struggled to do up the buttons on Joanie's dress ready to take her out for a walk in the push chair.

Six days later we spent Christmas Day back at Nanny's and Boxing Day was at number nine. There is no photographic record of anything or anyone around that time because the Kodak had been left with Uncle Percy in the pawn shop. Just before the new year the aunts and uncles came down to see the new house. They naturally made things worse for Mum by saying how much they missed us. With the occasional good comment on the bigger space, the bathroom and the fresh air.

Early in the new year, the Doswell family moved into the other half of our semi- detached. They were quickly followed, on our side of the road by the Uren's at Number three and Hanson's at five. Across the road the Knight's arrived and bit by bit a neighbourhood was being created. It took a few years before it really began to function as a community because each new arrival was viewed with suspicion by those already established. The phrase 'Keeping Up with the Joneses,' was coined around this time.

It was us kids who were forced to break down the barriers of 'keeping our-self to our-self' and it came about because we had to be educated and in that process, we had to mix with and get to know, the others in our age group.

At the beginning of the spring term, there being no local primary schools Beryl, who was eight, had to travel by coach back to her London school, while Chrissie, who would be five that year, went to an already established infants school in the older area of the Estate.

We older kids, aged from eleven to fifteen, had to walk about two miles to attend Redden Court School in Harold Wood on the other side of the A12 Colchester Road. It was there where the native children hated us Estate kids with an unremitting passion. Nearly all of the pupils who came from Harold Hill, were in the same boat as Jeanie and I. Their families had moved from small homes around the slums of London, into larger houses, so they had very little money. This meant that most of our clothes were a bit run down and raggedy. Well very raggedy actually. Back in the East End no one noticed because everyone was in the same boat. But down here, in middle-class land, the Harold Wood kids wore good un-patched clothes or a school uniform so while the bulk of the pupils were in Navy blue and red, us cockneys stood out in our myriad of grey shirts, trousers and coloured coats and frocks.

The Essex kids had decent shoes and un-darned socks that didn't have holes or were patched up. They had good books and shiny pencil boxes, they also had pocket money and warm top-coats. They didn't have to wear old overcoats or Wellington boots because their Mums and Dads couldn't afford shoes. So, we had the piss taken out of us at every given opportunity. Jeanie and I started there together but not for long. Because she hated the bullying so much, Mum and Dad agreed to let her return to Stepney where the Headmaster at her school in Cable Street offered to pay for her return fare on the Green Line. I, of course, had to be a fourteen-year-old grown up man!

I had been at Redden Court about six weeks and we were in the middle of double English, when two Police coppers came in and ordered all us boys to stand at the side of our desks. We had to raise each leg and show our shoe to be inspected. Policeman One walked up and down the rows looking at the soles of each boys' shoes. He didn't inspect the girls' shoes who just sat there wondering what was going on. I was in the second row and watched him examining the others until he got to me. I raised first my right foot and then the left, he looked down and I expected him to quickly pass on as he had done with the others. But no! He bent down to get a closer look.

'Would you mind going to the front of the class please, sonny?" He said, in a kind but firm voice.

I went to the front of the class and watched as he inspected the rest of the boys. There was one other pupil, a boy called Reggie also from Harold Hill, who was told to join me at the side of the teacher's desk. I stood in front of the blackboard going redder and redder as everyone, who wasn't watching the Policeman, was staring at me.

When the inspection had finished, all eyes turned to the front of the class. Miss Gower the teacher, were standing to one side by the door with Policeman Two. Policeman One crossed in front of us as he went towards number Two. They had a bit of a whispered conversation which Miss Gower was desperately trying to overhear. Number Two broke way and came to the centre of the class.

Speaking quite quietly, he said to Reggie. "Would you mind removing your shows one at a time please?"

Reggie took his shoes off one at a time and the copper inspected them around the outside, as though he was looking for mud or something. He returned the shoes to Reggie, with a 'Thank you, you will return to your desk.'

Reggie abandoned the area as quickly as he could, and the policeman stepped across to me.

"Would you do the same please, Lad?"

My heart sank. Shit and fucking fuck! I knew I had a great hole in the front of the sock on my left foot and my pink little toes were now going to be exposed for all those bullying bastards to see. Prolonging the inevitable I took off my right shoe first and handed it to the Copper.

While he was examining that shoe, I quickly whipped off the left one and hid my foot behind the leg I was standing on. I passed him the left shoe and took back the right and bent down awkwardly to put it back on. Still trying to conceal the exposed toes. I needn't have bothered because everyone in the classroom was looking at the Copper who was now poking about inside the shoe. A titter ran through the class.

With my right shoe now on I looked up just in time to see that clever bastard pull out from my left, the remains of a green and brown Woodbine cigarette packet! This had been folded over to protect my foot from the friction when I was walking. The hole was now glaringly obvious to the whole class. Especially because the soddin' Policeman had put his finger through the hole and wiggled it. Very witty!

I was fourteen and a half, standing in front of a class full of mixed teenagers, most of whom were just looking for something to hang me with. Looking at a policeman waggling his finger through my shoe hole and holding a withered Woodbine packet in his other hand. Needless to say, I was utterly, completely and devastatingly mortified.

The class giggled at the waggling finger through the hole.

"'Quiet please," said Miss Gower sharply.

The class fell silent as the Policeman handed me back my shoe. I took it and then, to complete my humiliation, he handed me back the Woodbine packet.

The memory of that moment still makes me go tense to the bottom of my buttocks. Not so much because of the holes in my footwear or even because I was using a cigarette packet to walk on. It was the fact that as I stood there, pushing the packet back down inside my shoe, I just wished and wished with all my heart, that instead of Woodbines, my Dad could have afforded 'Players' instead.

The Police said very little about what was going on and we only found out later, that someone had broken into one of the empty houses along Gubbins Lane, near Harold Wood Station, and they were looking for clues.

Apart from the bullying and the long early morning walks in the cold, I also got very bored. Most of what they were teaching I had already been through at Robert Monty Fury. This meant that I only went to school when I had to. Especially as I was more use at home. It was about three quarters of the way through the Spring term when the School Board Officer, who presumably thought that I had been playing truant, arrived at number nine to check up on why my attendance record was so bad.

Mum made me lie on the sofa and quickly covered me up with a blanket before she opened the front door and brought 'the gentleman' in.

"Well, he's always been a sickly child," lied Mum with tears in her eyes. "Suffers something chronic from sore throats and gastro enteritis all the time. I don't know where I am with him. He's not like my own kids. That's the worst of fostering. You never know what they are going to turn out like. I do my best, but he is a problem as far as his constitution goes. I've had no end of trouble rearing him. He's always so lethargic. But what can you do? I sometimes wonder if he'll ever come to manhood let alone get back to regular schooling."

God knows where she got all these phrases from but by the time she had finished, and I was acting sickly, the Inspector was almost crying and went on his way with an apology to my 'devoted carer' and a detailed report about my 'near death' condition.

"Silly old Bastard," was Mum's comment as she shut the front door behind him. "Now help me get this washing on and then you can take the baby for a walk while you go to get the shopping."

Soon after that I tried to leave the school. Not just to get away from the unfriendly and nasty attitudes, but because Dad had broken his leg and our family had a genuine case of need. He had slipped on something while working and had been rushed to the London hospital. He arrived home on Tuesday afternoon, driven by Terry Lyons in our car, with his leg all plastered up and obviously in a great deal of pain. I never found out what had happened but whatever it was, he got no compensation and lost his job. He was a very proud man and refused point blank to go on 'The Bun' as he called it. This meant that we had no money coming in at all.

"If you think I'm going down there to fill in all those forms," Dad argued from his propped-up position. "Just so they can take the rise out of me for the few bob they'll throw at me, you've got another think coming. Me leg will be better soon and then I'll get another job."

After the shock, we realised that we were going to be in desperate need of money until Mum could get a job back in London. On Thursday evening about four o/clock, with money all gone and the weekend approaching, it was decided that with the money we had left, I could get a half fare on the bus to Manor Park and then walk to East Ham to borrow enough money from Uncle Arthur. Just enough to get us through the next couple of weeks. It was a good plan as we were all convinced he would lend us a few bob.

It all went well, and I got to Arthur's house, in Burges Road just past East Ham Station, as it was beginning to get dark.

Unfortunately, there was nobody home. I knocked next door, but they had no clue as to where he or Aunt Margie were or when they might be back. I didn't like to ask them to lend me half a quid as I had no idea who they were. I sat on Arthur's step not knowing what to do and feeling like John Howard Davies in Oliver Twist. It was getting colder and would soon be getting darker and I realised that I had to come up with a plan. I arrived at two alternatives.

One: was that I could walk back home and arrive with no money.

Two: I could walk towards London and get to Nanny's in Stepney.

I knew that once I was there I would at least get my fare back home and maybe some money to see us through to the weekend. Deep down I knew that I could not possibly face returning home empty handed. It had to be the walk to Nanny's.

The problem was that I didn't know the way! However, due to my desperation, I had a brain wave. I would follow the bus route! A number forty bus went to Watney Street Market along Commercial Road. If I followed them and checked out the stops along the way, I would be bound to get there eventually. Having got that sorted in my head I stood up and walked back to the Barking Road and started to walk.

It slowly got darker and colder and then it started to rain I tried to walk quicker then it started to rain harder. It was horrible. By the time I got to Plaistow I was wet through. I didn't dare stop or take shelter because it looked like this

April sodding shower was going to go on all night. I knew that I had to keep going. Although at one point, along the East India Dock Road, the rain got so heavy I just had to wait in a shop door way until it eased off a little. All through the journey, I had no idea how much further I had to go or how long it was going to take. It was only when I got to Lime house and saw the sign saying Commercial Road, that I knew I was getting near.

Fortunately, I didn't know that I still had an hour's walk before I arrived at Planet Street. I got there just after nine o/clock and knocked at number sixteen. When Nanny opened the door, she was shocked to see me standing there soaked and dripping on her door step in the pouring rain. She was even more shocked when I burst into tears.

"We ain't got no money," I sobbed. "So, I went to Uncle Arthur's and he was out and I didn't have any fare home and I didn't know what to do so I had to walk from East Ham to you so that you can give me my fair home and some money for dinner tomorrow. 'Cause Daddy's broke his leg and we ain't got no money and I don't know what they are gonna do if I don't get back with some money."

I was taken into the warmth of the house, stripped off, wiped down and my clothes dried in front of the fire while I was wrapped in a blanket. Uncle Aggie and Aunt Kate were there with Joycie and after I had been sorted out and given something to eat and drink, he drove me home to Harold Hill with enough money to keep us going for a few days.

By the following week, Mum had managed to get a job at a dress factory in London. Even with Mum working we were still desperate for money, and that was when they applied for me to leave school three months early. I was actually due to leave in July, but the Redden Court School authorities refused, saying that I would have to get an Act of Parliament, or something like that to finish schooling before the end of the term. I wouldn't have minded but the previous year I could have left at fourteen with no questions asked. It was a stupid idea to put the leaving age up to fifteen.

Somehow, we managed to survive and I continued to sporadically attend the wretched Redden Court. It was during one of my infrequent attendances that I got involved in the school drama group and appeared in the end of year production playing a film director who wore a thick pullover and hugged himself a lot and that's all I remember about that.

I did take the exams and as they had mostly been subjects that I had already done well in at Valance Road, they gave me a certificate to say that I had I passed in everything. Even Metal-work, which I didn't even take!

I did take an interview with a Career's Officer who came to talk about the work we might like to do and the sort of job we could apply for when we left school. The interview took place in one of the small offices near the headmaster's room. I knocked and was called in.

'Good Morning John. How good of you to come. Sit down."

I sat down. The Officer in a tweed jacket and a false smile, sat behind his desk and waved me to a chair in front of him. He introduced himself, but I have no idea who he was because as soon as he said it the name went right out of my head.

"Now have you got a plan as to what you would like to do when you leave school?" He smiled in a patronising way. It was as though he was talking to one of the fathers of a local posh kid.

"No. Not a bleeding idea. I want to go on the stage, but I have a family at home and they need help to feed each other. My dad has been off work with a broken leg and my Mum is having to go to London to earn a few bob a week by working as a presser in a factory. The kids get me down and I have no idea what I want to do because I don't have time to think. I am good at acting and things like that but they all say that is a sissy job and I should be an engineer and do something manly. I haven't had a lot of time to think about what I want to do and no one to talk it over with. I have to help look after the kids and do the shopping and try to help make ends meet. So, all in all I suppose I ain't got no idea."

That is what I wanted to say: but what I actually said was: -

"Yes. I would like to be an engineer."

"An Engineer?" He asked. His eyebrows lifted up a little and his voice sounded surprised.

"That's right." I paused. "Or failing that, I'd like to go on the stage."

It was out! I had never said anything like that before. Even when Miss Fagg at Robert Monty Fury has suggested going to a drama school, I had never come right out and said I would like to do it. Now it was out. In the air and into the ears of the Careers Officer. Whose eyebrows reared up and tried to disappear into his bald skin line. What was left of his hair being too far back for an eyebrow to reach.

"On the stage?" he asked in a tight high-pitched voice. "What as?"

I now had to elaborate, even though I had never thought about putting my reasons into words.

"Well, sir, I'd like to do what they do in the pictures. Pretend to be someone else and get paid for it. I've done one play at this school and some stage stuff at my other school and for the Church that I used to go to in London. People said I was very good and my teacher Miss Fagg in London, said that I had a talent for it. She said I ought to go to a drama school. So, I think I would like to go on the stage and be an Actor."

He looked at me as though I was a snail lying in bits after he had just trodden on me. He shook his head, paused, leaned forward, spread his mouth wide with lips together trying to smile. He pursed his lips, sat back in his chair as though he had no idea what to say or do next. Eventually he put his hands together and made a clapping sound and buried his head in the papers on his desk.

"An Actor? No, I don't think so," He said, looking up at me. "No. You don't have the look of an actor and certainly not the voice. And as for engineering, well that would entail going to college for another couple of years to study mathematics and technical drawing among many other things." He paused and looked down at my records. "I see from your records that you tried to leave school early because you are needed at home to help out financially."

"Yeah," I answered already hating him.

"Well John, under the circumstances," he paused. "What I suggest is something that will bring in a certain amount of money to you and your family very quickly. Therefore, I would advise shop or office work. Maybe in an office which would eventually lead to a career if you worked hard and earned your way up. In fact, I have here a vacancy already submitted. It is for a young junior to be a solicitor's clerk. Would that interest you?"

A solicitor's clerk! I tried to work out what that meant. The only clerk I knew was the bookmakers clerk that helped out Dutch Harry of Stepney, when he was taking bets on the street corners. While the only solicitors I had heard of were the tarts 'up the Dilly,' as Mum called the whores in the West End. So as a solicitor's clerk, I imagined O would stand on the corner while a woman tried to get a bloke to have a shag. And if I saw a Rozzer I had to let her know. I was wise enough not to react straight away.

I paused a moment before asking. "How d'ya mean sir?"

"Well John," he said. Sounding more relaxed because he got on to something he knew about. "A solicitor when he goes into court or works in his office, has to have certain people around to help him. They are called clerks and they would be there to type out reports, file cards s well as read things or to run errands. All that along with the other duties that are required in any office. This work is usually done by what we call a junior clerk. That is to say, someone who would like to go into the Law and would benefit by spending some time learning the trade from the bottom up, as it were. I have such a vacancy in an office at Stratford along the Romford Road. If you are interested in applying for the post, I could arrange an interview."

"What about the whore's? I asked.

He took the question in but couldn't understand it. His eyebrows tried to kiss each other as he ignored my question.

"Shall I arrange an interview for you?"

"What would I have to do? I said. "I mean, if I went for an interview?"

"Well John," he smiled. "That would depend. Usually they talk to you about what you like doing and what you have done. They would then ask you some questions about your education followed by a bit of a chat about your hobbies and pastimes. Not unlike what we are doing now. After that and if they thought you might be suitable; they would offer you a job."

"What there and then?"

"Well no, John. Not necessarily there and then. They would have to consider you and the other applicants who were applying for the same post. After they had completed their deliberations they would possibly write or telephone you."

"We don't have no phone."

"In that case they would write to you if they thought you were the sort of chap they were looking for. After that John, they would call you in and offer you the post. At that meeting they would give you the conditions of work and pay and offer you a starting date."

"What? Then I just go and start work? I asked.

"Yes John. Would you like me to arrange an interview for you?"

"Yes," I said. "Why not? Thank you." I had nothing to lose and I had had enough of him by then.

"I will do that then," he said as I stood up to go "And John, I wouldn't mention the acting when you go for the interview. Let's just forget all about all that. Shall we? It really isn't for you."

Although I didn't tell him. I left the office thinking, 'What a waste of fucking time that was!'

In early in June, just after my fifteenth birthday, I prepared to go for my first job interview. Mum and Dad had impressed upon me that I must to look smart. So, I wore a clean white shirt and put a black tie on. I even cleaned my shoes which still had the hole, but I put a new fag packet in and doubled the thickness. I didn't have a suit, so I wore my best jacket which was a bit frayed round the cuffs, but it was set off with a pair of grey flannel trousers that Mum had managed to get me second hand from one of the women in her factory. I put a bit of Brylcream on my hair to help it lay flat and keep the natural curliness out of it. Having got myself, all dolled up, I set off for Stratford.

Thinking back to what I looked like, I must have presented a sad prospect for the Law industry. But I didn't know that then, so I went to the interview with confidence and just a natural touch of first job nervousness.

I found the office at the end of the Romford Road, just before it turns into Stratford Broadway. It was a tall Georgian house with two steps leading to a wide black door that had a grey stone column on either side. They are still there to this day. I lifted a big brass knocker and it banked on the door echoing in the passage behind it.

An older woman answered and ushered me into a waiting room on the right. After ten minutes I was called into an office across the hall. I entered and saw a plump man sitting behind a large desk smothered in papers and books. He was dressed in a pin striped suit, a white shirt with a stiff collar and striped tie. He told me to take a seat. He looked over his brass rimmed glasses and suggested that I tell him all about myself. I gave him my biggest smile and told them that I was John Ross and had come to be a clerk for the solicitor.

I could tell straight away that the pin stripe did not see me as a potential candidate to become a clerk in his office. He immediately informed me that they really wanted a girl and the fact that I could not type or do any shorthand did not go in my favour. He didn't say it but I instinctively felt that because I spoke with a cockney accent and looked frayed around my edges, it did nothing to inspire him to engage me.

He was polite and finished off the interview by telling me that they would write to me with their decision and thanked me for coming. They never did write to me and so ended my career in the Law.

In July when it was almost time for me to actually leave school Mum thought it would be best if I got a job back in the rag trade and perhaps train as a Hoffman presser or even a suit cutter. I agreed because it was a line of work I knew something about, having worked in Dad's factory after the war and I had been around the dress making business for years.

Dad suggested that I try to get a job in men's tailoring with Nossek and Nathan because Mum knew Barney Nathan and could get me in to see him. The next morning Mum took me to his factory in Cavel Street. When we got there at eight o/clcok Barney was standing behind a table laden down with papers, invoices, bits of cloth, pictures and a huge overflowing ash tray. The interview took place with us all standing and was short and sweet.

"Well you look an intelligent boy," he said in a comforting Jewish accent. "So long as you work hard and don't cause me no trouble you should be getting on alright. So, listen, you can start on the Monday, after you leave your school. You want to be a cutter? So, you learn the trade from the bottom up and you end up making a lot of money as a wonderful suit cutter for me. So, don't you worry you will always have a trade. You work from eight till five-thirty, five days a week, ten minutes tea and forty-five minutes for dinner break and I'll start you at two pounds ten shillings. So, what do you say?"

What could I say? Two pounds ten a week! A fortune!

"He'll take it," said Mum, as I stood in shock. "And thanks Barney."

"My pleasure. For a nice gel like you Nelly, what else? He looks a good kid. So, listen Johnny, when you come to start go straight up to the first floor and ask for Lily. You got that? Lily? She will put you right. Remember, no lateness and no soddin' about you get me?"

"Yes," I nodded.

Mum gave me a telling look. I quickly added.

"And thank you very much, Sir."

"Sir he calls me! No. It's just Mr. Nathan, but Sir is nice. Now before you go, a piece of advice. So, get yourself a good pair of scissors. No cheap shit, you'll pardon my French, a good strong sharp pair of scissors. Spend a bit of money, it will be worth it in the long run. Cheap tools are never worth it believe me. Now go, I have work to do. And don't be late!"

I said goodbye to my schooldays on a Friday afternoon and on the following Monday morning I started work at the men's tailoring factory in London E1 as a trainee cutter.

27 WORKING BOY WITH CAR TROUBLE

After Dad's broken leg had almost healed he had managed to get his job back, driving at Harris's, which was very handy for me because that meant that he could give me a lift to work every morning and that would save on my time and fares. Well that was the idea but didn't always work out that way. It was at this time in my life that I actually loathed poverty. Apart from the obvious lack of food and decent clothes there was also the shame and the constant inconvenience it caused. See below.

Dad and I travelled to London in our old Austin car which, quite frankly, was not in very good condition. The engine was incredibly temperamental and always difficult to get started. This meant that Dad had to swing the starting handle, accompanied by a lot of effing and yelling at me to pull the fucking choke out. Then he would yell louder because I had not guessed the correct length of the fucking choke which in any case was a matter of trial and error. He would continue yelling and swinging until we heard the satisfying splutter and it sparked up. He would quickly remove the handle, rush round into the driver's seat, throwing the handle into the back and pull away.

Apart from that, the main trouble with the car was the tyres. They had to be inflated by inner tubes and all the inner tubes were beginning to rot. We couldn't afford to buy one new ones let alone five. This meant that the journey to Stepney Green each day was a continuing saga of travelling with hope and trepidation. Rather like 'The Archers' on the Light Programme only without the music.

If it was the first one of the journey, it meant that we had to exchange flat tyre for the spare wheel. We would feel the clump, jump, clump, jump, of the car as it leaned in a slight list to the side of the car it was on. Dad would pull into the kerb and almost before he had stopped, I would be out of the near-side door ready to get the jack and then the wheel out of the boot. Dad would be out of his side, almost as quick and would quickly start to jack her up. He would then undo the nuts, we had no hub caps so that saved precious seconds, which I would catch and place on the running board ready to hand them to him after he had hung the fully inflated spare wheel on the chassis and was ready to screw them back on. While he was doing this, I would carry the punctured wheel into the boot and wait to replace the jack. As I was doing that and shutting the boot, Dad would be in the car and starting her up which with the engine being still warm, didn't usually involve the handle. I would return to my seat and we would be on our way again. Eventually as you can imagine we had our routine down to a fine art.

If it was the second puncture that meant that the spare wheel had already been used. So, the punctured inner tube would have to be mended at the side of the road. We would go through the early stages of our wheel changing routine up to taking the wheel off. After that the split inner tube would have to be removed from inside the tyre and the hole sealed ready to be pumped up by Dad. I would have already got the bowl and poured water into it from an old lemonade bottle which we carried for the purpose. The inner tube would be immersed into the water and Dad would use the foot pump to blow air into it until bubbles appeared in the bowl and we knew where the hole was. Once found, it would be a case of drying it and patching it with a rubber square that had to be glued on. We would then have to wait a certain amount of time for it to 'take.' As soon as it had taken and was sealed, Dad had to ease the tube back into the tyre without damaging the rotting rubber, foot-pump it up to fully inflate it, before putting the whole thing back onto the chassis. As you can appreciate two punctures on the same journey meant that we always had to allow ourselves an extra half an hour a day for inflation duty.

I don't think there was more than a mile stretch from the west side of Romford Market right up to Bow Bridge, where we didn't get a puncture during the next few months.

So, as I intimated above, you can stuff poverty. Right up your arse.

Luckily on my first day at Nossek and Nathan's we didn't break down at all. Dad dropped me off at Nanny's at quarter past seven, explaining that this was the one and only time he would do this and in future I would be dropped in the Whitechapel Road. I waited for half an hour with Nanny telling me that I was going into the big wide world now and as a man I had to look after my Mum and the little ones. Like I didn't know! What else had I been doing for the past fifteen bleeding years. I didn't say anything. I just agreed with her and said I would. After all she meant well, and I got on alright with her.

At ten to eight it was time to go to Cavel Street and report for work to Lily, the manageress. I arrived at the factory door at the same time as lots of women and a few men who rushed past me and went running up the stairs. I followed them into the factory area.

It which was much bigger than I was expecting, and I stood to the side to take it all in. There was a small back window and a large cutting table to the left of the door with three tailor's dummies standing like sentinels behind it. Near to them were a couple of Hoffman pressing machines which stood in front of shelves stacked against the far wall loaded with bales of suit materials, in different shades of grey and dark colours. To the far left of these, were three ordinary ironing boards supporting heavy steam irons on long electrical leads. Directly in front of me and covering the rest of the floor, right up to the big iron barred windows overlooking Cavel Street, were two rows of Singer sewing machines. About twenty from what I could see. These were facing each other with a trough between them to catch the completed work. Most of them had pieces of clothing already under the needle foot. In the far-right corner was a sink and a draining board with a large urn on it and above this were two shelves holding cups, mugs and tea making essentials.

As more people came through the door I was obviously in their way, so I moved further into the factory floor bewildered by the rush and strangeness of it all. I stood there, feeling like a lemon, without a clue as to where to go or what to do next. Meantime trying to figure out which one of the ladies rushing, to their machines, was Lily.

I didn't have to wait long before a woman, in heavy make up with two thin lines drawn on her forehead pretending to be eyebrows, came over to me.

"You must be Johnny. I'm Lily," she said, in a hurried voice. "I'm gonna show you the ropes. Do you know how to thread a machine? Don't worry I'll show you from the beginning. Come over here."

She led the way quickly across the floor towards the back wall. I could feel myself blushing as the other workers sat and looked at me. She took me behind a row of machines and pulled out a swing seat from under one of them and plonked herself on it.

"It's nearly eight. I'll unthread this one and we'll start from scratch when Harry turns the power on."

She took the reel of grey cotton off of the spindle on the top of the machine and the thread followed as she wound the cotton round the reel.

"Any minute now," said Lily, nodding towards the clock over the door as she shouted to a man across the floor. "Standing by Harry!"

I followed her look and saw that the big hand was almost at the twelve and the second hand was moving upwards. As it hit the top for eight o/clock, Harry pulled a large leaver on the side of a chrome box. Instantly all the lights went on, the radio started to blare out music and the deafening noise of machinery starting to fill the room. It frightened the shits out of me! At the same time the cutters, the Hoffman pressers, the button hole makers, the hand pressers, the sewing machinists, the packers and the shifters, in fact everybody started to work. I was shocked by the suddenness of it all. It reminded me of the time, when the school took us to see a live classical concert at the Troxy cinema and the bloke at the front raised his stick and they all started to play their instruments at once.

Lily didn't seem to notice anything at all.

"Right, you are going to be on pockets for the first couple of weeks, that way you can cause the least damage," she yelled above the noise. "So, you will need beige cotton. Over in that drawer you'll find a reel go and get it and I'll sort out a spare bobbin."

I collected the cotton from the glass fronted drawer which contained about a hundred different coloured reels and returned to Lily. She showed me how to thread it through the various cotton holders down the side of the machine and into the eye of the needle above the foot. I did know how to do this because of when I had worked in the factory at 51a, but I let her show me so that I wouldn't make any mistakes. She then drew back the footplate and showed me how to put the bobbin in the case under the needle.

"Now Johnny, when you do this always take your foot of the treadle. Then you won't accidentally push on it and start the machine going. If you do that you are more than likely to catch your finger. Mind you, you can't really call yourself a machinist until you've caught your finger and drawn blood."

It suited me not to draw blood because I didn't want to be a machinist anyway, I wanted to be a cutter and designer. I showed Lily how well I had learned to thread the machine and she expressed her admiration as to how quickly I had picked it up. She then led me to a counter that had pile of cream cloths that had been cut into a scimitar shape.

"Right these are your trouser pockets. You just machine down the side, round the bend and up to that slit. Don't go beyond the slit because it won't give the trouser machinists enough room to put them in the trousers. Bring some over to your machine."

I picked up a couple of dozen.

"No, more than that. Take about a hundred." She picked up a huge pile. "These should see you through the morning."

We returned to my machine and she showed me the route round the pocket. She positively shot round it in about two seconds and before I could even look at it she had sewn another one. We swapped places and I put the two pieces of cloth together and slowly machined round the edge, trying to get a nice smooth seam. I looked up at her. She looked down at me.

"Well it looks nice Johnny, but you ain't here to make a wedding dress for Princess Elizabeth, you are here to make a hundred pockets in a couple of hours. So, you'll have to get a move on if you want to make your money. Just swing it round under the foot and don't cut the cotton after each one is finished, just run them all together, then when you've done about thirty or forty, you can fold them, make a pile and cut the cottons all in one go before you put them out of your way. Have you got your own scissors?"

I took my new scissors with the black shiny handles from my inside pocket and showed her. I had bought from a stall in Romford Market on Saturday.

"Yeah, not really the best but they're good enough I suppose," She said in a disapproving way. "O.K. I've shown you as much as you need to know for now, just get on with it. If you want me I'm over there on the facing table, but don't bother me too much as I've got my own work to do. I'll see you at the break. We get ten minutes. Have you brought a mug?"

"No. Mr. Nathan never said anything about….."

She was on her way and shouted back over her shoulder. "Never mind, there's bound to be a spare, if not, you can…" The rest of her advice was drowned out by the noise.

I settled down to make my pockets.

The machine I was working on was actually a great deal faster than the ones I had been used to at home. So, I made quite a few mistakes to start with. The man next to me, Morris, was very helpful in telling me to cut them off and throw them in a big waste bin at the back along with all the other waste cloth. He also helped me get my tea, when Harry blew his whistle, and everyone rushed to the tea urn which was now boiling.

Morris found me a cup and brought me some tea with two sugars. By the time he got back to our machines and we had drunk it there was no time to talk except to exchange names and for me to say thanks. The machines and music started up again and with a thumbs-up from Lily I returned to steering the pockets through my Singer. I worked as fast as I could and was getting to the end of my pile of material when it was time to stop for dinner.

When the Greenwich time signal came on the radio at one o/clock everything stopped. I mean stopped Dead! Everything! Followed by an incredible stampede for the door as the workers grabbed their bags and coats and tore out. By the time I had realised what was happening the place was empty; apart from one or two machinists who were still there but had already got their sandwiches out. I sat at my machine in bewilderment. It was a short while before I realised that I had only forty-five minutes to eat and get back.

I had arranged to go to Nanny's for dinner and I arrived exhausted after my brisk five-minute walk. While I ate I told her all about my morning. She just told me not to worry as I would get used to it and it would all get easier to understand. I just had enough time to almost finish my pie and chips before it was time to rush back to carry on running the needle around those bits of cloth. Nanny was right. It did get easier and by the end of the week I had got used to it. I can't say I liked the work, but I did like my wages. Although, getting my first pay packet turned out to be a huge embarrassment.

In the dinner break I had gone down to the ground floor office with most of the other workers, to sign for my money. When I got to the front of thee queue I gave my name to

Irene the wages clerk. She flicked through the envelopes, but she couldn't find my mine! After going through the wage packets again, she asked me to give her my national insurance number.

This number was on the card that had been sent to me by the National Insurance Office. I had to keep this number until I retired, and I would have a stamp put on my cards every week when I was working. This would pay for my health care and count towards my pension when I retired at 65 years old.

While everyone was waiting impatiently behind me, Irene went to her filing cabinet and found that my name of John Ross, did not tally with the name on the card which was Michael Peter Ross!

"Never mind sweetheart," laughed Irene. "I don't always know who I am either. 'Specially after a couple of drinks on a Saturday night. You've go lovely coloured hair. Ain't he got lovely coloured hair Maureen? You should have been a girl. Anyway, now that we've got that sorted out what do you prefer us to call you?"

"Well, everyone calls me Johnny at home," I explained.

"O.K. then Johnny it is. Just sign there Johnny and make sure you put your real name."

I did as I was told and Morris, joked that he would call me Mike from now on to remind me of who I was. We had become a good friend during the week especially when people shouted at me. Or called me a fucking pest because I was in their way or if I had put something down in the wrong place.

He took the time to explain that they didn't always mean it, it was just that tempers often got a bit frayed in factory life.

Being the youngest person on the floor I came in for a great deal of teasing. Lily and a lot of the women were always going on about my hair colour and how jealous they were of it. I suppose they meant it in a nice sort of way, but I got embarrassed by it and would blush bright red. Which made them laugh and then they would flirt and try to kiss me. It wasn't malicious or anything like that it was just their way. They would go on about whether I had carroty hair down below and try to get a close look at the tiny bit of bum fluff that was around my chin to see if that was also ginger.

During their teasing Morris, who had quite a nice head of jet black hair himself, told me not to worry and that it was none of their business what I had 'downstairs.' He was a twenty-five-year-old Jewish man who had been in the Catering Corps towards the end of the war. He was very sophisticated and smoked Kensitas cigarettes which he carried in a silver cigarette case.

During my second week he asked me if I wanted to go with him to a club up west and offered to lend me some of his clothes. He always looked very smart and had some excellent clobber. I didn't tell him that I wouldn't know what to do in a club or that I couldn't afford it, because most of my wages had to go towards the family. I just politely refused.

I never realised just how much he thought of me until one afternoon during the tea break. I had rushed straight up to the factory toilet for a piddle. I was half way through when he came in and stood at the bowl next to mine.

"You must have been bursting for that Mike," he said as he opened his fly. "You were off the floor and out that door like a whippet at Walthamstow, I was bursting too but you beat me up here. Been drinking a lot?"

"I suppose I must have been," I said. "Although I only had a glass of lemonade at my Nan's with me dinner."

"No. I meant were you out on the piss last night?"

"No! I don't go out of a night," I confessed. "There's nowhere to go on the estate. Besides I can't afford it. My Mum needs as much of my money as I can give her."

"Fuck me, look at the size of that," said Morris jerking his head in the direction of his own groin. "That's what you call piss proud ain't it?

"Yeah I reckon so," I said without actually looking at his pride. I was blushing just the same."

"Yours look good too," he said.

"Ta," I said not knowing what else to say. "It's o.k. I suppose."

"Its more than o.k.," he whispered. "Its lovely. Hey Mike, would you mind if I had a feel?"

And then, without waiting for permission his hand was already on it. There was a bit more conversation before one thing led to another and we ended up playing with each other.

After that we met for sex on a semi regular basis and as far as I know, no one at the factory suspected a thing. Morris became a good mate and taught me a lot. Not just about sex but about lots of other things as well. A couple of times he asked me to spend the night at his house in Jubilee Street, but I refused. I don't know why. I could have easily have told Mum and Dad that I was going to stay with my mate, but I just never really wanted to.

At the factory I progressed from the pockets and on to the canvas reveres that go under the collar and lapels of the suits. By the beginning of August, I was occasionally allowed to work on the Hoffman to steam press the trousers legs and give them a good crease. There was also the occasion when Benny, the cutter, was laying up a new batch of material to cut and I was called over to watch him. Just to watch, nothing else. He was far too temperamental to allow me or anyone else to do more than that.

"What I do here on this table is the basis of the whole enterprise," he told me, as he rolled a bale of striped serge cloth up and down his long cutting table. "If I make a mistake in my laying up not only does it cost the firm a fucking fortune. If I don't notice the mistake the firm could easily go bust, by my life and I don't make no joke. So stand well clear. Over there you can observe what I do but touch nothing. Do you understand? Do and touch nothing! Do I make myself clear?"

"Yes Benny," I replied. "I wont touch nothing or do anything. I promise."

Lily was looking at me most of the time and when my first instruction was finished she called me aside.

"Don't be put off my him, Johnny," she said. "He is a cantankerous old git but he is the best at what he does. Like most of us, he's not going to give you the benefit of his experience too quickly in case you get too good and take over his job and he ends up out on the streets. So don't take anything he says personally. It's just business. You're doing very well. I am thinking of letting you learn the button hole machine soon."

I continued to watch Benny realising that I had a lot to learn and came to the conclusion that things were never as easy as they looked.

So, it was that my life fell into four categories. Work. Home. Leisure. Sex.

Work. Was with Dad and the punctures. Having breakfast and dinner at Nanny's then in the factory till the hooter went.

Home. Once indoors I would play with the little ones or go for a walk with Jeanie and Beryl over the fields to explore the area.

Leisure. If I stayed in Stepney, I would hang around with Betty, in her house or go to the church clubs. Sometimes I might meet up with Itchie and we would go to see a film up the Troxy or the Rivoli.

Sex. I occasionally saw Kat although it was a bit difficult to do any love making because summer meant it was hard to find somewhere to be alone. If I got desperate I would occasionally visit Uncle Ben or go with Morris during the day.

It wasn't a particularly exciting existence but as everyone said. 'That's what life is all about. When you grow up. Work home and bed. With a little bit of pleasure thrown in. That is if you can find and afford it.'

It was a way of life that I would have continued quite happily because I enjoyed it and quite frankly I knew no better. I never had the feeling of being dissatisfied with my existence. I had been brought up to get through and survive to-day because there wasn't much point in thinking about tomorrow which may never come. Despite my ultra sensitive side, which caused me to worry and get anxious, I was an optimistic young man who enjoyed life and lived in the moment. So what did I have to complain about? Nothing! Nothing that is until the hop picking season began.

Our family was still in desperate need for money. Even with Dad and Mum working and my meagre wages coming in, there was never enough. No mater what we did and how we skimped and scraped, there was always something that was needed to ensure that we were broke by the end of the week. Consequently, it was decided that the family would go hop picking. It was our usual way to get a bit of extra cash and if there was anything to spare it would go towards Christmas.

Dad told me, in no uncertain terms, that I would not, repeat not, be able to go with the family this year because I was now working and had a responsibility to my job. This did not please me at all. 'Hopping' was the one thing I thoroughly enjoyed and to be suddenly 'a man' and have to forgo that pleasures was too much of a wrench. I broached the subject when we were gathered in the kitchen on Friday night after work.

"I don't see why I can't go at least for a week or two," I argued.

"Johnny, are you gonna be a fucking pratt all your life?" Demanded my father. "What makes you think you can go hopping? You ain't bin in that job two months yet! So what gives you the idea that they're gonna keep your job open while you sod about down in Kent?"

"But I've been there over six weeks now and I could do with a holiday. I started straight from school remember."

"Do you really think they're gonna give you time off for a holiday?"

"Dad's right, Johnny," said Mum, as she was washing our clothes in the sink. "How can you ask for time off? Barney will tell you to piss off and to take the job with you. You ain't been there long enough to get any holiday pay. And besides we need your money. It's not much but it does help and if you work hard you may be able to ask for a raise by the time it gets to Christmas."

"But Mum," I said. "I can earn as much picking as I can machining and I won't have to pay me stamp. Besides, I've never missed going hopping. Not since I've been going with Nanny when I was eleven."

"Then it's about time you stopped going and gave yourself a rest from it," said Jeanie. She thought she was being so sodding clever!

"You mind your own business," I snapped back. "It's nothing to do with you. I'm having a private conversation with my own Mother and Father and I don't need you poking your bleedin' nose in."

'Now shut up the pair of you, you'll wake the baby," said Dad. "There's no argument, Johnny. You are not going hopping and that's that. You're gonna stay at your job and start to grow up. You can't remain a kid all your life. You've got to face up your responsibilities."

"Daddy's right son," said Mum. "And anyway, he'll be able to bring you down at weekends in the car. When all's said and done you really do have to study your job. Come and give us a hand to wring these shirts out."

And that was the end of that. No hop picking for me.

On Saturday the first of September the bedding, the beds, the clothes and all utensils that were needed to make a home in the huts, were packed on to the back of Harris's borrowed lorry. Mum and the girls drove off to Five-Oak-Green. Leaving me stuck in number nine to clean up the mess they had left all over the house. Betty came down in the afternoon, and although our love was too pure to go the whole hog, we had a swell time together in the house alone.

Dad returned on Sunday having got the women settled into the huts and we continued in our daily routine. The five days passed with no arguments and only two punctures. These particular punctures were an even bigger worry because the car's road tax had run out on the last Friday in August. We did not have the money to renew it so we weren't taxed or insured, meaning that if a copper had come along and seen our 'out of date tax disc,' while we were changing the wheel he could have taken us off the road. Dad could have been in for the high jump as well as a heavy fine. But what else could we do? It was not the most important thing to spend money on when the family needed food, clothes, petrol and hot water. Now the hop-picking session had started, Dad was going to get a sub from the farmer at Ploggs Hall. Then he would be able to tax and insure the car when we came home on the following Monday. It was going to be a busy weekend because he was also going to fix the faulty brakes once we got to the farm.

28 FATE TAKES A HAND

On Saturdays I arrived at his firm carrying a change of clothes for me and two bottles of sterilised milk left by the milkman that morning. After collecting the key from the office, I sat inside the car reading the Daily Mirror. Just after twelve thirty Dad came around the corner and we set off for Five Oak Green in Kent.

It was a tense journey. Dad drove with extra care in case he had to pull up sharp by using the handbrake, yet not so careful as to cause suspicion to passing Rozzers or worry to the other road users. To give him is due Dad was, despite all his other failings, a very good driver.

There was a lot less traffic on the roads in nineteen fifty-one but nevertheless, it was still busy around the East End on a Saturday afternoon. As a result the pressure on his driving didn't ease off until we had gone through the Blackwall Tunnel and into the South East. It was only then that Dad could put his foot down and get up a bit of speed. He was aiming to get down to Mum and the girls by three o/clock.

It had started to rain but everything went well until we had just come over the brow of Wrotham Hill. I could see through the windscreen, as I sat next to Dad, that we had a clear road ahead. Clear that is except for a large green van parked on the right-hand side near the bottom of the hill just before the road flattened out into a bend. Dad was using the handbrake to slow us down a little because our speed had increased as we descended the hill. We had got to about four hundred yards from the parked van, when a lorry came around the bend and started to overtake it. Thereby blocking both lanes of the road. It was obvious that the lorry driver hadn't seen us because, to our surprise, as it got level with the van it stopped, and the lorry driver started talking to the other driver through his cab window.

I had no ability to judge speed or anything like that but even I knew that there was no way we were going to get through. It was also extremely obvious to both of us that with our brakes being in the condition that they were we were not going to be able to stop before hitting either the lorry or the green van or both!

I knew something horrible was going to happen when Dad pulled hard on the handbrake and began to swear and share his thoughts aloud with me.

"Look at that stupid fucking Bastard! What is he doing?" he said. "Hold on Johnny we'll have to mount the bank. Fucking shit. I'm going to have to go up the side of the road. Hold on Son. I'm turning the wheel," he shouted as he turned the wheel and we continued moving forward. "Here we go! Fuck we're nearly at the lorry. Hold on. We're going up the verge. Hold on! Hold on! Watch out! Fuuuuck! Here we go! I'm turning off the engine."

I stared through the windscreen gritting my teeth harder and harder as the two vehicles got closer and closer to our car. Dad's voice was seeping into my brain, but my eyes were fixed ahead. I was willing the lorry to disappear so that we would pass through and not crash into it. Just before we were about to ram it, our car veered to the left and began to mount the steep grass verge at the side of the road. It climbed up a little way, slowed down when it got too steep to climb any further and it stopped. We hung there for a second or two before gravity took command and the car rolled over on to it's side and slid down the almost vertical bank. We slipped down accompanied by the sound of crunching metal, breaking glass, people yelling and me screaming. We landed in the road on with the driver's side resting on the tarmac. I was flung to my right on top of my father who was pressed up against the door with the surface of the road on the other side of the window. Everything came to a halt.

Silence.

"Johnny, are you alright?" Dad asked in a tight voice, as he tried to move my body that was hanging all over him.

I wasn't sure whether I was alright or half dead. I was in shock and could feel myself loosing consciousness.

"Don't faint. Whatever you do don't faint." I was thinking to myself. "If you faint now he will never forgive you. Keep in your senses and get yourself sorted out."

I noticed leaves and bits of twig stuck behind the wipers that had got stuck on the windscreen which mercifully was still in one piece. I could see raindrops on the glass.

"Yes Dad. I'm alright" I said. "Are you o.k.? I'll try to lift myself off of you. If I can."

"It's alright there's some people coming to help," Dad said.

Through the windscreen I saw a man climb up on to our car using the front bumper as a step and walk along the bonnet to get to the door above me. He leant over and with a bit of an effort managed to lift the door up and open. Another man was helped up and the two of them reached down into the front passenger seat to help me out. More people gathered around the car and bent over to watch their efforts through the windows.

I reached up and grabbed the hands that were searching for me. I had no way of levering myself up and did not want to put any more pressure on Dad. I let them drag me out like a limp dead rabbit. They lifted me up as carefully as they could and passed me to some other people who had come to the side. The side that was the underneath of the car. I was still trying to keep conscious as they laid me on the grass verge. A large woman in a leather jerkin came over to me carrying a Thermos flask cup that she put to my mouth.

"Here son," she said, in an Irish accent. "You'd better have a drink of this."

I watched as the men, who were still standing up on the side of the car, reached in and pulled my Father out. He helped himself by standing on the back of the seats and as his face appeared above the running board he looked bewildered, pale, frightened and confused. The men lowered him down the side of the dust filled chassis and on to the wet road. Another bloke held his arm as he came over and sat on the bank next to me.

"You o.k. Johnny?" he asked quietly.

"Oh yes he's fine that he is," said the woman with the flask. "Not a mark on him. Got a charmed life that one has. Here now friend have a couple of mouthfuls of this tea. It's nice and hot."

Dad took the tea and we sat there in shock. Not quite knowing what to do.

One of the men, in a battered trilby hat, who had helped pull us out, climbed down from the side of the Austin and came towards us.

"Thank God you're alright boys," he said. "My engine cut out as I got level with that van and when I saw your car coming down the hill out of control, I had no power to get out of your way. Thank God you're alright!"

"Lord be praised," said the flask lady. "They're both alive and it just needs getting the car back on its wheels to see what's been a going on with that 'un."

She turned to the men and women standing in the road. "Come on all you dirty layabouts, get off yer arses and get this 'ere vehicle back on it's right way up."

At her command more people appeared from behind the lorry and they formed a circle around the Austin. Men and women stood staring at it not quite knowing what to do as it lay on it's side in the wet road like a dying hippopotamus.

"Derek get down from off the car and put the door back in its place," ordered the lady. "Now the rest of you's, get this into your stupid heads. It will be no good just turning the car over. If you do that you're more than likely to break its shaft. It has got to be picked up so as not to cause any damage. So gather yourselves around it and prepare to listen to me. It must be lifted up from the road by the lot of you's, turned in the air and then put down on it's wheels, so it must. Have you all got that?"

The men and women standing around the car all agreed, by grunting nodding and confirming, that they had indeed got it.

"Right then, some of you's come round this side ready to take the top side when it comes down. We'll need the strongest at the back and the front. I'll give the count to start lifting. And mind this, I want no fecking about! We want this car back on it's wheels and away before any nosey parkers arrive. If you get my meaning. Right now, prepare to lift. One… Two…Three…"

Dad and I sat on the wet grass and watched our car being lifted up in the air and turned the right way up. It was quite a feat but thanks to their combined efforts, under the control and the determination of the tea woman, the car was lowered on to the road standing on its four tyres.

"Right Mate," said the Man in the battered trilby. "You'd better get in and see if she'll start up. I've had a look round I can't see any petrol leak, so it should be safe."

Dad passed me the flask cup as he walked round to the front of the car and got in behind the wheel.

I sat staring wide eyed and frightened.

It was all very well for that bloke say he had looked around but what if there had been a petrol leak inside the engine? The whole thing could blow up when Dad turned on the ignition. Before I could say anything, Dad had turned the key and the car spluttered into life. Accompanied by a damp cheer from the onlookers.

"Alright," said the Irishwoman. "All back in yer conveyances and let's get the road cleared. You in the car, if you can back up a bit we can get our lorry around this van and we'll all be on our way. Give me that cup boy."

I gave her the cup and went around the car to speak to Dad. I could see lots of grass and mud and stuff down the driver's side of it and the door handle looked a bit buckled.

"Shall I get in or wait till you've backed up?" I asked Dad.

"I think you'd better get in Johnny," said Dad, nodding in the direction of the lorry. "I don't like the look of what might happen."

I looked over and saw the man in the trilby and the lady in the jerkin, coming towards us with rather different expressions on their face. I quickly walked round the front of the car and got into my seat. Dad wound down his door window as the couple arrived.

"I don't see any point in taking this any further do you?" said the man. "I noticed that your tax is out of date and as you're not insured, for all the best reasons in the world, it would be wise to just carry on driving."

"Sure, and he knows that don't you Sir?" said the lady. "There's very little harm done. We are all alive. Your car is going and there is absolutely no call for anyone else to get involved. Best we keep it just between ourselves. I'm sure you see the sense of that. Don't you Sir?"

It was said with great reasonableness but with just enough of an underlying threat in the voices, to make it clear that no arguments were to be entered into. And so, very sensibly, none were.

Dad backed the car far enough up the hill in front of the green van. Leaving enough room so that the lorry could move forward and around both vehicles. The driver waved to us as it passed on it's way towards London. Along it's side in gold and green paint were the words 'Tate and Lyle.' Obviously, it was being used for a bit of moonlighting and the driver in his trilby hat, wanted no trouble or interference from any authority. Nor, as was the case, did we. Dad then changed gear and moved forward past the van and we continued on our way.

We travelled in silence. Neither of us yet able to take in all that had happened in such a short space of time. The thoughts of what might have happened were obviously playing around in both our minds. The enormity of the situation hard to comprehend. The silence was eventually broken when we got to a spot in the road where Dad could pull over.

"Right, I've got to have a piss." He said as he put the handbrake on, left the engine running and got out.

I felt the same, so I got out and we pissed up different sides of the same tree.

"Are you sure you're alright Son?" asked Dad, using an unfamiliar tone of endearment.

"Yeah! I'm O.K. But I was a bit scared to start with. I really thought we were gonna crash. You done good there Dad."

"Those silly bastards, I don't believe that their engine cut out. I think they just stopped to talk," said Dad. "I thought we'd had it. Going up the bank was the only thing I could think of doing to save out lives."

"It was a good job you did," I said. "Otherwise we would have been goners. It was good that the bank was just steep enough for us to get up it and not go straight over."

"I didn't have time to think of things like that. I just turned the wheel and hoped. I wondered where the fuck we were going when we rolled over."

"Me an' all," I added. "What was all that crashing sound?"

"I think it must have been the tools in the boot. I reckon we ought to have a look at everything properly now that we've stopped. Don't you?"

We returned to the car and opened the boot. Dad had been right. All the tools had been thrown all over the place, spanners and wrenches, the jack and the tin bowl we used for the punctures. But the most amazing thing was that the two bottles of sterilised milk were still intact. We looked over the rest of the car it was dented in places down the driver's side and the off-side indicator was having a bit of trouble coming out of its holder but otherwise it seemed in a reasonable state. The running board had been bent up a bit, so Dad jumped on it to push it down flat.

"I'm a silly bastard, should have done those brakes last night or before we left," Dad said. "It's gonna be the first thing I do when we get there."

"Perhaps you ought to do them now." I suggested.

"No fuck it. Come on, lets get on. She'll be wondering where we've got to. We'll just have to take it slow and careful."

We retuned to the Austin and I remember thinking to myself. "A trolley bus, and a car crash. Maybe I do have a charmed life."

The rest of the journey was completely uneventful. Things only got difficult when we arrived at the farm and Mum started nagging because we were late and she wanted Dad to drive her to Paddock Wood so that she could do some shopping.

"You mean you drove all the way down here with weak brakes," said Mum with her hands on her hips and her eyes blazing. "And with him in the car an' all. What is the matter with you Ted? You're fucking crazy. You could have both been killed and then what would we have done? We lost one kid in the canal, we don't want to lose another on the bleedin' road."

"Nelly," Dad tried to explain. "I was working till late last night and I never had a minute to do them before we left. It was just bad luck that the lorry pulled out."

"That's true Mum," I said backing him up. "We were doing fine 'till that happened and once it did, Dad didn't stand a chance. And anyway, he saved our lives by going up the bank."

"Saved your fucking lives," she continued. "Some fucking life I'd have had if you'd both ended up splattered in the road!"

"Well, we didn't end up in the fucking road. We are here and if you'd shut your bleedin' mouth and give us a cup of tea and something to eat we can get to Paddock Wood and get the shopping as soon as I've done the soddin' brakes."

We moved away from the car and into the hut. Mum, still nagging as gave us a plate of mutton stew and some bread and margarine.

Once we had eaten, Dad did mend the brakes and with such a good story to tell he managed to get help from a couple of men who liked messing about with cars. I didn't offer help. It would have been too embarrassing to be turned down.

I needed to acclimatise myself to my new surroundings. Instead of living in our usual tin huts, we were now billeted on a site at the back of one of the smaller hop fields and were living in were known as 'the Brick Huts.' Our quarters were in two of the sixteen huts that were in two rows of eight backing on to each other, with a communal cookhouse at the end of each row. There was enough room outside the huts to have our own fire to cook on, so the cookhouse was used mainly as a communal meeting area because it had a roof and was shut in on three sides. It also had a large indoor fireplace.

I showed off quite a bit round the fire that night telling all the youngsters the story of the crash, with embellishments and building up the role of the Gypsy Queen and the roughness of the geezers from the lorries.

When I got to bed I did have bad dreams that my life was over, and I was chained to a machine making buttons. I must have been making a bit of noise because I was shaken awake by Jeanie who told me to, "Shut you mouth, I'm trying to get to bleedin' sleep!"

29 THE FIRST GIRL

On the following morning, I had come to the realisation that I didn't want to work in the factory any more. I don't know what brought me to that conclusion perhaps it was due to the accident. I just knew that I had to get away from the work I was doing. It wasn't just because I wanted to stay down hopping. It was something deeper! That I had to change direction because there might just be another alternative.

During Sunday dinner I settled down to persuade Mum and Dad, that I'd had a big think and it would be better if I stayed on the farm rather than go back to Nossek and Nathan's.

"Don't get me wrong," I explained. "I do enjoy working in the factory, but I can't see where it is going to get me. It's gonna to be years before they let me get on the cutting table and although I enjoy machining a thousand pockets a week and occasionally using the Hoffman, I think I've had enough of it and it ain't gonna get me anywhere. After all I was machining when we had the factory in 51A. and that was years ago."

"But the machines weren't as fast as they are at Nossek's and you are learning other things as well," said Mum as she dished up the sausages, mash and fried onions.

"Yeah, well I've done the buttonhole machine and that was dead easy once I got the hang of it."

"But what about your wages?" Dad asked. "We need that money, you know we do."

"I reckon I can earn as much as I am getting from Nossek's by working down here. And I won't have to pay my stamp. And let's face it Dad, now that I've got a bit of experience I should easily be able to get a job in another factory when we go home. I might even try something else, something away from the rag-trade."

"It's a shame there ain't no work nearer to Harold Hill," said Mum.

"Yeah. It would be better for him to work nearer home," said Jeanie. "Save on his fare money."

"What d'ya mean home? Dulverton Road ain't home! Stepney's home," Mum insisted.

There was no point in arguing with her. It would be years before she referred to Harold Hill as home.

I continued to put my case with lots of pleading and the occasional touch of pathos and by tea time I had worn them down. It was agreed that I could stay 'down hopping' and get a new job when we all returned home at the end of the season.

"But you've got to pull your weight," said Dad. "No larking about all day. You've got to be up the fields first thing and keep at it till the last measure. Just keep it in your head that you are not a kid anymore so keep your mind on the job. And if I hear that you've been soddin' about, when I come down next week, you'll be straight home my lad and back to the factory. So don't think you've got it made. Because you ain't."

That was Dad's threat, as he left us on Sunday night. All ready to drive back to Essex with no tax or insurance but ready to pay it, with a sub in his pocket and fully working brakes.

So I stayed. Having spent years during the war of not knowing if we were going to be alive the next day let alone the next few weeks I had grown up learning not to worry to much about the future. So I didn't give much thought to what I would do when I got home. I was down hopping, and it was time to work hard and enjoy myself. Which is exactly what I did.

We got up about seven to be on the field at eight. I would wash outside in cold water or under the communal tap, while the kettle boiled for tea on the primus stove. Mum and the girls would have a wash in a bowl in the hut where it was a bit more private. After breakfast we would gather our stools, bags, along with anything else we needed for the day, put Chrissie and Joanie in the pushchair, and make our way to the picking field.

Living in the brick huts, we were now further away from the fields that had to be worked, which meant a longer walk at the beginning and end of the day. We had to follow the track round the side of our field, lift the pushchair and stuff over a stile, cross the road and go down a slope into the main common and make our way to wherever the current picking was taking place. Once there we would go to our row, pull down a bine and start to pick off the hops into our bin. This year we would be getting five-pence a bushel. This money would be collected at the end of the season. Minus any subs that we would have had to take to live on. This was the life I had given up the factory for. I loved it.

Another reason was Brenda. She had been my girl friend the previous year and her family were also living in the brick huts three doors along from us. Brenda like me was fifteen and was going to get a job in an office when she got home because she was clever. She was also beautiful, blond and I really liked her. We picked up from where we had left off the previous year when we had been 'hopping sweethearts.'

On the Wednesday evening we went to a dance, organised by Miss Whitby. It was in the big hut on the main common. We had been doing some waltzing and quick steps to the records they were playing on the gramophone and had got very close and easy with each other. About twenty minutes before the dance was due to finish, we both agreed that it was time to leave because it was quite dark, and we hadn't brought a torch. We said goodnight and thanked Miss Whitby, waved to our friends who were still on the dance floor and left through the big doors at the back which were open because it was a warm night.

We walked away from the lights and made our way past Nanny's hut, where she and Aunt Alice were sitting outside enjoying the music and the air.

"You off back home now you two?" asked Nanny.

"Yes, Mrs. Skelton," said Brenda. "Goodnight."

"Goodnight, dear," said Nanny.

"Don't you be up to no tricks and get up late for snatching 'em off, in the morning," said Aunt Alice, with an unnecessary amount of innuendo in her voice.

"Goodnight Aunt," I said, emphasising the word Aunt, as we walked past the glowing embers of their fire, towards the road.

As soon as we got beyond the huts is was much darker. We took each other's hand a swung them in time to the tune we could hear coming from the big hut and started to sing along. We were still singing when we got to the bank that led up to the road. I scrambled up first then reached down to grab hold of Brenda's hand to pull her up. But she thought it would be a good idea to pull me back down again, before I knew what was happening she had yanked on my arm and I skidded down the bank and we fell onto the grass together.

"You bleedin' cow," I laughed, as we rolled over and I pushed myself on top of her.

"I thought you might enjoy it," said Brenda. "Seeing as how you rolled down a bank in a car last Saturday."

"That's not very funny Brenda Branson," I said. "I could have been killed in that car. So shut your mouth."

"Make me shut it then. Go on!"

I didn't need telling twice! My mouth was on hers and my tongue between her lips before she could draw breath to get any more words out. We lay there kissing and holding each other close for a few minutes. I put my hand on her face, then slowly drew it down to her breasts which felt warm and soft under her pale green blouse. Her tongue went further into my mouth as she pressed against me. I stroked her and then tried to move my hand under her blouse.

"No, Johnny," she said.

"Why not?"

"Not here. They'll all be coming out of the dance soon," she reasoned. "Let's go somewhere a bit more private. Come on."

As she said that she laughed, pushed me onto my back and crawled up the bank. I rolled over and ran after her across the road. We climbed over the style into our small hopfield that was still waiting to be picked.

"I know," I said, as I jumped from the style. "Let's go round the back of the cookhouse."

"Yeah," said Brenda. "But we'll have to go the long way round, because if anyone's sitting outside their huts they'll see us."

"Sod 'em." I said. "They know we're together."

"No I don't mean it like that. I mean if my Mum's there she'll ask me to do something or want to know where I'm going. So will yours. It's safer if we go the long way round."

So we did. Stopping along the way for more kisses and caressing until we drew near to the row of huts and could see through the bines the glow of the fires. We crept through the foliage and down the side of the path towards the end of the cookhouse. It was much darker now as we carefully avoided the bottles, tins and bits of sacking that were strewn about the area. With my teenage passion rising and in the excitement of the moment, I almost pushed her through the wall as we fell against the black painted bricks.

It was just like all those pictures that I'd seen up the Troxy. I was Robert Taylor and she was Jennifer Jones. Our lips and tongues explored each other while our hands roamed all over our bodies. Our clothes were pulled up or pulled down so that as much naked flesh as possible could touch other naked flesh accompanied by subdued moans of pleasure all round. Very little was said but a tremendous amount was being expressed. However, when it came to the point, nothing could progress.

"I ain't got no French Letter," I gasped with shocked realisation.

"Never mind we'll use our hands then," said Brenda accommodatingly.

So we did, and it was super. It was great! However not as great or as super as when, two nights later we did the whole thing again. By then I had managed to get hold of a packet of three from Ronnie Ford and the full, exquisite pleasure of being at one with a girl made me almost fall over with exhaustion after we had finished.

It turned out to be a very good year not only for me but also for the harvest. The hops were big, and we managed to earn a good bit of money. In fact, I did actually earn more than I would have done if I had stayed at the factory. However, come the end of season it was time to say goodbye to Brenda along with our hopping friends and return home to face the reality of getting a proper job again.

30 TIME TO GET A TRADE

When we returned to Harold Hill, in early October, two big changes had taken place.

The first one was that the Local Council had finished building a prefabricated school on the land at the back of our house. This was called Broadford School and its intake would be five to eleven years olds which was exciting news to Beryl and Chrissie, because it meant that they wouldn't have to travel around the estate to their schools. To Jeanie it didn't mean much because she was still travelling to London and to Joanie, it meant nothing at all because she was just over two and was at the stage in her life when nothing mattered except getting her own way.

The other big change was that Dad's firm had moved out of Stepney Green and now had offices in Enfield. This meant that he had to travel further and leave home earlier. Fortunately, the car was now taxed and insured, until Christmas, and had a couple of new tyres which were bought with some of the hopping money.

The one thing that hadn't changed was that we were continuously low on cash. We had a family conflab. It was decided that because Mum could earn more money than me, it would be better if I stayed at home to look after the kids, do the shopping and cooking and she went to work. Mum, who never liked being 'stuck in Harold Hill,' was all for the idea. Within a couple of days, she had managed to get a job at Lyons Tea Shop in Cheapside just up the road from the Bank station.

I enjoyed being at home to begin with. Once the three eldest had gone to school Joanie and I had the house to ourselves and had a good time. This arrangement worked well for just over a month then I really got bored at having to rely on Mum for pocket money and being stuck in the house all day and night. Not to mention being at the back and call of everybody all the time. Having to get the dinner cooked, get the shopping done, clean up the house and be generally treated like a servant by everyone began to get me down. Heated arguments often ensued.

During one of the many rows we had at home, I shouted at Mum and Dad,

"I want to get a proper job again! If we got someone to look after Joanie, it would mean that Mum could still work, and we would have my money coming in as well. Beryl is capable of doing the shopping and Jeanie could take a couple of days off school a week. Why shouldn't I look for work? I'm sick of being treated like a slave"

The arguments continued until eventually it was decided that I should try to get a career.

The idea came about because after church on Sunday, I had gone back to Nanny's and had a conversation with Farver about what I ought to do for work. He had never really got over the general strike of the twenties. or the poverty and depravation that his and a lot of families had gone through in those days. He was convinced that I ought to learn a trade. Nanny who was also listening agreed.

"Or even better," Farver went on. "Get a steady job and be like Uncle Ted. He's in the Post Office. He's doing well up in the city. He'll never want for anything and look how he managed to survive the really bad times before the war. Not like the rest of us. And all because he had a regular job with regular money coming in."

"That's right," said Nanny. "A trade will always stand you in good stead!"

"You could no a lot worse than try for the Post Office," Farver continued. "It's a job for life. Once you're in you're in. They can't sack you. Well not unless you do something terrible. Why don't you have a go and take the exam. You've got a brain on you. Not like the likes of me. You can add up and read, you can even talk a bit of French. You'd be mad not to have a go. It'll be much better than pissing about in a factory or poncing about down with your Mother. Why don't you have a talk with Uncle Ted? If you like, shall I sound 'im out for you?"

On the following Sunday, after church, I went to see Uncle Ted. He lived five doors up from Nanny and Farver's house, at number six. Because they were well-to-do, it had a brass number plate, knocker and letter box on the door which was painted in two tones of glossy green. Great Aunt Nell answered my knock and led me down the passage to the back room. Uncle Ted, a younger version of Farver, except that both his eyes were good, was sitting at the table having tea and biscuits. Aunt Nell poured me a cup of tea. No biscuits were offered.

"She's got the best bone china out for you, haven't you Nell?" Uncle Ted laughed. "Come on John, we'll retire to the parlour."

We went back down the passage to the front room where the window looked out on to Planet Street.

Everything in this house was much more affluent that at number sixteen. The glass wear was glittering, the furniture highly polished and the carpets were fitted to the wall. It didn't reek of money, not like some of the homes I had visited when I was on the Black Market for Aunt Betty, but it smelt of comfort and time to care.

"Now then John, what's all this?" Uncle Ted said, as he plonked himself in a big armchair at the side of the fireplace. "Charlie tells me you're thinking of taking up a career in the Post Office. Is that right?"

"Yes. I think so. I am certainly thinking about it Uncle Ted." I replied.

"Well you could do a lot worse. You get a regular wage which will increase as you grow up plus there are always lots of opportunities for promotion as you get a bit older. I'm now an, E.O. that is an Executive Officer at The King Edward Building. But I started at the bottom, as a postman and I've worked hard to make my way up to where I am today."

"Where would I have to start Uncle Ted?" I asked.

"Well I reckon you, being only fifteen, would have to start as a telegraph boy. A messenger boy as they are commonly known. The beauty of that job is that you wouldn't have to worry about clothes. Your uniform would be provided. Everything from shoes to a hat and all things in between. Although not your vest and pants obviously, but you would get an overcoat for bad weather and socks. That would mean you would have more money to spend for yourself, or to give to Nelly and the kids. After all, you ought to look after them now you're growing up. Remember they took you when no one else wanted you. Otherwise where would you be now."

"I've always tried to help...."

"In Bernardo's that's where you'd have ended up. God knows what would have happened to you then. If this family hadn't taken you in and treated you like one of our own."

"I am gonna help. I was already giving ......"

"One of our own." He interrupted. "We've always made you welcome haven't we. Not only us Skeltons, but the Browns as well. Even the Halsteads, when they can be bothered to came and visit our Nelly. You could never say that you've ever had cause to complain about your treatment at the hands of this family. Can you?"

"Well no. But ..."

"And I for one and I don't think I am completely alone in this thought, think you ought to look forward and see what you can do to pay the family back."

He carried on saying how marvellous the family had been and how he in particular had been so generous towards me. When in point of fact, he had done fuck all for me. He had never given me as much as a three-penny bit for Christmas as a kid. I had never even been asked inside his house until to-day. So what the fucking hell he was going on about? I don't know. As he was droning on I suddenly remembered that in the family he was known as 'Tight Ted, tight as a cat's arse.

I didn't say anything. I just sat there and listened until he got on to what I really wanted to know. How I might get to work into the Post Office.

"What you've got to do my boy is to write to the Recruitment Officer at the King Edward Building at London, EC1. I've written it down for you. He's a good friend of mine. Tell him that you're interested in making the Post Office your career and that you have a relation already in the service. You can mention my name but remember that it is Edward Skelton, not Ted. You give them your address and then they will send you some forms. You fill them in and before you know it they'll ask you to go to the Head Office to take an exam and do a bit of an interview."

"Is the exam very difficult." I asked.

"Well I didn't find it so and they tell me it is a lot easier now, so I don't suppose you'll have much difficulty in getting through it. After all you ain't a complete idiot, are you? Charlie tells me you're quite bright, but then in comparison with him, no one's an idiot." He laughed.

I didn't laugh because I didn't get the joke. He looked at me and we finished our tea. With nothing more to say we both stood up and I said thanks for the tea as he showed me to the front door. Remembering my manners, I called down the passage in my best cockney voice because I knew it would annoy him.

"Fanks for the nice cuppa char, Aunt Nell, cheerio."

This set a precedent that has followed me for most of my life. Whenever I am faced with any form of pomposity I revert to being extremely common and coarse.

"You're very welcome lad," said Uncle Ted. "Good luck with it and if you have any problems let me know. We have got a phone, so you can call me. Charlie's got the number for emergencies. Don't forget to mention my name."

He shut the door behind me. I left heaving a huge sigh of relief.

I went back to Nanny's and had another cup of tea out of her chipped cup and enjoyed the buttered bun she put on the table. I told Farver what his brother had said. About joining the Post Office and we all came to the conclusion that it would be a good thing. I left out all the shit about me being fostered as I knew that might cause trouble. Farver suggested that instead of sending away for the application forms, I try to get them from the Eastern District Office at the bottom of

Cavell Street. This suited me very well because I was going to see Betty in Raven Row, which backed on the EDO on my way home.

"How I kept my fucking shitting poxy temper with him, I'll never know!" I said to Betty when we met. "No one in the family has ever referred to the fact that I had been fostered into it. And here was this pratt who had nothing whatever to do with bringing me up, going on about how grateful I should be. Like he didn't even care that most of the money I ever earned went to Mum, Dad and the girls. Like he wouldn't give his shit to the crows if they were dying of starvation on the wing. And he's got the bleedin' cheek to lecture me. Fuck 'im!"

"Yeah. But never mind Johnny, I'm really glad you're gonna do this," Betty said. "I reckon you ought to do well in a career like that. If I get my exams and become a Nurse, we'll both be professionals.

She came with me to collect the forms from the sorting office at the back of the building because the front counter area was shut. The postman on the door kicked up a bit of fuss but Betty smiled and tossed her fair hair at him, so he eventually went into another room and came out with some forms and an envelope which he grudgingly handed over to me.

We returned to her house and, despite most of her family talking and interfering, we managed to get it all filled in. Not completely because I had to take it home to get Dad to sign as I was under eighteen. Betty wished me good luck as she walked me to the bus stop. We had a bit of a snog in a shop doorway while we were.

When I got home, Mum and Dad seemed pleased and we went over the forms together after which Dad signed them and Mum took them with her to work the following morning so she could post them in the City. Her café was local to the King Edward Building.

On the Thursday morning a buff envelope with **O.H.M.S.** on the front and addressed to John Ross Esq., came through the letter box. It was from the King and said that I had an appointment to see some bloke at the City Head Post Office and would I call to confirm. So off I went, with Joanie in the push chair, to the phone box outside the shops and after putting my two-pence in I dialled the London number and pressed button 'A'. I confirmed the appointment, with the woman on the line who told me, to report to the information desk at the E.D.O. at nine thirty the following morning. She also told me that I should be prepared to take an examination, an intelligence test and to bring my employment cards with me. I agreed to all this, thanked her and said goodbye.

There was lots of excitement that night. Fortunately, my cards had been retrieved from Nossek and Nathan by Mum when we got back from hopping. She had ironed my white shirt and I even considered having a bit of a shave.

"Don't make me laugh," said Dad. "What are you gonna shave? You've hardly got any fluff there to take off. Shave! You won't have to shave for another year yet. And when you do, you ain't borrowing my razor you can buy your bleedin' own."

I opted out of the shave.

The following morning, I got up early to catch the seven twenty-five, workman's train with Mum. Dad couldn't give us a lift because he had left to get to Enfield by seven. It was dark and cold when we shut the street door behind us and walked to the station to join a queue for the last cheap day workman's ticket. After that the fare would double as an ordinary journey. Mum already had her weekly ticket and as soon as I got my return, we went down to platform three which was crowded with workers. I thought it looked rather romantic in the early morning light from the station lamps. The romance didn't last.

"Don't get it in the first two carriages," said Mum moving down the platform through the waiting workers. "We'll stand more of a chance of getting a seat a bit further back."

We managed to get a seat next to each other and as soon as we pulled out of Harold Wood, Mum started rattling on about Lylie, her workmate from Dalston.

"That Lylie is a bit of a laugh and yesterday afternoon she accidentally dropped a large spaghetti pie on the floor in the kitchen. Instead of picking it up she then proceeded to kick it around 'till it crumbled into bits."

Mum's voice could be heard by lots of the other passengers and I could see some of the blokes smiling to themselves. Mum could always make a story funny, I'll say that for her.

The thing was, I didn't want to hear all about Lylie and her stupid spaghetti games. I was going for a job and I should be trying to relax and concentrate. There was little chance of that because by the time we got to Ilford, she had finished the story about Lylie and had started giving me instructions.

"Now you're looking very smart so don't be too shy," she said, in a voice that the packed carriage could hear! "Speak up for yourself and if they ask you questions, make sure you give them the right answer. He's going for interview to get a job in the Post Office," she told the man strap hanging above us who had just turned over his Daily Sketch and had caught her eye. "He's a bit quiet but he's got to learn to stand up for 'isself. Ain't he?"

The man agreed with a mumble and I wanted to crawl under the seat.

"Alright Mum," I whispered. "You don't have to tell the whole world our business."

"What's the matter with you?" she demanded even louder. "There you go again. It's nothing to be ashamed of just because you're going to get a job. Everyone has to get jobs. Half these people in this carriage had to go for interviews to get their jobs so what are you so worried about?"

I could sense everyone looking at me and thought it best to keep quiet as I lowered my face to check that my knees were still in the middle of my legs.

She took a break from her talking just after Manor Park. Only resuming as the train drew into Stratford Station.

"Now you could get off here and get the Central Line to Saint Pauls, 'cause that's the nearest station to where you're going. But as I say, it's better to stay with me as it's your first time. We'll get the twenty three bus at Liverpool Street. Then I can get off at the bottom of Cheapside and you can stay on 'till you get to Saint Pauls that'll suit you fine."

Now everyone knew where we were going. I wouldn't have been surprised if she had asked them all to come along with us.

"We'll soon be there now. Don't worry. You're not nervous, are you?"

"No Mum, I'm fine. Just don't keep going on about it," I quietly urged her through gritted teeth.

"You look a bit pale to me. Perhaps it's the getting up early. You're not used to it are you. Well not since we was down hopping."

"Mum, I'm O.K.," I insisted. "Just leave me in peace for a bit will ya?"

"Oh, that's nice, ain't it. I'm only trying to take your mind off things in case you're nervous."

"I'm not nervous. I just want you to shut up for a bit and let me think."

"Well sod you then," she said. She then clamped her mouth together, sat upright and coughed as she patted the carrier bag on her lap. Mercifully she stayed like that until the train slowed down and went into the sooty tunnels that led into Liverpool Street Station.

"If you don't mind me talking to you now," she said, oozing sarcasm. "I think we ought to start getting up to be ready to get off the train. If you get lost in the rush, I'll see you at the twenty three bus stop. Ask anyone. Or perhaps you can hang on to my coat tails like you did when you were a little boy. I suppose you think you are too grown up now. You think you're a man."

I didn't take the bait and we both stood up.

The carriage was by now jammed packed with workers who were standing nose to nose and nose to back of head. As the train jerked to a halt the whole mass moved as one towards the doors. Mum and I joined them and were almost carried out on to the platform. Once there we were forced to walk quickly towards the ticket barrier. A porter was standing there throwing his arms about in all directions as he tried to collect the tickets and check the season tickets that were being thrust towards him by the commuters.

Once through the barrier everyone went rushing past to get to their offices or their other connections. We went up a steep staircase that led out into Bishopsgate and crossed the road to the bus stop where there was a long queue. Here most of the men were in suits, bowler hats and carrying brief cases. The young girls were in grey raincoats with their tits sticking out sharply because their belts were pulled in too tight.

It being the rush hour, busses were arriving frequently and often together. Deep down inside I was finding it all rather exciting especially as Mum was too busy looking out for our bus to be nagging on about our private concerns.

"Here it comes, Johnny," she said, as if I hadn't seen it. "Here's a number eight. This'll do us. Now get ready to get on Son. Try to get downstairs as I haven't got too far to go. Be-low here we go."

Despite the press of the other passengers, we managed to get on and push our way inside the lower deck. We stood up for a couple stops before some seats became available as workers disembarked in Cornhill.

"Johnny, you take that seat down the front," Mum instructed. "Because you've got a bit of a way to go yet I'll sit by the door."

I moved down the bus and took the front seat, next to a woman who sitting behind the driver. I started to feel relieved and happy to get away from Mum. I did love her but why did she have to be so loud? I sat staring through the window at the people as we slowly moved through the early morning traffic. I relaxed.

"Johnny, don't you worry about the time," yelled my Mother down the bus. "It takes a bit of time to get through this lot then it'll speed up when we get past the Bank. If you feel like it, after you've done your test, come back to Lyons and I'll save you a nice bit of Spaghetti pie. That's if Lylie ain't kicked it all over the floor," she screamed with laughter. "D'ya wanna do that?"

I wanted to disappear. I pretended I wasn't with her. I stared resolutely out of the window. The woman on the inside seat near the window, nudged me.

"I think your Mother's talking to you," said the woman.

Mum saw this happen.

"It's alright dear," she shouted. "I know he can hear me. He's just a bit nervous. He's going to try for a job up the Post Office this morning and he'll have to take a few tests. It's only natural he'll be a bit languid. He's not used to getting up this early."

I couldn't believe it! She was telling the whole of the lower deck my business. I turned around to glare at her.

"Yes, alright Mum," I hissed, hoping to shut her up. "I'll come to see you after I've finished but only if I feel like it."

"Alright then darlin'," she called. "I'm getting off at the next stop. You do your test well and I'll see ya later. If you don't come to see me and you get home first, you or Jeanie get the chops on and do some greens with 'em. Oh yes, there's some potatoes in the carrier under the sink."

She was doing it! She was actually discussing our food in front of a bus load of office workers! Would we never get the to Cheapside so that I could be released from this humiliation?

"Alright Mum. Yes! Alright!" I glared.

A short lull in the conversation. Off she went again.

"Johnny, Johnny! I'm getting off now," she was like a racing commentator on the Home Service. "Speak up for yourself and If I don't see you at Lyons I'll see you at home. Mind how ya go Son. Tat-tar. Don't rush the test. I'm getting off now."

"Oh, for fuck sake go!" I thought to myself as she left the bus. Only to run along the kerb to the front of it to knock on the window and wave goodbye.

"Bye Darlin'. Good luck. Mummy loves ya! Johnny!"

I knew I couldn't avoid it. I would have to recognise her. I looked across the bus and smiled with tense teeth. Nodded my head and waved the fingers of my right hand in greeting as mercifully the bus pulled away. I settled into back into my seat. Hoping that the burning vermillion colour of my face, that I could see in the reflection behind the driver, would soon cool down and clear because I felt that everyone, in the whole of the City of London, was looking at me.

I had managed to calm down by the time I had got to Saint Paul's. I found my way to the Post Office I went through the big imposing door of the King Edward Building. The time on the large clock in the centre of the wall indicated that I was a quarter of an hour early.

At the information desk I told the receptionist that I had come to do an exam for a job and I was sent to wait on a leather backed chair over by the staircase. I sat there watching the scores of people coming and going. Those who knew what they were about went past the Statue of the King and up the wide staircase, others went to the receptionist who gave them directions but most of them went straight through the swing doors that led to a Post Office counter. It was a world completely different from what I was used to at the factory and bore absolutely no resemblance to school life whatsoever. Growing up was strange.

My interest perked up when a messenger boy came in and smiled as he went past me down the staircase. I paid particular attention to his navy-blue uniform that had red stripes down the leg of his trousers and a badge with a number on his label. He was wearing a peaked cap like those worn by an officer in a Jack Hawkins film and around his waist he wore a leather belt with a pouch attached to it.

I had been sitting there about ten minutes when a man came up the stairs and went to the receptionist, who pointed to me and he came over.

"Good morning John," he said and held out his hand for me to shake it.

"Good morning, Sir," I replied.

"My name is Alf Willis. I am the officer who is going to supervise your two tests this morning," he said. "Come downstairs and we'll go into the reception room. I don't like to call it the examination room because that makes it sound a bit too daunting."

He led me down the staircase. It was much less ornate once we had passed out of sight of the public and moved towards the lower ground floor. We walked along a wide passage with mysterious corridors leading off of it until we arrived to a plain brown wooden door.

"It's in here, John," he said as he opened the door and ushered me in.

I was expecting a huge room to match the size of those upstairs, but it was just a small space with two desks facing a bigger desk at the end of the back wall.

"This is where the dirty deed is to take place," Alf said. "There are two tests. The first one is an intelligence test and the other is general knowledge. They're not too difficult. When you have answered all the question, and do try to answer them all even if you have to guess, you then sign it and put the date the bottom of the page. Have you got your cards with you?"

I handed over the envelope containing my National Insurance cards.

"Thanks," he said. "Now if you sit at that desk with the Intelligence Test paper already on it you can begin. We give you half an hour for the completion of that. After which will be a short break and then you have another quarter of an hour for the General Knowledge. I'll be sitting here but I am not allowed to communicate with you except in emergencies. If you want to use the toilet you must do that between the tests. Is that all clear, John?"

I told him it was and we both sat down to begin the first test. There was a pen on my desk by the inkwell for me and a copy of the Daily Herald on his.

I had never seen, let alone done, an intelligence test before. So I was more than a bit bemused when I opened the paper and saw lots of shapes and drawings as part of the questions. I read a bit of the instructions and was confused by questions like which is the wrong shape and how many words are similar to the main one? What angles go in what multiple shapes and if you turn things round which would be the right way up for the dog in this picture to climb? Lots of stuff like that.

I must have wasted precious minutes in trying to figure out what the bloody hell it all meant before I realised that I would not be able to take it all in. So I decided to just do one question a time as it came and work it out as I went. The first was about the months of the year and then another about the alphabet so that gave me confidence. I started to tick the boxes. As the test progressed I realised that it was really just a question of working things out and not having to answer actual questions, which is what I had been expecting.

I hadn't quite reached the end of the test by the time Mr. Willis, told me to stop, sign and date the paper because the half hour was up.

"Bloody hell that went quick." I said as I signed, John Ross, added the date and handed it over. "Can I go to the toilet now?"

"Course you can, Lad." Said Alf. "While you're gone, I'll just look through this and put your National Insurance number on it. You go out of the door, turn left down the corridor and the Gents lays back in a small alcove."

I went out feeling glad of the break and a bit of exercise. I did what I had to do and returned to the room.

Mr. Willis was looking a bit disturbed.

"I'm sorry John but don't quite get what's going on here. What's happening with your name?"

'Oh, fucking hell,' I thought. 'I've ballsed up the signature.'

"On your cards your name is Michael Peter Ross and yet in your application forms and now on your intelligence test you have signed John Ross. Surely you know your own name? Don't you? I suppose you are Michael Ross? Or are there two of you?"

"No, well you see," I spluttered to explain. "I was fostered, and they didn't like the name Michael. Because my Nan thought it was too Irish and they had just lost a son called John, so they thought it would be a good idea to call me John and I have grown up thinking that my name was John and it was only when I started work that it came out that I was Michael Peter. So that's who I really am but sometimes I forget. I'm very sorry. Will I have to do the test again?"

I stood there like a gibbering idiot and feeling like a right pratt knowing that my head must look like a Belisha beacon with my ginger hair and blushing face.

Alf Willis was smiling. Not in a piss taking sort of way, but in a kindly way. As though I was someone who needed to be in a special care school.

"No son, you won't have to take the test again," he said. "Once you've done it you would know the answers. However, you will have to cross out the John Ross signature and sign it as Michael Peter Ross, in whatever way you like, as long as it is the name on your insurance cards. I'll countersign it and that should be alright for the examiners. Although I must say this is the first time in my experience that I have had a candidate for an intelligence test who didn't know his own name."

I rectified the paper and signed it M. P. Ross, so that I could get it over quickly. Which is how I sign to this day, although dear Alf Willis, who I never saw again, would never know that.

I did the General Knowledge Test soon after and was very particular about signing M. P. etc. as I handed the paper over to Alf,

"Thanks Michael," he said. "I call you by your proper name now, so you can get used to it. Although if you get the job and with that mop of hair I've no doubt that you'll be called 'Ginger,' by the other boys. Just between ourselves," he dropped his voice conspiratorially. "I've looked at your Intelligence Test and I shouldn't think you have anything to worry about at all. If you do as well in the General Knowledge, then I reckon you could go on to be Postmaster General in no time at all."

We did our good byes and I thanked him as he led me back to the reception area. I went out into the cold air of the City of London and found my way down Cheapside. As I was now feeling rather relaxed, I decided that I would go to visit Mum in Lyons. She was really pleased to see me and introduced me to Lylie who brought me a big piece of spaghetti pie and a cup of tea. Mum then went on to tell the staff and most of the customers all about my interview.

The following week, I received a letter from the G.P.O. which informed me that I had passed both tests and been accepted as a Telegraph Messenger. It instructed me to report to The King Edward Building on the following Monday morning, where I would be issued with my uniform and badge. Following that I would be taken to start my on the job training at Fenchurch Street Branch Office, which would be my permanent place of work. I would be expected to work a forty-eight-hour week, from Monday morning until Saturday lunchtime. I would also be allowed 'day release,' once a week to further my education. The letter gave me a phone number to call it if I wanted to accept the post.

I called them soon after I read the letter and took the job at two pounds, twelve shillings and sixpence a week. Plus luncheon vouchers.

31 A TELEGRAM BOY

On Monday morning I reported to the King Edward Building, or K.E.B. as it was known because everything was always an acronym in the P.O. This time I went to an office at the side in St. Martin's Le Grande, where a postman took me to the clothing store. I was instructed to take off my own clothes and put on a white shirt, navy blue trousers and jacket with red stripes on them plus a pair of socks and strong walking shoes. Lastly I was given a peaked cap and a leather purse that slipped on to a leather belt that buckled round my waist.

Even though the war had been five years ago, clothes and shoes were still in short supply so new clothes were a luxury that I hadn't been used to, in fact hardly ever. One of the luxuries I didn't appreciate was a big rubber cape that went over our uniforms in wet weather. They were made to accommodate all messenger boys, including those in areas where riding a bike was essential. In bad weather these capes blew around us like sails billowing above a pirate ship.

I was taken to sign the Official Secrets Act, three times. This was presumably so that if I sold the secrets of any telegram to the Russians, they could blindfold me in a corner and shoot me. Having thrice sworn to keep Britain safe and secure, I was issued with a pair of badges with my number, 14433 on them. One for the cap, the other for the lapel of my jacket. Fully kitted out and clutching the carrier bag containing my civvy clothes, I was led to a post office van and driven to Fenchurch Street Branch Office known as Fen. Street B.O. My workplace for the next three years.

The van came to a halt in London Street where the driver led me through the side door of the B.O. along a passage and into the Telegraph Room. Sitting behind his desk sat the Postman Supervisor of Messengers known as the P.S.M. Facing him was a glass partition where I could see machines with tubes coming out of them, filing cabinets, racks of bookshelves and trays of orange envelopes.

"Here you are Harry," said my driver. "Another one for the slaughter. I leave him in your very capable hands. Mind how you go Ginger and good luck."

As he left, the door in the glass partition opened and a fair headed boy, with rolled up shirt sleeves, came out carrying a hand full of telegram envelopes.

"All yours Mr. Cave," he said as he handed them to the P.S.M. and returned quickly into his room.

Mr. Cave turned to me and indicated a bench along the wall beside him.

"Sit there a minute Lad," he said. "I'll just get these dispatched."

I sat down and put my carrier bag between my legs. My new uniform was feeling stiff against my body and I was feeling excited by the new situation I found myself in. I knew already that being a telegram boy for the Post Office was going to be very different from being a trainee cutter for Nossek and Nathan.

Four messengers who were sitting on benches reading the daily paper's and comics, looked over at me but said nothing. The P.S.M. sorted the telegrams by putting them into one or other of the twelve partitions in a rack in front of him. On the backs of the partitions were lists of the streets around the Fenchurch Street area that made up 'a walk.' A messenger would deliver the telegrams to the offices in those streets. While Mr. Cave was sorting the envelopes two of the boy's got up and took their hats and belts from pegs on the wall. By the time they were ready the P.S.M. had finished sorting and was logging the telegrams into a ledger. He looked up and across at a scruffy looking boy who was still sitting reading,

"You too Hawkins," he said, while he continued to write. "You're next, aren't you?"

"Yes, you're right, Mr. Cave Sir," said Hawkins, as he put his comic down and got ready to go out. "I was gonna get up anyway."

"Of course you were, you lazy little git. I could see that from here," Cave replied.

The P.S.M. handed a few telegrams to each of the other boys and just one to Hawkins. They stared at me but still didn't say anything as they bantered among themselves and left the room to do their deliveries.

Once the boys had left the room, Mr. Cave opened a drawer in his desk and turned his attention to me.

"So you're Michael Ross and you have just been kitted out up at K.E.B. is that right?"

"Yes sir," I replied, with a slight smile.

"I am Mr. Cave as far as you are concerned," he continued. "My first name is Harry and due to the moustache I have on my upper lip, I am known to the boys as 'Hairy Harry.' I would prefer not to hear that name mentioned in my presence after to-day. If I do hear it, then the boy that utters it will be given a few days of 'late's' which tends to shut him up in no uncertain terms. For the duration of your first week, you will be taken around the various walks with one of our senior lads who will show you the ropes. Downstairs we have our own canteen. In there, should you so desire it, you may purchase a lunch for four pence half-penny. I'll get someone to show you how to go about that pretty soon. That room facing us is the Tube Room and this door, to the left of my desk. leads to the despatch room and from thence you enter the rear of Post Office counter."

"Is that the Post Office Counter we passed when we pulled up outside?" I asked.

"The very same," said Cave. " You do NOT! I repeat NOT, go through that door unless you are specifically ordered to do so by your P.S.M. That is to say myself or my opposite number Mr. Frederick Lambert. Or indeed any other Officer who is deputising for either of us due to leave of absence or illness. Where don't you ever go to Michael Ross?"

"Through that door to the counter Sir."

"Correct young Ross. You learn quick. I like a quick learner."

A tall, dark haired, messenger came in through the passage door.

"I'm back Mr. Cave," he said, as he hung his hat on one of the pegs and took off his belt.

"Yes, Williams I can see that," said Mr. Cave. "But kindly shut up your cake hold because, as you can see, I am in conference with Mr. Ross here. Mr. Ross has seen fit to join us in our endeavours to keep the City of London moving in the deliverance of the telegraphed message. As I was saying Mr. Ross."

"Sorry Sir," said Williams and sat down opposite me and smiled in a confiding way.

"Quiet!" Cave barked at him before turning back to me. "Mr. Ross, to continue. Your duties will be delivering telegrams on all of the various walks in the Fenchurch Street area. Of which there are twelve that is to say, an exact dozen. These deliveries will occur as and when myself or Mr. Lambert feel that it is time that the mail needs delivering. When you are not out on a walk, you will wait here in the Messenger Room unless you are on a break. If you are on a break, you will wait downstairs in the comfort of the Boys

Room. There you may laze around and play with yourself to your heart's content, until it is time to return up here to resume your duties."

"The bogs are down there too, aren't they Mr. Cave?" Said Williams with a wicked glint in his eye.

Mr. Cave got up from his desk. Crossed in front of me and stood facing Williams while the other messenger, who had been taking no interest in our conversation, looked up with sudden awareness.

"Take my place Mr. Williams," said Cave. Waving his arm in a flamboyant gesture. "The desk is all yours. You obviously feel that you are in a better position than I, to instruct Mr. Ross as to the ways and intricacies of the General Post Office. I therefore relinquish my position and allow you to take over my seat."

"No. That's alright sir," said Williams. "You seem to be coping very well on your own. Please you carry on."

"And how right you are, you ignorant little git," said Mr. Cave, sarcasm dripping from his mouth, as he resumed his seat. Saying as he did so. "And seeing that you deem to know so much about the layout of the toilets and obviously wish to impart you extensive knowledge to our newest recruit, perhaps you will condescend to be Mr. Michael Ross's partner in his instruction for this week."

"I would be truly honoured, Sir, "said the messenger.

"Excellent Williams," said Mr. Cave, as he took a locker key from his desk drawer and handed it to me, "In which case, piss off downstairs the both of you. You can give Mr. Ross his locker and show him the ropes while you make him a cup of tea. I've got work to do."

The boy from the Tube Room had come out carrying a big wad of telegrams, which he handed to Cave, who began sorting them as Williams and I were leaving the room.

"Be back here in fifteen minutes," Cave called after us. "Take him round to Rene and get a dinner sorted out for him. If he wants one."

Three messengers came up the stairs, pushing and shoving each other as they returned to work.

"My name is Sidney Williams, but they call me Willy here," said Williams, as he led me back along the passage and down the stone staircase into the basement. "Don't worry too much about Hairy Harry, his bark is all bark and no bite. He's a good bloke under all that showing off with his language. These are the locker racks. They're not just for us but for the counter clerks and the cleaners as well."

I put my carrier bag into my locker and we walked towards a room at the end of a short corridor.

"This is the Boys Room," said Willy as we entered. "When we're not on duty we can come down here to relax. There are some games and a pack of cards. The sink's over there, as you can see, and we can make tea on that gas ring. That door is the P.S.M.'s room. It's locked at the moment because

Harry's on duty and Fred Lambert isn't in yet. I'll put the kettle on and then I'll show you the rest of what goes on down here. You can take your hat off now, it's allowed."

He filled the kettle at the sink as I removed my hat and stood watching him.

"Will you want to have your dinner in here to-day?" said Willy turning around. "Fuck me, you ARE a ginger bonce ain't ya?"

"I ain't though about eating so I don't know." I said. "Where else is there?"

"Well there's a few good café's around, especially the one in Billingsgate, but it's much cheaper here. It's only four pence halfpenny and Rene the cook, does s very good meal. Tell ya what, while we're waiting for the kettle, I'll take you round to her and book you in for a dinner. I'm staying in today, so we can have it together."

We left the boys room and went back down the passage and into a kitchen at the end. Off to the left of this was a small dining room with three tables in it.

"Rene, can we come in?" Willy called out.

"Course you can Luv," Answered a woman's voice with a slight northern accent. "What are you after?"

"I'm not after anything," said Willy. "This is a new boy, Mr. Ross."

"Michael," I interrupted him, remembering to use my proper name.

"Hello Michael Luv," said Rene, drying her hands on a white tea towel with G.P.O. stamped in red on it. "What gorgeous coloured hair. I've never seen anyone with such a colour. Most women would kill to have a head of hair that colour. Will you be wanting a dinner to-day dear?"

"Yes please," I said. "Who do I have to pay?"

"Well normally you pay in advance and book in at the end of the week for the following week. But as it's your first day or rather your first week you can settle up on Friday when you decide what you want to do about next week. Will that suit ya Duck?"

I said that it would suit me.

"Right then. Frankie, we'll need a couple more taters," said Rene.

A boy emerged from a passage down the side of a large store cupboard. He was holding out a large potato in his hand.

"I am already on to it cook," said Frankie.

"This is Frankie Simmons," said Willy. "He is Cook's Boy. Which means that he comes in early every day to help Rene prepare the dinners. When he's finished doing that he comes up do his proper job."

"And very helpful he is too." Said Rene. "I don't only have you boys to cook for Michael. I also cater for the counter staff and the cleaners and one or two postmen who just drop bye for the grub."

"So you are gonna 'ave one of our delicious dinner are you Ginger?" said Frankie. "I'll do it specially for you."

I looked away from Rene in her green cross-over apron and focussed on Frankie Simmons.

He was a good-looking boy about my height but perhaps a couple of years older. He had thick dark brown hair and deep blue eyes with pale skin and a red mouth. He was wearing his shirt, undone at the collar, with no tie and tucked loosely into his messenger trousers. I took all this in as he looked straight at me with a flirty openness that was quite disturbing.

"Yeah, I will have a dinner thank you very much," I said. My voice sounding rather unsteady. I didn't know why.

"It's beef stew and boiled potatoes with suet pudding and custard for your afters," said Rene. "Now off you go the pair of you, we've got work to do. Frankie have ya cut up those carrots yet?"

"I'm just getting on to it cook. Don't you worry about that. See ya later Ginger." Frankie said with a wink as Willy and I turned to leave. When we got to the door I looked back at him and smiled.

Willy and I left the kitchen and, he pointed out the functions of the rooms we passed along the corridor.

"By the way." Willy said, on our way back to the Boys Room. "Don't be upset by Frankie he is a bit camp but he's alright. They say he's Fred Lambert's bum boy, but everyone says that about everyone else. He's leaving soon be to become a postman before he goes to do his national service in the army."

I didn't know what 'camp' meant, so I assumed it would be something to do with Frankie going to do his national service under canvas.

When we returned to our room there were two other messengers in there. Willy introduced me as 'Ginger' and them as Terry and Dave. They were both older than me and brim full of confidence. Willy made the tea and the four of us sat drinking and them doing most of the talking like boys do. Using a lot of swear words without saying very much. We sat until a buzzer sounded in the corner of the room and Willy got up from the table.

"I reckon that's for us," he said. "Hairy must be thinking it's time to get some work done. Come on Ginger lets get up there. Don't forget your cap."

We went upstairs to the office where Mr. Cave welcomed us with open arms.

"How kind you are to honour us with your presence," he said. "Welcome back. Both the new boy and his mate. Did you think you were having the rest of the day to sit about looking at the pictures of Jane with her tits out? I don't think so. The work is coming in thick and fast. Therefore, I think it is about time for Mr. Ross to experience the joys and the smells of the E.C.2. area. That we all know and love so much."

"I've shown him the kitchen and he's put his name down for dinner," Willy informed our supervisor.

"I have very little interest in your social life below stairs Williams. Please don your hat and your belt and instruct Mr. Ross in the intricacies of the 'Crutched Friars Walk', as you endeavour to deliver these messages. And please Mr. Williams, do make an effort to distribute them to the correct addresses for once."

Harry put five telegrams on the desk. I moved over to pick them up as Willy got his hat from the hook.

"I see no reason, Mr. Ross," said Cave. "Why you think you ought to take these telegrams before your instructor has had a chance of telling you how to lay them in. Do you, perchance, know how to lay in a walk?"

"No sir, I don't," I replied, having a vision of myself lying in the gutter while office workers walked over me: yet instinctively knowing that that wasn't what he meant.

"Mr. Williams," he said. "For the edification of Mr. Michael Ross and for the entertainment of myself and your four fellow skivers lying around this room, would you perchance, explain to our new recruit how you would lay in a walk?"

The boy from the Tube Room came out with more work.

"And," said Mr. Cave, pointing in the direction of the boy. "Our esteemed colleague Mr. Arnold James the Tube Boy will, I insist, stay here to study the benefit of your expertise. Pray proceed Mr. Williams."

"Certainly Sir, I will in your own inimitable style," said Willy with a flourish of his hat and suiting his actions to his words. "I take the telegrams to be delivered and peruse the address on each one. Then with my knowledge of the walk gained from previous experience, I lay one behind the other in the order that I think will be the most efficient way of delivering them at the offices to which they are addressed. Hence the tern 'laying in.' I then leave the room to complete the delivery."

Willy bowed, and the other boys gave him some mock applause and whistles.

"Thank you for that Mr. Williams," said the P.S.M. "I assume that Mr. Ross is now fully aware of the work involved in laying in. So get your arses out of here, the both of you."

Arnold went back to his tubes as we left the office amid cat calls and laughter from the others waiting to go on delivery.

Willy walked me round to the various offices on the walk, explaining that later part of the morning was often the busiest time of the day, because the city had woken up and trading had begun. He showed me a choice of short cuts through the many alley ways and when went into the foyers of big office blocks he taught me where to look on the address boards for the particular firm we had a telegram for. After that it was a short walk up the stairs or taking the lift to the relevant office.

Once there we would go to the reception desk with a quick 'Hello" to the girl, it was always a girl, give her the envelope and leave. We didn't to wait for any replies, nor did the girl receiving the telegram look worried or shocked.

The telegram boys who did the domestic work mainly delivered telegrams that contained bad news. Us City messengers got very few of those. Neither did we get many 'Greetings Telegrams.'

The delivery took us about a quarter of an hour and on our way round we passed other boys on their walks around the delivery area. Even on this, my very first trip, I found I enjoyed the freedom and fresh air as well as the feeling of being my own boss. Willy was a good instructor and very chatty about the city as well as the other boys. By the time we arrived back at the office I had begun to feel much more relaxed. We did two more trips until just after half past twelve when we were given our dinner break.

We collected our food from Rene and carried it along the passage to eat in the boys' room. We were not allowed to sit with the grown-up workers because that they thought the boys were too rowdy and vulgar. This suited the boys very much since they could be as vulgar and rowdy as they liked in the comfort of their own area. Dirty jokes were the order of the day as far as conversation went along with jokes and taking the piss out of each other. Everything from looks, clothes, sexuality, and sport, to health and education was fair game to be sent up by the boys. I've found that this is usual when men are thrown together in an exclusive masculine environment and I reckon it's because it saves us from the embarrassment of having to converse about serious things like personal problems and real feelings. However, I could be wrong.

Over our dinner, which was very good, I got to know a few more of the lads. They came from all over London each with a pride in their own area and their football team. I was much prouder of coming from Stepney than I was of Harold Hill, which was still an alien space as far as I was concerned and as I had no interest in sport at all, I kept quiet. Most of the lads seemed to get on with each other even though there was a bit of friction between a couple of them. But it never got really nasty. Not like it had in the factory where many a time it had exploded from vicious threats into stand-up fights. In the B.O. the aggression was just youthful posturing that flared up and just as soon cooled down again.

While we were eating our pudding, the door was flung open and a man, with a balding head and wearing an overcoat, burst into the room.

"What are you lazy lot doing down here," said the man, "Don't you know the King has urgent telegrams waiting to be delivered. The G.P.O. has got to keep this country moving forward and you lot are just laying about playing with yourselves when you should be upstairs doing your duty. And look at the mess in this room! You live like the sluts of Babylon. Charlie Hawkins, get your arse away from my door. I want to get into my office."

"Sorry Mr. Lambert, Sir," said Charlie. "I would never had been in your way if I had known that you were coming in so suddenly. I would have made sure that your pathway was completely clear of any obstructions."

"Don't' take the piss," said Lambert. "I know where your sister does her whoring so keep your moth shut or I'll report her to the law."

"You only know that sir, because your sister has the pitch next door."

"Very true Charlie, but remember my sister only deals in silver, not like the farthings and half pennies your sister charges."

We all laughed as he unlocked the door and went into the small room, known as the P.S.M.'s hole.

"And who is that carroty headed little sod sitting there all quiet?" Mr. Lambert asked, as he put his bag down in the room.

I wasn't even aware that he had noticed me.

"He's the new boy, just started this morning," said Willy. "I'm looking after him."

Lambert had taken off his top coat and hung it behind the door. He now stood in the doorway staring out at me.

"What's your name Lad?" he asked.

"Michael Ross," I said as the boys watched, hoping for an opportunity to come in with some witty remark.

"But we are calling him Ginger," said Willy.

"How very original. Especially as he is almost rust coloured and blushing to the roots of his ginger head," said Lambert. "I'm Mr. Fred Lambert, and despite the rumours I am happily married and not at all interested in your or any other boy's arses."

"But you are a Scoutmaster," said Charlie. "And we all know what they get up to in their tents."

"Like we all know that you spend most of your time off duty sitting in the bog pulling on your pudding," Fred said. "Don't be a wanker all your life Hawkins, give you cock a day off now and again."

"Only if you promise not to......." Charlie was interrupted.

"I wouldn't push it too far if I were you young fella-me-lad," said the P.S.M. "And changing the subject, has this new boy been told how to clean his red stripes yet? Have you lad?"

"No, sir," I replied. Thinking to myself that I didn't think we would have to clean the red stripes that ran down our trouser legs and across our jackets.

"Sidney Williams, what have you been a doin' with this lad," demanded Lambert. "Surely you know that the most important first lesson is to learn how to keep the red stripes on the new uniform bright and glowing?"

"We have been very busy, sir," said Willy. "Mr. Cave has kept us at it all the morning."

"Please don't flood my brain with your whining," said Lambert. Then turning to me he said. "Mr. Ross, if you want to continue to look as smart in your uniform as you do today, I suggest you mke a trip to the local ironmonger's shop. Tell him where it is Arnold James."

"You will find it just across the road," said the boy from the Tube Room. "It's behind this office, next to Fenchurch Street Station."

"Go in there," said Lambert. "And ask the man behind the counter, what is his name Charlie Hawkins?"

"Reggie Turner," was Charlie's immediate reply.

"Thank you for that information," said Lambert. "Now then Michael Ross, or Ginger as they call you. You are to go to this Mr. Turner and tell him you have been sent for a small bottle of Post Office Dragon's Blood and he is to put the charge for it onto the Post Office account."

"Yes Sir," I said, getting up to get my hat and belt.

"Shall I go with him Sir? Said Willy.

"I see no reason why you should, unless the pair of you are joined at the scrotum," Mr. Lambert replied.

I smiled at Willy and left the room. I made my way out of the building and turned left towards the station.

Turner's Ironmongers, was in a row of shops along the short road called Fenchurch Place. I pushed open the door and a bell rang. Mr. Turner, short, shiny and completely bald was standing behind his counter.

"What do you want?' he said sharply as though he was expecting the worst.

"I would like a quarter bottle of Post Office Dragon's Blood and please Sir could you put the charge on the Post Office Account," I asked politely.

"What the bleeding hell do you lot take me for!" Turner exploded. "They do this every-tine there's a new boy. Do you all think I have nothing better to do with my time than listen to stupid remarks like this. Don't you know that dragon's have been extinct for hundreds of years you stupid git? Do you think I have saved their blood just so that you and your soddin' mates can clean your silly red stripes? Just get out of my shop and don't come back until you want something that makes sense. And don't let those tykes take the piss out of you anymore. Grow Up!"

The doorbell clanged in my ears as I quickly left the shop. As I turned out of the doorway to return to the office, I was met by six of the lads all doubled up with laughter. They had been looking through the window. Their laughter was so infectious I just had to laugh myself.

"You rotten Bastards," I said, "You all wait 'till I know what I'm bloody doing! I'll get you all back for that. And that Mr. Fucking Fred Lambert."

"Never mind," said Willy. "We've all had it done to us on our first day so don't take it personally. I must say old Fred really did set it up for you splendidly. Even I was taken in for a minute or two."

It seemed that I had passed some sort of initiation test because on my return there was a different atmosphere towards me.

Willy and I spent the rest of the afternoon going out of various walks and I slowly began to feel more confident. Towards the end of my session he even let me lay in a few telegrams and I didn't make that many mistakes. Well, just a few on the walks that I had done already.

At about half past three Mr. Lambert, who was now on duty, told me that as I had been on duty all day I could go home and that I was to report in again at nine o/clock tomorrow morning. I didn't need telling twice. I was down the stairs getting my own clothes from my locker and out of that building as quickly as though I was back in the factory. It sure felt like a really great job. Even more important, it meant that I would be earning enough money to be able to buy everyone presents for Christmas.

I almost ran towards Liverpool Street Station via Aldgate and Houndsditch having picked up the way during the day. I was in a rush to get home and tell everyone all about my new trade.

When I arrived home, it was back to normal. Jeanie needed help with the kids and I had to get the dinner ready. I hung my civvy clothes up and kept my uniform on so that I could show it off when Mum and Dad got home but they were so knackered after their own days work there was only minimal interest in me. Eventually, after we had all finished our meal, I got my new cap from the hall and using it as if it was a top hat and I was Fred Astaire, I sang 'My Old Man said Follow the Van.' That got their attention and a small round of applause. Mum said that I looked very smart in my working clothes and Dad gave a non-committal grunt.By the end of my first week it had been decided that Mum would stay on at Lyons and because Jeanie would not be able to stay off school forever, Joanie would be looked after by Mrs. Rayner, who lived across the road and had a daughter Patsy, of the same age. On the days that Mrs. Rayner couldn't look after her, I would take her to Nanny's on my way to work and bring her home with me after I had finished.

Back at the B.O. I learned to get on well with most of the other lads and I was surprised to discover that none of them had as many sisters as I had and not one of them was an orphan. By the end of the week I was out doing the 'Walks' on my own.

I really liked our district. It covered the area between, Bevis Marks to Great Tower Street and from Gracechurch Street to the Minories. It didn't look big on the map, but it was in terms of the numbers of offices in the buildings spread around. I had quickly got to know all the short cuts around the streets. Streets that had great old London names like Crutched Friars, Seething Lane and Pepys Street. I loved the fact that I was walking around places that had been there for centuries. Even the buildings were very old and had lifts that had rickety gates that were a positive danger to be using. There was one place in Billiter Street, that had a lift that I had to pull up myself by heaving on to a thick greasy rope. Don't ask how it worked and don't even think about Health and

Safety! It was very different in the modern buildings that had been built in the Thirties. These had lots of shiny tiles and polished glass. Cunard House, in Leadenhall Street, was one I loved. There the lifts were chrome with doors that shut on their own and would speedily whisk me to the brightly lit, carpeted reception areas on the 9th and 10th floor. Whatever the building, I would flirt with the girls behind the desks.

I enjoyed the work and soon got to know most of the people in the offices I delivered to. Although when it was foggy, cold or pissing with rain it wasn't all that much fun battling around the city streets especially when the wind was coming of the Thames and whipping around the narrow byways and squares.

One of the really good things the Post Office did for us boys, was to encourage us to pursue or education by giving us what was known as 'day release.' I opted to go to City Day College, which was situated somewhere near Moorefield's Eye Hospital. I signed up to study among other things, English Language and French. This meant that I could study plays in the English classes and an accent from Mme. Poultrice our French teacher. She was a real Frenchwoman who was built quite large. She had a mass of grey hair piled up on top like Queen Marie Antoinette without the curls. Her clothes were variations of pale blue two-piece suits and white blouses with frills around the collar and cuffs. She also had a great sense of humour which was emphasised by her thick French accent and the little French I still have I can trace back to her. That college also helped me to get an appreciation of Shakespeare and literature, not that there was much time for reading away from the classroom, but it was a beginning.

A really excellent thing was the Luncheon Vouchers that helped pay towards our food. These were on printed paper to the value of a shilling, which had increased to one and six pence by the time I left. Most days I stayed in the office and had a dinner from Rene because it was cheaper than going out. This also meant that I could sell my vouchers for extra money to take home.

I occasionally went to the café in Monument Street, known as 'Stan's.' A lot of us boys went. It was run by Stan the counter man. He was Greek, and did lots of continental dishes as well as the usual English. His place was heavily patronised by the Billingsgate fish porters, which meant that although the food was cheap it was good. If it wasn't up to scratch the men would create a big fuss and a few of them would throw it back across the counter. Stains of food from all countries could be seen on the wall behind the till. It was at Stan's that I first tasted real spaghetti.

Chalked up on the Menu was Spaghetti Bolognaise. I was expecting Heinz spaghetti, like we had on toast at home, smothered in their familiar tomato sauce. I was completely startled and confused when I collected it from the counter. The stuff that lay on my plate was a white stringy mound covered in mince with lots of stuff mixed in with it! I didn't like to make a fuss neither did I know what to do with it. When I got to my table in desperation I just copied Willy. He wound the long stringing bits round his fork and used his big spoon to add the mince. I did all this only to be disappointed when I found that it tasted like wet wool and not at all like the soft strong tomato taste I was expecting. I didn't like it and only ate about a third of it before deciding that enough was enough. I was particularly surprised that not one of the porters had thrown it back at Stan.

By the time Christmas arrived I was a fully-fledged messenger boy and although most of my wages went to Mum, it was grand to have a few shillings in my pocket to call my own. I took Jeanie with me when I went to Romford Market to buy presents for the little one's and something for Mum and Dad.

It wasn't much of a Christmas, but it was better than we were expecting, after all, we were better off than we had been when we moved in a year ago. Mum still hankered after the East End, but the girls had made friends and with three of us working we managed to afford a large chicken which, stuffed with a bit of sage and onion tasted wonderful. And there was a tinned syrup pudding for afters.

Nineteen fifty-two came in with a big frost which made Mrs. Rayner ill, so I had to take Joanie to Nanny's everyday and then collect her after work. She was a good kid but because she was up at seven in the morning, by the time we came home in the evening she would be dead tired. No matter how I nagged and moaned at her, I would have to carry her most of the way home, with her fair hair blowing in my face as she nestled into my neck. The really annoying thing was that as soon as she got indoors she would be full of energy and start to play with Chrissie or Beryl. Crafty little cow.

32 LIVING IN HISTORY

It was on 6th February, a Wednesday just after nine o'clock, that I came out of the office with my pouch full of telegrams for the shipping firms in Plantation House and saw in big black letters on the news-stands - **"THE KING IS DEAD!"**

It was a big shock. I stood looking at the white sheet of paper, behind the criss-cross wire that was holding it in, for about half a minute until I came to my senses and realised that I had work to deliver. I walked up the street towards Aldgate with the realisation that I was actually living in history. This wasn't a film about a fictitious king dying or being killed in the crusades; this was our King George and he had actually died. When I got to my first delivery address I asked the girl behind the desk if she had heard the news about the King? She hadn't, so I told her and within seconds it was all over the firm with everyone looking stunned. On the way back to the office I bought the Daily Herald and quickly read that: King George the sixth had passed peacefully away in his sleep during the night.

In the delivery room all the lads were reading bits out of the various newspapers they had bought. It turned out that the King was alright when he said goodbye to Princess Elizabeth when she went to Africa. I knew about that because I'd seen it on the Pathé News at the Odeon. He was o.k. on the Tuesday night when he went to bed and then he had just died in his sleep. The news had not been released until the Princess could be told first. Now we were going to have a Queen. Queen Elizabeth the second. It felt really strange to think that we would have to say 'God Save The Queen' instead of 'God Save The King!' The papers said that Her Majesty had been informed while she was living in a tree house in Kenya and would be flying back immediately with her consort Prince Philip. She was only twenty-five. Just ten years older than me.

I was on an early shift, so when I got home that afternoon, I quickly turned on the light programme where there was lots of talk about the King and they only played classical music. Everyone was saying what a good man he had been and how he would be missed, and I agreed.

On Friday the new Queen got home from Kenya. When she got off of the jet plane, she was met by Mr. Churchill and some other blokes who all knelt on the tarmac to greet her. There were loads of photos in the papers showing her arriving. Also, hundreds dealing with what had happened during the Kings reign and lots of speculation about a New Elizabethan Age.

The King was to lie in state allowing us to go and say goodbye if we wanted to. As it worked out, so many people turned up they had to keep the chapel open till the early hours of the morning and despite this they still has to turn people away.

NO EXPECTATIONS

The funeral took place on the following Friday. There was a very dramatic picture of the three Queens. Queen Mary the Mother, Queen Elizabeth the Wife and our new Queen Elizabeth the Daughter. They were all veiled and draped in black on the steps of St George's Chapel in Windsor. I listened to the funeral service on the radio, but I don't remember whether we had been given the day off or not.

While all these things were happening to the country my own life continued much the same as usual. It was a case of going to work, sometimes going to Nanny's to pick up Joanie getting home, sorting out the kids before Mum and Dad came home and doing what was necessary around the house before going to bed. There were occasional trips to the cinema's in Romford. There was the Odeon, the A.B.C. and on rare occasions the Flea Pit in the Market. I would still go to the East End at the weekend usually staying with Alice and Ernie. As the weather got warmer, friends and relations came to see us and to have a nose round to see what we hadn't got.

Katrina came down but only the once on a Saturday afternoon in August. The Olympics were being broadcast and everyone was talking about Emil Zatopek. After we had our dinner, Dad took Mum and the girls on a trip to Southend. I took Kat out for a walk over the fields just before they left. After walking for a while we managed to get to lying in a haystack near Gallows Corner where we got very sexy. We went back to my empty house and started to make love in the kitchen, where things began to get really passionate. In the heat of the moment pushed her backwards over the electric cooker with myself on top. It was all going marvellously until, what I thought were moans of pleasure, turned out to be grunts of pain. Someone had left the grill on a low heat and Kat's back was burning. It had taken me so long to realise what was happening that she had got slightly scorched. The moment was ruined. I did apologise and explained it was an accident. She immediately decided that she ought to go home. At the green line stop, when I put my arms around her to kiss her goodbye, she jumped with pain because she was still sore. She pushed me away and told me to piss off. It proved to be the end of our relationship and I never saw her again.

Strangely I never really missed her because I still had Betty and not long after that I met Cathy, while I was on holiday at Ploggs Hall farm and we fell in love. The fly in the ointment was that Nanny didn't approve of her and kept trying to warn me off of her because she was a Roman Catholic. But I persevered because the Gemini in me was always urging me to have two girlfriends at the same time.

At work I had now been there long enough to be allowed to go on Express Deliveries. This meant being given a packet that was handed over the Post Office counter and had to be delivered by hand that day. Usually it was somewhere outside of our area. As an express delivery boy, I got to travel around London on the underground to out of the way places like, Chiswick or Brixton, which meant that I got my fare paid and gradually learned the tube map by heart. To be quite frank about it that wasn't all I learnt.

It was while I was on a delivery to somewhere in Knightsbridge that I was groped by a bloke on the Piccadilly Line. This came as quite a shock to me because it was during the latter part of the morning rush hour and was the last thing I was expecting. Needless to say I didn't follow it through. I just gave a surprised, quiet squeak and moved away through the crowd without looking back at the groper. As I did more of this work and early morning travel, I was surprised to find that there was quite a lot of sexual activity happening on the tube. For instance, one morning while I was delivering a small packet to the Elephant and Castle, on the Northern Line, it got so crowded that I found myself pressed up against the glass behind a double seat area. I happened to glance down and was astonished to see a young girl giving some bloke a hand job behind the Daily Mail. He was in a suit and bowler, holding the paper up as though he was having a quiet read, while she did the business underneath! It was a good way to conceal their activity from the rest of the train but from my vantage point, behind them, it was a bit too much of an eyeful. Especially as it was only half past nine in the morning!

I was so surprised and embarrassed I had to turn away. Only to find my face almost in a large woman's breasts who quickly swung them out of my way. I couldn't wait to get back to the office to tell the lad's all about that! Sex, in all it's forms, being the main topic of conversation during our breaks.

"The trouble with you lazy tykes," Mr. Lambert constantly told us. "Is that you've all got a one-track mind - a filthy dirt track. You'll all be blind by the time you reach thirty."

I liked Fred Lambert who, when he found out that I came from a large family, had taken a particular interest in me. He knew we were a bit desperate for money and one Friday evening he took me to his church hall so that I could check out the jumble sale stuff before it went on sale to the public. I bought a few toys for the kids and an imitation fur coat for

Mum, which cost me half a crown. I gave it to her with a promise that one day I'd buy her a real mink. A few weeks after that, Fred, he said I could call him Fred when away from the office, told me that they had got hold of lots of second hand children's books and if I would like to take some home I could have them for nothing. I returned to the hall to have a look and while I was going through them I got a brilliant idea that we could loan them out, around the estate, to make a bit of money. I suggested this to Fred and he said that he would be grateful if I would take them all off his hands.

I broached the idea to Mum that night and she thought it was a good one. Between us we managed to persuade Dad to drive to Bermondsey with me and returned home with over a hundred books.

Determined to start up a library I got very business like with my John Bull printing set and the use of a stencilling machine at work. I made enough tickets and return date sheets for the girls to stick in each book. After lots of arguments we decided to call it the 'Long Pencil Library' after a very long, yellow pencil that I had bought in Woolworth's. By the next weekend the L.P.L. was officially launched.

Helped by Jeanie, Beryl and sometimes Mum, we loaded as many of the books that could be squeezed onto our old pram and wheeled them around the streets knocking on doors to drum up some customers. It was a difficult job getting started but with hard work and determination, coupled with desperation, we managed to get over seventy families to borrow them paying three-pence a week. With the four of us sharing the delivery and collections we soon got a nice little earner going. It didn't bring in a lot of money just enough for

NO EXPECTATIONS

a few pairs of socks and knickers for the girls and some stuff for me. Our overheads were nothing, so it was all profit.

The business progressed excellently during the summer with Mum reaping most of the profits. When the weather turned colder, and winter came in friction began to occur in the work force. There were many rows and arguments when nobody wanted to go out on the rounds in the rain, the cold or the fog. Apathy reared its ugly head. Eventually the L.P.L. was abandoned and the customers that still had them, kept their borrowed books. The rest of the non-loaned stock hung around the house for months.

I had been at Fen. Street B.O. almost a year when, due to some of the boys leaving to do National Service and others wanting to change jobs, Fred and Harry decided that I should be given the job of Tube Boy. A job that was considered a definite, if unpaid, promotion and carried a lot of prestige. It had nothing whatever to do with the underground railway system. It was the G.P.O. system for passing telegrams under the city of London in canisters through a network of pipelines.

In the tube room the most impressive things were the two large tube Capsules that were part of the Pipeline. There was a green one for incoming telegrams and a red one for the outgoing ones. They were rather like a space capsule contraption. There is nothing like it nowadays and not a lot of people knew about it even then.

The Capsules were made of solid steel with a tube, wide enough to take a can of baked beans, coming up out of the floor going into the Capsule at one end, out the other side back and down into the floor. The contraption had two handles acting as gates at either end to seal off the frantic high-speed air that was blowing the telegram canisters, at great velocity, beneath the streets of the streets. In the centre of each capsule was a viewing window which enabled Tube Boy, to check the colour of the canister being held against the out gate. If it was blue, our office colour, the capsule would be sealed by closing off the air with the incoming handle. It was then safe to pull open the capsule and remove it. If it wasn't for us the outgoing gate would be opened to blow it on towards Aldgate. B.O. One canister could contain up to a dozen telegrams, which would be date stamped and put in envelopes before delivery to the P.S.M.

When there were telegrams handed in over our Post Office counter, I would be alerted by a buzzer for me to collect them. I would enter them into a manual, put them into a blue canister and send forward in the red despatch capsule to a Telegraph Officer somewhere down the line I never knew where. He would stick ticker tape the words on to a sheet and forward them all over the country. If they were for London, then they would be despatched via the tube network to the various offices around the City. All in all it would take less than an hour for a telegram to be delivered from counter to any office in the Kingdom. The London system continued in use until the early sixties.

Being the Tube Boy was a very responsible job and I was determined to do my best. It also meant that I would be working indoors most of the time and not have to go out in all weathers, an added bonus with Winter fast approaching.

NO EXPECTATIONS

It was early in December nineteen fifty-two when the 'Great Smog' occurred.

I had taken Rosie to the Troxy on Wednesday night and had stayed in the spare bed at Aunt Alice's in the Tait Street overnight. It was quite early on Thursday morning when Uncle Ernie shook me awake to go to work.

"Come on Johnny," he said. "You'd better get a move on. There's a lot of fog about. It looks like it's surrounding the whole of Stepney."

I had a quick wash under the cold tap in the kitchen and left the house after a hurried cup of tea. Outside the fog was yellow and thick, like walking around in a filthy bridal veil. The fact that it was still early morning dark made it worse. I knew the streets up to Commercial Road like the back of my hand so that part of my journey didn't worry me. But when I arrived at Commercial Road and turned west to get to the City, it became a different matter. I knew that if I kept walking in a straight line I would eventually get to Aldgate. I also knew that if I lost my sense of direction I wouldn't know where I was going or where I had been.

As I walked I overtook the busses that were crawling along with the conductors walking ahead carrying an oil lamp or a torch. I screwed up my eyes as the sulphur in the atmosphere stung into them. All the time I was trying not to breathe in the sooty air too deeply. I like so many other people, tied my handkerchief around my mouth and nose as I prepared to battle my way to Fenchurch Street. It took a lot longer than I thought it would and it was very tricky finding my way round Gardener's corner.

It was a Mafeking relief to eventually get to work and in the warm. Everybody arrived late and at a different time with different stories of their journey's, but we managed to keep the Post Office open and telegrams going through. Everyone thought that the fog would clear as the day wore on, but that ghastly great smog hung around until the following Tuesday. Five days! Five days that almost brought the capital to a standstill.

It was brought about by the thick winter coal-smoke coming from the chimneys causing extra pollution and at the same time there had been what they called a freak anticyclonic fog, whatever that was. But whatever it was, it was lethal. It killed about four thousand people who had chest infections or asthma. The great smog of fifty-two as it became know, helped clear the way for some clean air legislation. Four years later in 1956 a private members bill by Gerald Nabarro brought in the Clean Air Act, asking for smoke control areas which the council began that year. But it wasn't until the early seventies, after the countless coal and wood burning grates and boilers had all been converted, that it began to have an effect. (*London in the 20th century. Jerry White.*) We continued to have bad smog right up until 1974, but thankfully there was nothing as cruel as that one ever again.

Our Christmas in that year was much better than the previous one, we even had a Tree and a Christmas pudding. When nineteen fifty-three came in everything in the Kingdom was about getting ready for the Coronation of Elizabeth the Second. Songs on the Radio, historical things in the papers, the secrets about the coronation dress and the significance of all the rituals of the ceremony were being written and talked abut everywhere. There were going to be big open-air street parties with flags and food for all the kids. A great number of people even bought new televisions sets to see it. We couldn't afford anything like that. On Coronation Day families who didn't have a television and knew someone who did, went around to their house to watch it. I had seen Uncle Ted's set in his front room, he never asked us to watch it, I saw through the window. It looked amazing was just like having your own little cinema screen in a wooden box in the corner.

Feeling that I was now a bit too old for all the street party nonsense I decided that I would definitely prefer to see the coronation in person. Well, not exactly in the Abbey! You had to be invited for that but to be one of the spectators along the route. All workers had been given the day off and I thought that I might as well make the most of it because, let's face it, a coronation doesn't come along every day of the decade. With this in mind and me liking a bit of company, I got Willy, Itchie and Rosie to come with me. Betty couldn't come because she was helping with a party.

The big question facing the four of us was where to position ourselves to see the procession and at what time? We had lots of arguments about it but eventually decided that we would go to Whitehall. Rosie read in the Star newspaper that after the ceremony itself, the newly crowned Queen would be returning to Buckingham Palace along that route. Itchie reckoned that with the Cenotaph in the middle of the road, it would mean that the golden coach would have to pass close to the kerb on one of its sides. It was just a question of which side l it would be. The whole point was to get a good close up view when she passed. It was eventually decided that we would sleep on the kerb-side and get a place as near to Horse Guards Parade as possible.

The weather forecast was 'very warm and possibly rain.' Willy and I worked out that if we took our huge post office capes buttoned them together and put an umbrella up the centre it would make a small tent for the four of us to get in and keep dry.

We met on Monday, Coronation Eve, in a pub near Aldgate Station. Carrying our supplies consisting of overcoats, jackets, lemonade, two flasks of tea and some sandwiches. Having finished in the pub we climbed aboard the top of a number fifteen bus to Charing Cross Station. As we moved towards the bottom of the Strand, we saw thousands of people from all over the world and the United Kingdom, camped across Trafalgar Square. We got off and pushed our way through the crowds along the pavements. As we moved across Northumberland Avenue, we could see hoards of people moving towards the Mall. So many people creating the most amazing open-hearted atmosphere that you could imagine.

Eventually we managed to thrust our way into Whitehall and claim our piece of pavement in front of Horse Guards Parade facing the Cenotaph. We had just enough room to spread ourselves.

Our nearest neighbours on the kerb were from Sweden and although we got on well with them we did get a little fed up with them constantly singing 'Wonderful wonderful Copenhagen' throughout the night.

NO EXPECTATIONS

Around about half past two in the morning, it got very cold and we all tried to snuggle up together to get warm and snatch a bit of shuteye. Rosie and I had a good snog to take our minds off of the discomfort. Actual sleep of any kind proved almost impossible especially when at about six o/clock in the morning, sailors and policemen arrived to line the route to guard the Queen and Prince Philip.

As the morning wore on we got quite friendly with our nearest policeman called Archie. The sailors, on the other hand, had strict instructions to watch the road and not to talk to the crowd. Not long after they arrived, the horse drawn carriages started galloping towards Westminster Abbey. The crowd tried to figure out who was in them but as they had their hoods it was very difficult, especially as they were on the other side of the road from us. We took comfort from this assuming that if they went into the Abbey that way, they would come back on our side and we would get a good view.

As the day got brighter the rain started to fall, but we kept cheerful. There was a huge cheer as Princess Margaret and the Queen Mother went by, waving graciously, accompanied by Guards in full regalia. We never saw the Queen going towards the Abbey because she was taking another route so that more people could see her.

It was a long wait before it all kicked off in the Abbey and the Queen became the crowned monarch. I think we were entertained by an outside broadcast, although I wouldn't swear to this.

After the ceremony the great Coronation Procession left the Abbey and passed by us. Passed by us on the other side of the bloody road! After doing all that research, we had chosen the wrong fucking side. It was a huge disappointment. Once the front of the procession passed us we talked about trying to rush to the other side of Whitehall and push our way in there. We quickly decided that it was impossible because the sailors might shoot us and the crowd over there would have lynched us rather than let us in. So we watched from where we were.

The members of the armed services marched by to the music of their brass bands and there were troops from all over the world, including the Ghurkhas who got a massive cheer. Between the forces there were the visiting Kings, Presidents, Lords, Ladies, Princes and lesser royalty wearing their coronets in their coaches, who waved at us through their closed windows. However, when Queen Salote of Tonga came by in her open landau with her huge smile and small husband, she got the most fantastic cheer. Although we didn't know who she was, we wanted to show our appreciation because she was sharing in our wetness.

At last, when Queen Elizabeth the Second and her Prince Philip Consort came by in that amazing gold coronation coach, with all the pomp of history travelling with her, the roar and the emotion of the crowd was so overwhelming it almost made me want to cry. That moment was an unforgettable experience. Even all these years later.

As the last of the rest of the parade went by with the brass band disappearing towards Trafalgar Square to return the Queen to Buckingham Palace on the Mall.

NO EXPECTATIONS

The sailors who had been on kerb guard formed up and were marched away. Soon after that the policemen allowed the crown to move and we, along with thousands of wet but jubilant, spectators made our way home. The four of us said our goodbye at Aldgate and I walked down Commercial Road to Nanny's arriving there exhausted. I fell off to sleep in the upstairs back room while the Coronation Party continued in Planet Street without me.

I bought all the newspapers the next day to keep as souvenirs, one of them, the Daily Express, even had their front page printed in gold. The film of the coronation itself called "A Queen is Crowned" was in the cinemas by the end of the week. I took Rosie to see it and although we never featured in the crowd scenes, it was great to see in close up all the things we had missed. The ritual was amazing and the crowds wonderful we felt great about it all, even more so because we had actually been there!

33 THE NEW ELIZABETHAN AGE

Despite all the clap-trap about the New Elizabethan Age, not a lot changed after the coronation.   No one discovered Tobacco or potatoes like in the old Age, although Edmund Hilary did manage to get to the top of Everest with Sherpa Tensing.

At work Frankie told me that he loved me, but I didn't believe him I thought that he was just saying that to get me. As far as I was concerned, love was between boys and girls. It was only sex that went on between boys and men. Frankie and I didn't get it together, not because I didn't like him but because I was getting enough from other sources.

In those teenage years I got loads of sexual attention from men.

I think there must have been some vulnerable or needy energy coming off of me. I certainly didn't consider myself very attractive. I was ginger haired, skinny, pale with a freckled face and a broken tooth. Perhaps it was because so many of the blokes were trapped in repression due to the laws of the time? On the other hand maybe, I looked a bit easy. Who knows? I just know that as soon as I was out on my own, some bloke would make eyes at me or try to touch me up. It even happened once in Romford Market!! And I was with my Mum!

Frankie left to do his National Service and I became Cooks Boy. It was a job I thoroughly enjoyed due to working with Rene. She was known as 'quite a girl,' flirted with the counter clerks outrageously and was a complete law unto herself. She taught me how to count out the vegetables and weigh up just the right amounts needed to feed the number of people who had ordered lunch that day.

I got to know the older staff when I was helping dish up their food. A couple of the more randy men and one of the women, wanted to get to know me a bit better than I thought was necessary. I mentioned this to Rene who explained the best way to deal with unwanted attentions was to give a polite refusal, which I found worked very well.

That is, it worked on most people apart from on Alf. He was one of the cleaners. He wore filthy navy-blue dungarees and a grubby shirt, was overweight, smelled and had blotchy hands. He was aggressively persistent in trying to grope me at every opportunity and completely refused to take no for an answer. His attentions continued despite me telling him to fuck off. Until one morning he popped out from behind a row of lockers with his dick poking out of his flies.

"Well look at that," I said, quite loudly. "It's just like a cock, only smaller."

Then I gave it a good thwack with a pencil! He never bothered me again.

It was strange where sexual encounters would rear heir heads. The next one was one that came right out of the blue and was the last thing I would be expecting.

I'd got home from work and as it was a nice afternoon I was helping Dad, do a bit of digging in the back garden. Being new to this sort of physical activity, I left myself open to a lot of criticism.

"Just dig the shovel in as far as it will go for fuck sake," said Daddy in his helpful way. "Then bend it back towards you. Now lift it up and turn it over back on the ground."

"Alright! Give us a chance," I snapped back. "I've never done any digging in me life."

"No! Cause you're a lazy bastard! Now put your back into it!"

Well I put me back into it to such an extent that by the time we stopped for a cup of tea I had got a severe pain in the groin. I went to check it out in the downstairs loo and saw that my left ball was all swollen up. It was too embarrassing even to tell Mum and Dad. I just took it easy hoping it would go away.

Unfortunately, the pain continued and eventually got so bad that I was almost sick. I knew I had to stop and rest or do something. I dropped my shovel and leaned against the wall.

"I've got to stop," I said. "I'm in agony."

Dad of course was wonderfully sympathetic.

"It's 'cause the lazy sod has been doing a bit of hard work for a change," he said to Mum who was looking through the kitchen window. "There's nothing wrong with 'im."

"Shut up and give it a rest, will ya," I replied. "You don't know what you're talking about. This is really hurting me and when I went to the lav, just now, I saw that it's all swollen up down there."

"What on your bollocks?"

"Edd don't use that word," said Mum. "You know I don't like that sort of swearing!"

"Yeah," I said. "The one on the left is really big and it's murdering me."

After a bit more arguing and Dad having taken a look, it was decided that I ought to go to see a Doctor.

I hadn't been to the doctors for years. It had always been cheaper to look after ourselves and get stuff from the chemist than pay anything up to half a crown to see a Quack, unless it was really serious. But now we had the Health Service, which meant we could see a Doctor for nothing.

We were registered with Dr. Jones. Mum insisted on coming with me.

His surgery, was in a two-bedroom council house only a five-minute walk away. The front door was open when we arrived. We went into his waiting room. I was surprised to find that there were no mats on the bare tiles and nothing to sit on except three kitchen chairs and a frayed wicker work settee with an armchair to match. On the wall facing us, above an electric fire, were two large black and white framed pictures. One of Lenin and the other of Stalin and selotaped on the wall between them was a large hand-written notice which read;

TO ALL MY PATIENTS.

I RESPECTFULLY ASK THAT YOU STOP YOUR SLUTS OF CHILDREN FROM PICKING AT AND DISMANTLING MY EXPENSIVE FURNITURE.

THANKS!"

Mum pulled a face at me as we both read it then she sat on one of the chairs and got into conversation with the three other patients.

"You might have to wait a bit," said a woman with a large boil on her neck. "He tends to doze off a lot which make the waiting time longer. But he is good, he knows what he's doin' and we don't have to pay now."

"If he dozes off, Johnny," said Mum. "Just give a loud cough enough to wake him up."

I sat in there, slowly moving to ease the pan in my groin, for over an hour before it was my turn to go in. Mum came in with me and knowing what she was like, I thought, "For fuck's sake don't let her stay in there!"

However, after introducing herself and me to Dr. Jones. She explained my problem in great detail, with many a colourful aside, before she left the surgery to wait outside with the other sluts.

Dr. Jones was a tweed wearing narcoleptic with glasses and a bald, freckled head. He asked me for the usual details of name, address date of birth etc, and wrote them onto a new card. He asked me to explain my symptoms in my own words.

"I was helping me Dad do a bit of diggin' and when I had finished I got this terrible pain in me boll... me ball. When I had a look, it was all swelled up and Mum said I ought to come to see you."

"In that case we had better have a look," he said. "If you would like to hop up on to that couch, I will ease your rousers down to examine you. Just unbutton your flies before getting up there as that will make things easier for me."

He came from behind his desk and helped me on to his consulting couch. I lay there feeling very embarrassed with my flies wide open. He then pulled my trousers and pants down and stared down at my naked groin.

"Ah yes," he said to himself. "I will have to return that to its rightful position. This is going to be a little uncomfortable but bear with me for as long as you can."

He then gripped my swollen left testicle between his thumb and forefinger and twisted it back into its natural position. It was extremely painful and once he had done the twisting he continued to hold it in position between his fingers.

He then fell asleep.

I didn't know what to do. I mean here I was on a couch with my pants down and a doctor leaning over me nether regions. He was fast asleep. His head was bowed, and his breath was exhaling onto my pale thighs, just above my knee. After what seemed about half an hour I got a bit desperate and despite the fact that it might make my ball swell up again; I gave a loud, pretend sneeze. It caused a severe pain to shoot up my stomach but mercifully the ball stayed where it was. Probably because his hand was still on it. He woke up, stood up and returned to his desk as if nothing had happened. He diagnosed a strangulated hernia.

He told me that I could go to a hospital to have an operation, but at the moment it wasn't necessary. Suggesting that we should see how it went. He ordered five days rest and gave me a proscription for a small pink truss.

"Wear that until you feel secure enough to leave it off," was his advice. "Here is a certificate for work and some pills to help with the pain."

Despite the pills and the truss, the pain at times was desperately severe. Nevertheless, I left off the truss as soon as I could because it was too embarrassing. But the problem continued, on and off, for quite a few months.

When it got too bad I had to return to Dr. Jones. Once I got into his surgery, we followed the same routine as we had on the original diagnosis, except that he didn't always fall asleep. On a couple of rare occasions, he did fall asleep with my privates in his hand, he slowly worked at getting me hard. I can only assume that he was either dreaming or doing it deliberately. I quite enjoyed it so learned to just lie back and think of the N.H.S.

It all came to an end on a Sunday morning. I was attending the eleven o/clock Mass at St. Phillips with Nanny and Betty. As I got up from a kneeling position, out it popped again. I tried to cope with it, but during the next hymn it all got too much, and I collapsed into a heap. St Philips being situated just behind the London Hospital, I was helped out and taken to the emergency room. After about fifteen minutes a doctor arrived and tried to twist it back, but it refused to say back and was so painful that I eventually passed out again.

I knew nothing more until I was being shaken by a nurse who was urging me to wake up and taking my temperature. A little later the short, stocky, red-cheeked Sister came to my bed to inform me that I had been operated on for a strangulated hernia. She also told me through pursed lips that while I was coming around from the anaesthetic my language had been a disgrace! Nothing new there then! The following morning, I learned, from the visiting doctor, that the cord inside my body, that had been causing the strangulation had been twisted back and stitched up so it would now keep the testicle permanently in its place. I was discharged after a couple of days having to return a week later to get the stitches taken out. That wasn't nice at all!!

While I was recovering I decided that I would like to do some acting again and during a trip to Romford Market, I hobbled into the Library to find out if there were any local Drama Groups I could join. The beige dressed woman behind the counter went through her list and suggested an operatic society. I loved singing, but I didn't have enough confidence in my voice for opera, never having seen one. After a few more suggestions she gave me a list of groups that just did acting.

I read through them on the bus but none of them meant anything to me apart from the Co-Operative Players, because I knew Mum was a member and had a Dividend number.

I went to the shops and made a call to the secretary Jean Copping, who told me that the group met at seven thirty every Tuesday evening in a building on the Eastern Avenue. This sounded ideal. If I got off the train at Romford Station after work I could easily get there by bus. I told her that I would come along on the following Tuesday.

At seven fifteen the following week I arrived at a building that was curved and covered in white and green tiles which I now know was in the thirties style of Art Deco. Once inside I followed the notices to the room where the group was meeting. I was a bit nervous thinking that the other people might be a bit posh and were proper actors. I need not have worried because Jean Copping, a tall slim woman with a turn in one eye was there to meet me. She introduced me to Mrs. Connolly, the producer of the group who had been a professional actress.

Mrs. Con, for that is how she like to be called, was a small woman with faded auburn hair and bright sparkling eyes. She greeted me like an old friend.

"Hello dear John," she said, in a warm well pronounced voice. "You are very welcome. It will be splendid to have a younger man in our company, especially one with such lovely colour hair. Unfortunately, at the moment we will not be able to give you any acting parts as we are in the middle of our next production. But I can assure you that as soon as that is over, I will definitely find a play with something in it for you. In the meantime, I am sure you will be able to keep busy helping with stage management and props. I look forward to working with you."

By now the rest of the members had arrived and were getting coffee and spreading themselves around the room. They all greeted me enthusiastically and reiterated that new members, especially male ones, were always needed. They only had three men and a boy in the company. Les, who was tall and rather plump, Tim, very tall with a moustache and Bill who was the good looking one. The ten-year-old boy was Douglas whose mother Eileen was also a member. The other women were two older ladies, Rita and May and five younger girls who were all older than me. I soon learned that they were; Jean the secretary, Anne the treasurer, Joan who had a lovely pair of breasts and Tall Pam who did stage managing and was helped by Elsa the quiet one.

I soon relaxed and settled in very easily during the next few weeks. I was enjoying making props, painting bits of scenery and helping to look for costumes. I was kept busy and gradually got to know the other members as I watched rehearsals. The play they were doing was a modern whodunit, called 'The Veil. Les played the detective and Bill was the bloke who murdered Ann, his wife because he really loved Jean.

When someone couldn't get to the rehearsal due to work or other things, Mrs. Con. asked me to read in for them. I did and was given lots of encouragement. Mrs. Con. said I would definitely be given a part in their next production, which was going to be entered into a local One Act Play Festival.

I didn't have a clue what a festival was until Joan, with the tits, explained that it was where lots of groups came together to show their plays. The festival itself usually ran for a few nights and at the end of each performance some bloke, in what they called an adjudication would give each group some criticism. He would tell you what was good and what was bad, and marks would be given. When all the groups had been seen the play with the highest mark would be presented with a certificate or a cup or some sort of trophy. I took it all in but really, I wasn't much interested in al that. I just wanted to do a bit of acting.

During the early part of the summer the Co-Op arranged for us to go on a weekend acting workshop in a big house in Walthamstow called Hollybank. We were booked in on Saturday morning and stayed there until Sunday afternoon. During that time, we would do voice classes, acting exercises and scenes from plays. All directed by different producers. I absolutely loved it! Just doing acting for a couple of days, to me was fucking fantastic. We would also be sharing the house and the course with another Co-Op group from Hampstead.

One of our guest teachers was a producer called Joan Littlewood, who was running the Theatre Royal in Stratford. She wore a cap, had a warm smile and was already in the studio when we all trouped in for her class. She introduced herself as Joan and before we did anything else, she asked us all go out of the room and then come in again just exactly as we had when we first arrived. She made us do it a few times and eventually explained that we had to do it without acting or demonstrating. Just simply come into the studio just like we had when we first arrived. She also made us play games in a circle using a ball and saying our second names and later we did things with props. I didn't always get what she was going on about, but it was enormous fun. I especially liked the bit towards the end of the evening when she made us do scenes. Not from a script but from stuff we made up on the spot and in our own words. Improvisation she called it.

It was a marvellous weekend, with other teachers giving us movement and dance things to do. It was a great way of getting to know the other personalities of our group. I was a bit shocked when Joan and Les, who was her fiancé, had a flaming row at the breakfast table on the Sunday morning. He was a big bloke and for one minute I thought he might hit her and I wondered what everyone would do if he did. But he didn't. He just stormed out of the dining room. She burst into teas and was comforted by the other girls. I thought if they are like this when they were only engaged, what was it going to be like when they were married? Although I was used to rows at home I just wasn't expecting that sort of thing in front of strangers in a public place. Especially from people who owned their own houses. Bill told me that they were always like that and not to worry because by lunchtime they would be friends again. Which is exactly what happened.

Sometime after coming back from that glorious weekend I arrived home from work one day and Mum called me into the front room.

"Johnny, I wanna have a word with you," she said, in a tone that told me that this was not going to be any ordinary conversation.

"What's the matter?" I asked, as I sat on a dining room chair and she stood with her back towards the French window. I assumed it was going to be about money or rather the lack of it.

There was a bit of a pause. This in itself was unusual. In our family because nobody paused, otherwise someone would jump in and you wouldn't get a change to speak at all.

"I think I'm pregnant again and I don't know how I'm gonna tell your father."

I most definitely was not expecting this. I took a pause of my own to collect myself.

"What d'ya mean you don't know how you're gonna tell 'im," I eventually asked. "Its as much his fault as yours. Just tell him."

"But it's the last news he'd want to hear right now. Not when we're just getting on our feet a bit."

"Well, he's gonna find out sooner or later," I said. 'It's not something you can keep hidden for long. Well not longer than a few months."

She looked at me and said, "Will you be there with me when I tell him. Just in case he starts doin' his nut?"

I thought for a moment.

"I don't think it would be a good idea if I was actually in the room with you," I said. "But if you let me know when you're gonna tell 'im. I'll be standing by just in case. I'll get Jeanie with me, as well."

"Don't tell her why, will you?"

"No course not. I tell you what. If you tell him tonight, I'll make sure we're listening in the passage. Just like we did when that old geezer came to complain about our language."

"He was a nosy old bastard,' she said. "Alright I'll tell Edd tonight. But make sure you are standing by. And for fuck sake come in quick if he starts shouting. Shut up now, there's the girls coming down the path.

That night after the young 'uns had gone up to bed. Mum looked at me and gave me what was called 'an old-fashioned look' and said to Dad, as she turned off the cooker.

"Edd, I wanna have a talk to you in the front room."

"What?" He said, surprised. "A talk? What sort of talk? I hope you ain't gonna ask me for money. I've only got enough to get me through to the end of the week."

"No," said Mum, "It ain't about that, its something else. Come into the front room. I don't wanna talk in front of these two."

Dad looked at me and Jeanie, frowned, got up from the table and left the kitchen. Mum pulled an apprehensive face at me as she followed him into the front room.

"What's going on?" Jeanie asked.

"Nothing," I lied. "Just shut up and be quiet. Let's go into the hall."

She opened her mouth to say something else, but I raised my finger to stop her. We went into the hall and waited. We were standing next to the row of coats hanging on their hooks with the kids' shoes underneath them. It was quiet, but I could just hear Mum talking in a low voice. I couldn't actually hear the words. Jeanie put her mouth close to my ear.

"What's happening?" She whispered

"Be quiet!" I whispered as I elbowed her in the ribs to shut her up. She did.

"Pregnant!" I heard Dad shout. "Pregnant? What the fuck are you doing getting pregnant you silly mare? We can't afford any more kids we can hardly keep up with the ones we 'ave got!"

"Its no good shouting Edd," Mum said. I've been to the doctors and he told me I am expecting, and it'll be due sometime next March."

"Well, it had better not be another fucking girl then," said Dad.

Thus, a new unborn baby was welcomed into the family by its father.

The following year, on March tenth to be precise, the baby was born. It was a boy! We called him Billy. Proper name William Edward, which was brother Eddy's name only the other way around. At last I had a brother! Eddy would have been seventeen by now and I still missed him. Nevertheless, Billy was a big blond bouncy baby boy and I loved him.

Meanwhile back the co-op group it had been decided that we would enter the Walthamstow Summer Drama Festival with a one act play called 'The Thin Red Line.' There were only two parts in it and I was cast as a young French Soldier, who escapes from the Foreign Legion and while hiding in a barn he gets caught by an English Officer, played by Bill. The part gave me a chance to perfect my French accent which I copied from Charles Boyer and Mme. Poultrice at the City Day College.

With only a couple of hours a week the rehearsal period was quite long. The play was going to be produced in early July. This caused some of concern. I would be eighteen years old in May and after that would be eligible for National Service. If I was conscripted quickly it would mean that I may not be available to do the play? Mrs. Con, Bill and I had a conflab and decided that I would continue with the part and hope for the best.

To keep the women in the group happy they began working on a one act play with a totally female cast. It was called 'Mrs. Grundy.' Mrs. Con decided that we would put on both plays, for three nights, in a hall in Ilford. This would give us a run in before the festival. It wasn't a very big hall and we managed to sell enough tickets to almost fill it every night. I was thrilled that Mum, Dad and the girls managed to get to see it, as well as quite a few friends from the post office.

Itchie, was on leave and came too. He was six months older than me so was already in the Army. He was on leave having just finished doing his basic training in Salisbury. He turned up wearing his Army uniform. I tried the jacket and cap on and immediately decided that I would join the Royal Air Force.

I really loved doing the play and got a good few laughs as well as lots of praise. Some people even told me that I ought to take it up as a career. All this feedback gave me a lot of confidence for when it was time to do it at the Walthamstow festival. At the festival, I was a little disappointed because although the adjudicator liked Bill's and my acting he didn't like the play! He positively hated the costumes and thought the set was shit. Although he didn't quite say it in those words. So sod him! I decided that I would like to take up an acting career.

In 'The Thin Red Line,' which finished on Saturday night, I had played an army officer in the Napoleonic period, and on the following Monday morning. Guess what? I received a letter On Her Majesty's Service, ordering me to report to a National Service Recruiting Office.

Now that I had reached the age of eighteen, it was mine and every young mans duty to serve his country in the Army, the Royal Air Force, or the Royal Navy. The bulk of national servicemen went into the various regiments of the British Army while a smaller percentage went into the Royal Air Force and fewer went into the Royal Navy. Having given it some thought and with the Itchie experiment, it was obvious that Khaki did not suit me. I returned the letter stating my preference for the R.A.F.

The following week I arrived at the Recruiting Office, in Romford and was given a warm welcome by a young officer and an even younger corporal. They told me all about the joys of being an airman and informed me that under no circumstances would I be called upon to fly a plane. However, as a serviceman I would be taught a trade which would benefit me when I was discharged. I could learn: cooking, motor mechanics, engineering, supplies, shorthand and typing, logistics, accounting, even driving. All that and other things I had never heard of. They also said that, while it was compulsory to serve my country as a National

Serviceman for two years, I might like to consider the option of signing on as a Regular Airman, for three years or more. If I did become a Regular Airman, I would receive a higher salary. The officer continued selling the joys of the R.A.F. by extolling the joys of service life with comradeship, education and healthy living. I left. Taking away various forms to fill in, some leaflets and an order to return the following morning to sign on.

At home we had a long discussion as to the pros and cons of becoming a regular Airman, until it was decided that I would sign on for one extra year, thus enabling me to send more money home to help the family. Secretly I thought that I might be able to save a bit towards going to acting school when I left at twenty-one. With this in mind I decided I would learn to type and do shorthand as this might help me get temporary work while I was a drama student.

I reported back the following morning and handed in my forms to the smiling Corporal who led me to a room where there were other recruits waiting to start out on careers as Aircraftmen second class, known in the Royal Air Force as an AC2. This was how several thousand young men every month were enlisted in a process that took from three to four days.

In 1954, all air force recruits went to one of two Reception Units, either RAF Padgate, or in my case RAF Cardington in Bedfordshire. It was there, three days later, we were welcomed by corporals and sergeants with open arms and told to line up to be kitted out with underwear, socks, cap, two jackets and two pairs of trousers, belts and a kitbag as well as canvas packs to put over our shoulders and held up by stiff canvas belts known as webbing. Everything was blue with brass buttons and fittings. Everything that is apart from the cream vests and pants and the boots. The boots were black with a toecap that would have to be polished bright enough to see our faces in it.

The following day, having experienced the joys of dormitory sleeping and the N.A.A.F.I., we were escorted to a Medical Centre. We were politely asked to do a hearing and sight test, have our chest and heart examined. We had to drop our new blue trousers and cream under pants so that the doctor could grab our balls as we coughed. We were then ordered to turn round and bend over while our arses were inspected. That done we pulled up our trousers did a short walk up and down and we were pronounced A.1. fit for service.

Now that the government knew that we were fit we were entitled to our number. Once we had it we were ordered to learn it by heart and remember it for the rest of our lives. I remember it to this day. We were later taken to an aircraft hanger and encouraged to wander around some tables that were set up and talk to the officers who would help us chose a trade. I had already decided on a clerical trade but I had a look at the trades on offer just to get to know the other lads.

After our warm, friendly and considerate introduction into the RAF, where everyone was approachable and always ready to answer any question we asked, we were dispatched from Cardington in a specially chartered train to West Kirby: No. 5 School of Recruit Training, in the Wirral, near Liverpool.

Immediately the train pulled into the station, even before it came to a halt gangs of corporals, sergeants, and flight sergeants tore open the carriage doors and shrieked at us to disembark. To say that we received a shock would be a massive understatement! They bellowed and yelled at us to move on the double with no talking and herded us like cattle dragging our kit with us, to an aircraft hanger where we were screamed at to fall into lines. Once in line we were marched towards eight barber's chairs where our hair was shorn off as close to our scalp as possible. Feeling utterly bewildered we were marched out onto a parade ground and sorted into flights. There were four flights to a squadron, and two squadrons to a wing. Which of course meant nothing to us young AC2s. as we wandered around like headless chickens till told to stand still and form ranks.

We were then made to run, on the double as they called it, to a hut and given a bed space in the dormitory. Our flight would be supervised by a Corporal drill instructor that would sleep in a separate room at the end of the hut. This was the place that would be our prison, for the next six weeks, while we suffered the hell of what was laughingly knows as square bashing.

Of course, the experience, in retrospect, was one that I would not have missed. Sometimes it was extremely hard and at others hilarious. There has been enough written about the forces experience. I will just say that I never completed my three years before I was invalided out. My life as a man had begun in the care of the military. I was loaded with vivid expectations, fears and worries churning around in my mind as I fell asleep in my billet, for the first time as an Aircraftman Second Class.

Now this book must end, as did my childhood.

NO EXPECTATIONS

Printed in Great Britain
by Amazon